GÉRARD HOULLIER
THE LIVERPOOL REVOLUTION

Stephen F. Kelly

Dedication

To four young Liverpool supporters:
Nicholas, Emma, Naomi and Ben

First published in Great Britain in 2003 by
Virgin Books
Thames Wharf Studios
Rainville Road
London W6 9HA

A catalogue record for the book is available from the British
Library.

ISBN 1 85227 067 5

Typeset by TW Typesetting, Plymouth, Devon

Printed and bound in Great Britain by
Mackays of Chatham PLC

CONTENTS

1. CRISIS IN THE DRESSING ROOM

As Houllier lay in the ambulance, the paramedics placed an oxygen mask over his face. The seriousness of the problem was beginning to emerge, but Houllier could not then have realised that at 54 his life was hanging in the balance, that his whole world was about change.

In hindsight, the problem should have been spotted a mile off. Against Alavés in the UEFA Cup final on 16 May 2001, Gérard Houllier sat on the sidelines chuntering to himself, his bottom lip vibrating repeatedly, his beady eyes rotating. It was as if he were mumbling a litany of Hail Marys, or reciting some magic mantra. Maybe he was; after all, this was one of the most dramatic European finals in decades, and watching your team throw away a commanding lead is enough to make anyone chunter to themselves. You could catch sight of this behaviour at other games as well. Whereas the exuberant Thompson would be out of the dugout and on his feet screaming at players, Houllier would sit quietly and respectfully in his seat, internalising all the drama and tension, chewing on his bottom lip, sipping from his bottle of water, occasionally shaking his head. It might have been better for him had he followed Thompson's example.

The visit of Leeds later that year, on 13 October, was a major event. David O'Leary's young side was showing championship form, unbeaten and top of the table. In the previous season they had twice had the better of Liverpool in the League, although the Reds had notched up a famous cup victory at Elland Road on their way to the FA Cup final. But this was the sort of game Liverpool had to win if their ambitions to win the Premiership were to be realised.

Houllier had been feeling uncomfortable all morning – that weary feeling. He'd been feeling that way for a few weeks. It wasn't like him. He was normally full of energy and drive. People always spoke of him as being a workaholic, but in recent weeks he'd felt tired. Although the season was only two months old, it had been unrelenting, a merry-go-round that seemed to stop only for the briefest of moments, and he had been following a hectic timetable since that UEFA Cup final. He put his listlessness down to old age creeping up on him and the fact that he'd not had a proper break that summer. 'I made a mistake by not taking a proper holiday during the close season,' he admitted. 'I went to the Confederations Cup in Korea to enjoy games without any involvement, but found I could not sleep.' Generally he never sleeps well, but in the Far East he was worse than usual. It was a trip that was really unnecessary and would prove to have dire consequences.

Liverpool had also kicked off the 2001/02 season early as they had to qualify for the Champions League. First up was a trip to Finland, followed by the Charity Shield opener against Manchester United. It might have been only a friendly, but try telling that to anyone in Liverpool when United are the opposition. Then came another major game, this time in the European Super Cup against Bayern Munich in Monaco. There, Houllier hadn't even felt like indulging himself in one of his favourite pastimes. 'We were in a nice hotel, with a pool and a gym. I like swimming, but I didn't feel like using the pool. Physically I felt something was wrong, but I did not show that to my players. If you show you are weak, the team will be weak. In my mind I could not allow that to happen.' By the time Liverpool lined up for their second Premiership fixture August wasn't yet over and they'd already contested five major games.

Pressures were steadily mounting within the squad, too. Michael Owen had been injured, Markus Babbel had contracted a mysterious virus and there was still the Robbie Fowler problem to be sorted out. Then, at the beginning of September, on his birthday, Houllier dashed to France with the club's chief executive, Rick Parry, to complete the £6 million transfer of Le Havre's two teenage stars Anthony Le Tallec and Florent Sinama Pongolle. The two lads might have been only sixteen years old but there was fierce competition for their signatures and Houllier reckoned their signings were so important to the club's future that he took total charge of events. 'When I got back from France I was absolutely exhausted,' he recalled. 'Usually, I would be tired the following day and recover, but this time it took a week, which was quite unusual.' Parry remembered him looking tired, and admitting to it, on that short trip to Le Havre.

The pressure continued to build throughout September with seven fixtures, including a derby game against Everton and energy-sapping European ties against Boavista, Borussia Dortmund and Dynamo Kiev. He knew he needed a break, and with an international week imminent and so few players around Melwood, he was persuaded to take a short break. But in the end all it amounted to was a three-day holiday in France where he even managed to find enough energy to play a 90-minute game of football with some friends. When he returned home he still did not feel one hundred per cent. 'When I came back I finally decided I needed a check-up and had some blood tests. I still did not really believe there was anything seriously wrong. I rested and felt fine again.' But as a precaution he arranged for further heart tests to be performed by his doctor in Paris. Unfortunately, an ECG and ordinary blood pressure tests would only ever reveal a problem with the heart, not the kind of problem Houllier had. He was given the all-clear.

After those tests he flew to Prague to meet Milan Baros, Liverpool's new Czech signing. He returned to London for meetings on 7 October, then went back to Liverpool the following day to supervise training and arrangements for the club's defence of the Worthington Cup. To everyone's astonishment, on 9 October Liverpool lost 2–1 to Grimsby Town at Anfield. Although they had created enough chances to win by five or six goals, it was still a humiliating defeat that produced some unwelcome headlines. Further pressure. That was on the Tuesday; on Saturday Leeds United came to town.

That morning he felt it especially. He'd had pains in his chest but put it down initially to indigestion. When Leeds arrived at Anfield, Leeds manager David O'Leary, an old friend, noticed that Houllier wasn't looking too well. 'I asked him how he was. He said that he didn't feel too good and I have to admit that he didn't look too good either. In retrospect you could see that he was carrying a touch too much weight. He looked tired, as if he hadn't had enough exercise. But at the time I thought no more of it.'

It was not a good first half for Houllier. Liverpool looked sluggish and had fallen a goal behind. The half-time whistle couldn't come a minute too soon. Emile Heskey had picked up an injury, and Houllier and Thompson needed to get to grips with the problem. As the two teams filed back into their dressing rooms, Houllier began to feel worse. It had been a stressful 45 minutes, and although he might have been inclined to put the increased pain down to the tension, he knew that something was not right. This wasn't indigestion and it wasn't stress. Houllier gave a quick team talk, far shorter than he had intended. He simply did not have the strength to say any more. The club doctor Mark Waller and physio Dave Galley were both close by, attending to Emile Heskey. It didn't look as if the striker was going to be able to make the second half. Houllier told Jari Litmanen to get himself ready.

In the pressure cooker of the dressing room, Houllier began to sweat. He decided to have a word with Mark Waller, who had now left Heskey to the physio. He told him that he wasn't sure what was happening; did he have anything that might help ease the pain? Waller and Galley took him aside into another room and decided to give him a quick examination. Houllier was a bit reluctant but went along with it. He was eager to get back out there to his seat in the dugout as soon as possible. Waller sounded his chest, then took his blood pressure. He didn't like what he saw. Houllier looked pale and drawn. Both were quick to realise that something was wrong. Former Liverpool player Brian Hall was in the corridor just outside the dressing room. 'I knew something was going on,' he said. 'There was a flurry of activity. I knew that Emile Heskey had picked up an injury and I thought it was maybe something to do with that. Then somebody said the boss wasn't too good.'

Houllier was now readying himself to go back to the dugout for the second half, so Waller had to make a quick decision. 'You simply can't go out there,' he insisted. 'Why not?' the Frenchman replied, ready to brush them aside. 'I'll be OK.' But neither Waller nor Galley was to be contradicted; they feared there was something seriously wrong. They had to be quick, and immediately called for an ambulance. They wanted to get him to a hospital as soon as possible.

As the two teams prepared to go out for the second half, Galley went back into the dressing room and pulled Phil Thompson aside. 'We're going to have to get Gérard to hospital. There's a problem. I think he might have had a heart attack, or it could be something else,' he told him. Thompson was stunned and at that moment was not quite sure what to do. 'Go on out,' they told him. 'There's nothing you can do here. We'll sort things.'

The second-half bell rang and the two sides emerged to make their way back on to the pitch. None of the players, as yet, was aware of the drama taking place nearby. Thompson had decided not to say anything to them. It would only have caused distress and confusion and would not have helped the situation. They would have to play on regardless.

Waller then sent someone to find Houllier's wife Isabelle in the stands. 'You'd better tell Rick Parry as well,' he added. Within a few minutes Isabelle was by her husband's side. 'We have to get him to hospital immediately,' said Waller. 'There's an ambulance waiting outside.' Houllier looked grey, his face was furrowed and he was clearly in some pain. Parry, still unaware of just how serious the problem was, had decided to remain in the directors' box. 'There was nothing I could do and I knew that he was in good hands,' Parry explained.

Everything was happening so rapidly; there was hardly time to think. Houllier and his wife were immediately ushered into the ambulance, and with the siren sounding it made for Broadgreen Hospital, one of the leading cardiac hospitals in the region, just a few miles down the road from the ground. Brian Hall had nipped out of the stadium and gone over to his office in Anfield Road. He was returning just as the ambulance pulled in with its lights flashing. He immediately put two and two together. 'I realised straight away it was for the boss,' he said, 'but it wasn't until after the game that I began to piece the jigsaw together.'

As Houllier lay in the ambulance, the paramedics placed an oxygen mask over his face. The seriousness of the problem was beginning to emerge, but Houllier could not then have realised that at 54 his life was hanging in the balance, that his whole world was about change.

During that second half nobody outside the club's staff had any idea of what had happened. The eagle-eyed in the stadium might have noticed that Houllier had not taken up his usual seat in the dugout, but for all they knew he might well have decided to watch the second half from the directors' box, or even have jetted off on a prearranged scouting mission. Even in the directors' box few were aware of the drama that was taking place. In the dugout Phil Thompson was, as usual, out on the touchline bellowing at his players. He, too, had had little time to take in just how serious things were as the game swung one way, then the other. Things still weren't going according to plan.

As soon as Houllier arrived at Broadgreen Hospital doctors crowded around him and began to carry out a series of detailed examinations to ascertain whether in fact he had had a heart attack. Houllier was tense, annoyed that he wasn't back at Anfield and didn't know how things were going, and irritated by the fact that this was happening at an important moment. The next day he was due to fly off to Kiev for a Champions League game. The doctors took a couple of hours to conduct their tests, and later that evening they gave him the bad news.

Back at Anfield, as the players trudged off the field and back into the dressing room the talk was of Danny Murphy's headed equaliser. Robbie Fowler was boasting about the fact that it was his long-range chip that had struck the crossbar to rebound for Murphy to score. Sami Hyypia was cursing his luck after Nigel Martyn had saved what looked like a possible winner. 'We deserved all three points,' he was claiming. Of course, one or two players were by now wondering where the manager was. In the heat of the game few had noticed that Houllier had not been sitting in his usual seat in the dugout. After a quick word with Dave Galley, Phil Thompson called them together and asked for quiet. 'I have to tell you,' he said, 'that Gérard Houllier was taken ill at half-time with chest pains and has been rushed to Broadgreen Hospital.'

There was total silence. Nobody could believe it. Emile Heskey, who had remained behind on the treatment table in the dressing room after half-time, was the only one who had any idea of what was happening. 'I couldn't sleep that night,' he recalled. 'I could see how bad it was and how concerned everyone was.' Heskey was now telling the others what he had seen. The players looked at one another in disbelief. There was now real concern that they might not see their manager again. The players bathed and changed quietly, each of them pondering on the potential consequences. If it was a heart attack, would Houllier be back? If not, who'd take over, and where would they go from there? They were told that the 24 hours following a heart attack were crucial. Another attack during this time could easily be fatal.

Suddenly, their season seemed in disarray. The result of the game was no longer important. Word quickly spread around Anfield. In the boardroom they were beginning to piece the story together and becoming increasingly alarmed. Rick Parry was immediately on the phone to the hospital. David O'Leary came into the dressing room looking very concerned. Rivalries were forgotten. Houllier had helped him considerably during his early days at Elland Road. Gary McAllister, as one of the most senior players, was pushed forward to do press interviews. 'The players are dazed. We know as much as you. At this moment our thoughts are with his wife and family. We just hope he gets through this,' he told the assembled journalists, who were now throwing away their match reports in favour of this even bigger story. Mobile phones were ringing, journalists were getting new orders from their newsrooms. Club officials were trying to get as much news as possible to help them. But nobody was quite sure what was going on.

By 5.30 p.m. the news was public. Fans driving home from Anfield in their cars were the first to hear that Gérard Houllier was ill in hospital with a suspected heart attack. As the evening wore on, the news grew steadily grimmer.

'Well, you haven't had a heart attack,' said consultant cardiologist Dr Rod Stables, sitting in a chair close to Houllier's bed, 'of that we're certain. But we think that what you have is a dissection of the aorta, a kind of tear in the main artery that takes the blood away from the heart. It's leaking, and it is a very serious condition. It has to be treated immediately and that means we shall have to operate as soon as possible.' If they didn't operate straight away, he would die. It was as simple as that, but even then Houllier did not fully grasp just how serious things were.

'What are the chances of recovery?' he asked.

Dr Stables looked him full in the eye. 'Well, I'm not going to lie to you,' he began ominously. 'The chances are good, but they are not one hundred per cent.'

'How long will the operation take?' Isabelle asked.

'Well, it's a difficult operation, so it could take as long as ten hours,' replied Dr Stables.

Houllier and Isabelle looked at each other. It was enough to shake even the most resolute.

The doctor then asked Houllier if he wanted to speak to anyone else. The Liverpool manager shook his head; he just wanted to have a few brief moments alone with his wife. 'Only then did I realise what he was saying,' said Houllier. What the doctor was implying, without spelling it out, was that Houllier faced a life-threatening operation. In a nutshell, he could easily die. He would also have to be induced into a coma in order to cool the body down. The blood flow to his brain would be halted and there was no knowing how that might affect him. It was quite possible he could end up with some brain damage. 'I didn't think twice,' recalled Houllier, 'I just told him to get it done. I've taken risks all my life.'

For a few moments the medical staff left Houllier and his wife alone to share their thoughts and prepare for the operation.

In the event, the operation took even longer than had been anticipated. Houllier lay for eleven hours undergoing open-heart surgery, which was conducted by the consultant cardiac surgeons Mr Abbas Rashid and Miss Elaine Griffiths, consultant anaesthetist Dr Jim Murphy, and Dr Stables himself. Outside the operating theatre Isabelle Houllier waited anxiously for any information. Houllier's brother, who was a doctor, was already on his way to join her.

In Liverpool's pubs and restaurants that evening the talk was of Houllier. It had by that time become clear that their manager was facing open-heart surgery. On the radio some commentators were reckoning that it would be the end of Houllier's days as Liverpool's boss. The curse of the Liverpool manager seemed to have struck again. Kenny Dalglish had resigned following a nervous breakdown, Graeme Souness had suffered a heart attack followed by bypass surgery, and now Gérard Houllier had been struck down, just three years into the job.

Parry had decided not to tell the press how long the operation would take as that would lead only to further speculation and panic, though this plan was wrecked the following morning when David O'Leary appeared on the hospital steps and in a most unhelpful contribution revealed all. Parry hadn't been able to sleep at all during the night of the operation. The hospital had told him to stay away. 'There's nothing you can do. He's in good hands. We'll do all we can.' At six o'clock on the morning of the 14th the phone suddenly rang. Parry went cold with fear. It was the hospital. 'He's come through it,' they said, 'but we won't fully know how he is until he's out of the coma. Only then will we know if he's OK.'

2. A CHANGE TOO SOON

Around the boardroom, after almost every game, heads were being shaken. Everybody knew that really it was not working. Liverpool were admittedly winning games, but they were never in serious contention for the title. Gaining points was sometimes like wringing blood out of a stone. They might have finished in respectable positions in recent years, but the likes of Arsenal and Manchester United were in a different league. The youngsters promised much, but some of the players they had signed and moulded into the side seemed to fall short in key areas. The days when Liverpool represented the gold standard of English and European football were long gone. Manchester United were now the benchmark of Premiership football.

They've never been very good at change in Liverpool. It's probably part of the city's personality – a belief in tradition, history, loyalty and, of course, sentiment. There's nobody outside Ireland more sentimental than scousers. And they're much the same with their football.

Little altered at Anfield in the three decades after the arrival in December 1959 of Bill Shankly. It was he who laid down the pattern of play, the training methods and the transfer policies. And why should they change? During that period they had won everything, and others had copied their system. Wherever you went in football there were bootrooms, five-a-side games, the same kind of training sessions and so forth. Managers and their coaches from all around the world came to visit Anfield and its Melwood training ground in their search for the secret ingredient. They'd look and be puzzled. 'What is it?' they'd ask as they watched a training session. 'Surely you do something else, something special we don't know about?' But there were no magic ingredients, other than ritual, tradition and purpose. They'd always done it that way and it had been successful, so why change things?

But Kenny Dalglish's dramatic resignation as Liverpool manager in February 1991 set into motion a spiral of appointments and events that would eventually lead to a period of change from which the club has yet to fully recover. Under Shankly, Bob Paisley, Joe Fagan and Dalglish, Liverpool had become the most successful club in English football, and one of the most feared in Europe. They had won four European Cups, two UEFA Cups, and countless League championships, League Cups and FA Cups. It had seemed that the conveyor belt of honours would go on for ever. Even the traumas of Heysel and Hillsborough had failed to upset the continuity of success. Until Dalglish resigned. But you could hardly blame him for what was to happen. Dalglish had quit the club suffering from exhaustion and stress, mostly brought on by the aftermath of the Hillsborough disaster.

Into the breach stepped Dalglish's number two and lifelong Liverpool bootroom boy Ronnie Moran, but it was to be only a brief sojourn. There was little support among the board members for a formal offer to be made to Moran. He'd been overlooked in the past when Dalglish stepped up, and as the late Sydney Moss argued when he was vice-chairman, 'if Moran had really wanted the job we would have given it to him, but he wasn't biting our hands off'. Results during his brief reign were also mixed. In hindsight, had Liverpool stuck with Moran, the next twenty years might have turned out very differently.

There was little doubt who everybody fancied as the new manager. The name of former Liverpool midfielder Graeme Souness had been suggested from the start. Souness was not only an insider like his predecessors, he had also proved himself as a successful manager at a top club. Who could possibly be more appropriate? What's more, he would have Ronnie Moran and reserve-team coach Roy Evans to support him. After leaving Liverpool to join Sampdoria, Souness had returned home in 1986 to take charge of the ailing Scottish giants Rangers. Having spent years in the doldrums, Rangers were dramatically revitalised by Souness and went on to win three Scottish League championships and four cups over the next five seasons. Souness was a winner. You only had to look at the way he played, and the way in which he had broken the mould of Scottish soccer, and in particular the sectarianism of Glasgow football. He had signed a Catholic player, Mo Johnston, when he was supposed to be on the verge of joining arch-rivals Celtic. Johnston was the first known Catholic to sign for the ultra-Protestant Rangers, but Souness didn't care if he was bucking history, nor did he care if people at Rangers didn't like it. He had also gone out and sensationally signed a number of English players, beginning with the England number two keeper Chris Woods and the national side's most inspirational player Terry Butcher. Others would follow as Souness battled to transform Rangers from a provincial Protestant institution into a cosmopolitan European football club.

Initially, Souness denied any interest in the Liverpool job. He still had work to do at Ibrox, and still had three years left on his contract. Word seeped down from Glasgow that he wasn't looking to move, so the Liverpool directors began to look elsewhere. John Toshack, the club's former striker, was reported as being high on their wanted list, and another name appeared in one or two papers: Gérard Houllier.

Peter Robinson, the then chief executive of Liverpool, had known Houllier for years; in 1985 Robinson had even recommended the Frenchman to Irving Scholar at Tottenham Hotspur as a prospective manager. Robinson had told Scholar that he knew Houllier well and felt that he was just the kind of man who would do well in English football. He was intelligent, spoke good English and was well acclimatised to the English way of life. 'He'll do a good job for Spurs,' Robinson had asserted. Scholar agreed, and an offer was subsequently made to Houllier, but by then he had joined Paris St Germain as team manager and was lost to English football. 'I didn't think I was ready,' he reflected. 'At least for the time being.' A year later, Peter Robinson invited Houllier to Anfield to watch a game along with another French manager, Arséne Wenger, both of whom come 2001 would be leading out their respective sides in an FA Cup final. By the time of his visit, Houllier had already led Paris St Germain to their first ever French title and become hot property. He was even pencilled in by Juventus as a possible new manager.

Robinson had remained friends with Houllier, and they'd met from time to time at various European football functions. As Liverpool searched around for a replacement for Dalglish, Robinson once more remembered his old friend, arguing that Houllier had the necessary qualities to lead Liverpool through a difficult period. Yes, he said, it would be a daring and adventurous appointment, but if they couldn't get Souness, who else would fit the bill? It was true there was no other obvious successor, certainly in the English game, and the only possible internal candidate was Roy Evans who had had no experience at such a senior level. No matter who they chose, it would always be something of a gamble.

It was a convincing argument, but a phone call to Houllier soon knocked it on the head. Houllier had not long been in his post as a coach with the French Football Federation; he wanted to wait until after the 1994 World Cup before he returned to club football, he told Robinson. There was a huge job to be done, and it was a task he felt he had to see through, especially as so much of it depended on nurturing a youth system designed not just to reap rewards in 1994 but to provide a steady flow of young French footballing talent for the foreseeable future. Houllier's role in this scheme was crucial, and not surprisingly it was something he wished to remain a part of until after the finals.

In the event, of course, Souness changed his mind. After a few days of thinking it over he decided that he had had enough of Scottish football with its then insular attitude. He was forever being hauled before the Scottish FA for one misdemeanour or another, and he realised that he was never going to achieve any kind of European success when your season's only major domestic fixtures were against one club, Celtic. English football offered so many more challenges, and to return to Anfield was an offer he could not in the end refuse.

Souness duly arrived at Anfield in April 1991 in a flurry of publicity, and began to survey the scene. Unsurprisingly, not much had changed since his days there. The bootroom was still there, with the same old faces. The training routine was much the same, too: a few gentle laps of Melwood, some sprinting, maybe some work on the boards, a little shooting practice and then the traditional five-a-side game. After that it was back to Anfield on the bus for a bath and a bite to eat. Even the food in the canteen was the same, and not always the healthiest. Fish and chips were bought by the manager on the coach home after an away game. It was as if he'd hardly been away.

But Souness was very much his own man, and unlike many of those at Anfield he had seen and experienced different methods and styles of management on the continent. As manager at Rangers he'd begun to adopt some of these new methods as well as instilling different ideas and attitudes into his players. Souness was not so stuck in the Liverpool traditions to believe that it was the only possible way things could be done. During Liverpool's five-year ban from Europe following the Heysel tragedy of 1985, the club had been overtaken in its thinking by the leading continental clubs who had developed new styles of play and training. It was obvious that as soon as Souness arrived at Anfield things were going to change.

The first public indication of this was the fact that he brought with him his assistant Phil Boersma. Boersma might have briefly played for Liverpool at the same time as Souness, but essentially he was a new face in the hallowed bootroom. Even Shankly had not brought anybody with him when he arrived at Anfield; it had always been a case in the bootroom of someone stepping up from one job to another. Roy Evans was the only person who could really have been classed as a 'new boy', and he had simply moved from playing staff to coaching staff. When Boersma walked into the bootroom everybody felt slightly uncomfortable and wondered if their own roles were being challenged. Would Boersma exclusively have the ear of the manager?

In time there would be many other changes, some for the better, some not so welcome. Training became more considered and regulated, and Melwood was transformed so that there was no need to travel back to Anfield to bathe and change. New dietary restrictions were imposed, too. 'Meat pies were suddenly off the menu,' Ian Rush recalled. Roy Evans was supportive of the changes. 'Graeme came in and he changed one or two things. We started to move the whole complex to Melwood. Anfield was getting improved and the bootroom itself was demolished. Graeme takes a lot of criticism that things changed dramatically when he got here. Some of the training routine was slightly different, but training routines have to change otherwise you can end up living in the past.'

Of more importance were the personnel changes. Out went a generation of legends including Peter Beardsley, Bruce Grobbelaar, Steve Staunton, Gary Gillespie, Steve McMahon, Gary Ablett, Barry Venison and Ray Houghton, many of whom had given long and sterling service to the club. Souness claimed they were too old, but though some of them were 30 or approaching it, they had plenty of energy left in their legs and would still be plying their trade in the top division several years later. Jan Molby was around Anfield during those early Souness years and thought that players were coming and going far too quickly. 'He made Mark Wright his first or second signing, shortly followed by Torben Piechnik, because he didn't fancy Gary Ablett. We had Ablett, Gary Gillespie and Glenn Hysen already at Anfield but he didn't fancy them, he wanted his own people in. Mark Wright proved to be OK, but they were always playing catch-up. The same thing happened when Nigel Clough was brought in – Peter Beardsley went. It wasn't a case of "Nigel might need a bit of time, let's play Peter".' John Barnes also thought Souness made his decisions too quickly, solely on the basis of 'four or five matches', and Roy Evans, too, criticised his eagerness, 'instead of looking at it and saying, "Yes, we'll change it gradually, maybe get a better quality of player in." But he tried, and I've never seen a man so distraught at not being successful.'

Souness sold a total of eighteen players for a cumulative sum of £12 million, but taking their places were a new bunch of players, many of whom were inferior to those they were intended to replace. In Souness's opinion, the team was just not tough enough; it needed to reflect his own determined character. So in came the likes of Neil Ruddock and Julian Dicks, two noted hard men unafraid to 'put the boot in' when necessary. The changes were designed to bring a new edge and freshness to the team; instead, they brought instability, confusion and misunderstanding. The players seemed barely to recognise one another. The natural telepathy displayed by previous Liverpool teams disappeared. There were some notable signings, such as Rob Jones, Mark Wright and Dean Saunders, but there were many that were not so clever. Dicks, Mark Walters, Istvan Kozma, Paul Stewart and Torben Piechnik, for example, were players who never deserved to wear the red of Liverpool. On the field the team struggled – not horribly, but by the club's high standards even second place was considered a disaster. In Souness's time at Anfield the side finished sixth in successive years. The only silverware he ever had to show was the 1992 FA Cup.

In many ways it was a clash of cultures and personalities. Souness was not always the easiest of people to get on with. He was uncompromising, determined, sure of his own destiny. He had seen it all before, and done it all. He had won European Cups, League championships, had even played in the World Cup finals. At his height he was probably the finest midfielder in European football, if not world football. On the pitch he had few equals, and although that alone is never a recipe for success as a manager, at least he could point to the medals and honours he had won in the game. That certainly demanded respect.

But at the same time he was feeling his way back into English football. Success in Scotland was no qualification for or guarantee of success in England. Rangers might have been hugely successful in Scottish terms and Souness might have won League titles with them, but he had not experienced English football since leaving for Sampdoria in June 1984, seven long years before he took up the reins at Anfield. What Souness had not realised was that English football had changed. It was not quite as simple as it used to be. It was now far more competitive.

For all his faults, Souness was a man with open eyes, always ready to face challenges. His two years in Italy had widened his horizons and taught him to respect other cultures and ways. He was not a man to sit in his Italian villa, eating fish and chips and yearning for English beer and Mars bars; he was always someone who would try to immerse himself in the local culture, be he in Liverpool, Glasgow or Genoa. The problem at Anfield was that Souness could not understand why his players did not have the same vision, commitment and determination to win as he'd had. Brian Hall found him alone in the dressing room one afternoon, head in his hands. Hall asked him what was wrong. 'I just don't understand it,' Souness replied. 'They don't seem to have the same hunger to win as you and I did.'

Hall retains a high regard for Souness. 'Out of all the people I've worked with, there's nobody who tried harder than Graeme to be successful, but it just didn't happen for him,' he said. 'He was impetuous, I have to say that, in his early days, but only because he wanted to be successful. If he had two or three players he didn't fancy in our squad, he'd want them out immediately, and sometimes you just can't do that. Sometimes I used to drive away from the games and I used to feel for him, I used to worry about him going away. He looked so very sad. He had nowhere to go, and that was a worry. Of course he had problems with his heart. Again, he was the bravest man in the world to carry on through that, and you have to remember that we did actually win the cup with Graeme in charge.'

Oddly enough, it was Souness's off-the-field changes that contributed most to his downfall in early 1994. In line with the Taylor Report, following the Hillsborough disaster, the order went out to tear down the terraces. And so the Kop, perhaps the greatest terracing in world football, was demolished and replaced by an all-seater stand. It was inevitable, and given that the disaster had involved Liverpool it was right that the club should institute the change without any opposition, but tearing down the Kop would always be associated with Souness. 'Shankly would never have allowed it; he'd have been lying on the road in front of the bulldozers' was the myth fans liked to believe. The legendary bootroom, home of so many vital discussions and decisions over the years, also went, ripped down in order to build a new press centre for Euro 96. You couldn't blame Souness for these changes, but as the team struggled, inevitably he got the blame for everything.

'Yes, Graeme got the blame for that as well,' admitted Peter Robinson, 'but others were involved. It was the same when we decided to stop bringing the players back to Anfield every day after training. We thought it would be better for the players to report directly to Melwood each day and to train and be fed there rather than to ride up and down in an old coach. At the time I don't think anyone in the club was opposed to that change. It just suited certain journalists to label Graeme and blame everything on him.' Melwood's upgrading did have its supporters within Anfield, and one of those was Roy Evans. 'It needed to be done,' he said. 'It was far more sensible and far more realistic and gave the players a chance to have lunch and, for those who wanted to, do a little bit more in the afternoon, do anything you wanted to do. Whereas if you were bussing them up and down it was a pain in the arse.'

Nevertheless, even current assistant manager Phil Thompson was shocked when the bootroom came down. 'You could feel it when they were knocking it down, you could feel it. I had gone by then, but shivers went down my spine. They should have done it like the London Bridge when it went to America. They should have taken it down brick by brick, numbered them and then transferred it to the other side. It wouldn't have been the same, but it could have been pretty similar. It was a very sad day, but life goes on I suppose. There were a lot of changes with moving down here to Melwood, but that was progress.'

Although most fans would never have been aware of any variation in the methods of training, once players suddenly started to miss games through injury questions were asked about that, too. For years Liverpool players never seemed to get injured. Partly that was because Shankly disliked players being injured and would shun them. He expected his charges to act like 'men' and to walk through the pain barrier. And mostly they did, although often to their own detriment in later life. Again, the charge was that these changes to the age-old routine were to blame for the rise in the injury rate. The cooling down on the bus back to Anfield had gone, and Souness had installed new weight machines and placed an emphasis on muscle building. Whether or not these factors contributed to the problem is a matter of conjecture, but, again, it was Souness who had introduced these changes so it was all his fault.

And then there was the heart attack. It had already begun to seem as if Liverpool managers were fated. Bill Shankly had left on the spur of the moment, Joe Fagan had quit after only two years, Dalglish had resigned as stress led to a nervous breakdown. Souness's heart attack and subsequent bypass surgery probably won him some sympathy, but that was dispersed by his article in the *Sun* in April 1992. For many Liverpool fans that was the crucial turning point in their relationship with the Scotsman. It was, after all, the *Sun* that had made outrageous allegations about Liverpool fans following the Hillsborough tragedy. Copies of the paper had been burnt in the streets, sales of the paper on Merseyside had plummeted, and in the city the newspaper became known as the *Scum*. For Souness suddenly to detail the story of his heart problems in this most vilified of tabloid rags was unforgivable. From that point on, Souness was irreparably damaged. Even a public apology was not enough.

There was also the bitter row between Souness and reserve-team coach Phil Thompson which resulted in the latter's sacking.

The former Liverpool defender had been appointed by Dalglish, and his dismissal did not go down well with most Kopites who saw a little of themselves in Thompson, a fervent scouser with a passion for Liverpool who had once been a Kop regular. As far as the public were concerned Thompson appeared to be doing an excellent job, and his sacking was interpreted as another illogical and impulsive decision by Souness.

Backstage, it was clear there was dressing-room discontent, something that had not been known at Anfield since the 1950s. Liverpool had never been a club for washing its dirty linen in public, but suddenly there were murmurings around the city. More than a few tea cups were being thrown, and some recently transferred players even went public with their grievances. Add all these problems to a run of poor results in the first half of the 1993/94 season and the inevitable outcome was the parting of the ways with Souness. But even then, it did not come easy. In the boardroom, there were split loyalties. At one point the directors took a decision to sack Souness, then changed their minds. The 'has he gone or hasn't he gone' debate lingered for a day until it was announced that Souness had in fact survived and would continue as manager. Then, in the wake of that turnaround, there was a split on the board that resulted in one director resigning. As a concession to the malcontents, coach Roy Evans was appointed assistant manager. That in itself was not a surprise; it was part of the deal, a compromise with Souness. Evans, the down-to-earth scouser, would balance the more impulsive Souness. The real surprise was that Souness was still there.

But it wasn't long before even that arrangement fell apart. Humiliation in the FA Cup at Anfield at the hands of Bristol City was one defeat too far, and at the end of January 1994 Souness's tenure as manager of Liverpool ended. It had been a turbulent few years. One trophy had been won, but Liverpool's dominance of English football had been squandered. They might never exactly have flirted with relegation, but any challenge for the title had rarely, if ever, materialised. The team had been torn apart and replaced by a side showing few of the qualities of its many predecessors.

Souness had gambled, and lost. He had decided that the club needed restructuring from top to bottom, but his radical ideas clashed with the traditionalists who argued on the lines of 'if it ain't broke, don't fix it'. In many ways, however, Souness was right. As former player David Fairclough remarked, 'I don't think Liverpool or English clubs were aware of what was going on on the continent. Liverpool have this attitude that we are Liverpool, we are the best, why should we change things, we've won trophies. We were always tempting fate.' Souness might have had the right ideas, but still, his methods of implementing them probably left something to be desired. He failed to win support for his ideas, and to carry others with him. In particular, many of the players he signed were not as good as those he sold. Had it worked on the field, he would have had no problem in convincing everyone that changes were necessary, but failure on the pitch made it all the more difficult for him. He had gone in for a radical restructuring at Anfield – indeed, it was almost certainly necessary – but there were few signs anywhere that it was working.

For some months before Souness's departure the call had been going out in favour of getting back to basics. Liverpool needed to rediscover the formula that had served them so well in the past. Somewhere along the line things had gone awry, and it was surely only a matter of time before it could be put right, especially with Roy Evans stepping into the limelight to take over. Evans was a safe proposition. He had been at Anfield all his adult life. Born and bred in Liverpool, he had been an England schoolboy international before signing schoolboy terms and then professional forms with the club. He'd made his debut for Liverpool as a full-back in September 1969, but his playing career was sadly cut short after just eleven appearances in 1973 following a serious injury. It had looked like the end of the road for him, but then, much to his surprise, Bill Shankly invited him to join the coaching staff. It hadn't taken Evans much time to make a decision, and by the time he took over as manager of the club he had twenty years' loyal service under his belt.

In July 1974, shortly after Evans joined the bootroom, to everyone's surprise Shankly quit. Instead of looking outside for a successor, the club decided to appoint from within, and Shankly's number two Bob Paisley found himself promoted to the top job, a job he had neither sought nor desired. As a consequence, Evans moved up a rung on the ladder. The same thing happened when Joe Fagan took over in May 1983, and under Kenny Dalglish (1985–91) he continued to serve the club in whatever capacity the manager wished. During those seventeen years there were few changes to the personnel in the bootroom. Phil Thompson had joined under Dalglish after Chris Lawler was sacked, and chief scout Geoff Twentyman was also sacked by Dalglish and replaced by Ron Yeats, but the biggest changes were made under Souness. Even then the continuity was maintained through Ronnie Moran, Roy Evans and ex-headmaster, now director, Tom Saunders.

The promotion of Roy Evans to manager came as no surprise, although yet again other names were mentioned, including, once more, that of Gérard Houllier. But there was only ever going to be one appointment, and it was Evans, the bootroom boy who had so steadfastly stood by whoever was in charge, always eager to help in whatever way he could. Evans was red through and through, a former Kopite turned player, and could surely be trusted to ease the club back to its winning ways. The fans, the directors, everyone craved a return to the evolutionary style that had suited the club so well over the previous three decades.

As ever, Evans was more than willing to take on whatever role the club deemed necessary, be it tea-boy, coach or manager. There was no haggling over salary, and it is doubtful he was ever paid as well as Graeme Souness. Still, no one was putting any pressure on the new manager to deliver trophies within any given period, though there was clearly an expectation that the silverware would soon be returning to Anfield. The club would be trying to get back to basics at a time when football was going through its most radical changes ever. While Liverpool were eagerly rediscovering the methods and philosophies of the 1960s, the game was taking up the challenge of the forthcoming twenty-first century.

The old Football League Division One had disappeared in 1992 and been replaced by the Premier League. Live television coverage had also arrived, bringing with it bucketfuls of cash. Off the field, new all-seater stadia were springing up with corporate facilities and dining areas; on the field, salaries and transfer fees soared, and super-rich foreign players flooded in. Suddenly, the English football set-up was comparable to those in Spain, Italy, France and

Germany. Money was no object; the stars of European football were just as likely to sell their services to England as anywhere. This culture of change drove the game forward quickly. More than ever, football was about being successful.

Evans made an encouraging start in the closing months of the 1993/94 season, but problems soon became apparent. His sixteen League games that season brought five wins and nine defeats, and by May Liverpool had conceded 55 goals, the same as the previous season, a far cry from the paltry sixteen let through during the 1978/79 season. They finished in eighth spot, their lowest position for 30 years. It was clear that new blood was desperately needed, but to everyone's astonishment there were no summer signings and barely any selling.

Evans was busy with his first task: to instil in his players a sense of loyalty, the age-old principle of the bootroom. After the turbulent years under Souness, stability was desperately needed; players had to know where they stood. A poor run of form was no longer a good enough reason for dropping a player. But there were limits to this policy in the Premier League environment, and at times Evans would have been far better off leaving a player out or claiming that he had an injury. Put simply, far too much loyalty was shown when perhaps a good kick up the backside might have been more effective.

Evans's greatest problem was his defence. A long-term injury to Mark Wright created problems, and Neil Ruddock was never really up to the task. There were moments when he showed international class, but he was never in the same league as a Hansen, a Lawrenson or a Yeats. Evans began a search for a new central defender, but none was forthcoming. 'It was my biggest downfall,' he claimed. 'Getting central defenders was a problem. The availability at that time was difficult. We tried to get Laurent Blanc, and others we tried to get were Matt Elliott and [Jurgen] Kohler. We knew that if we could stop the aerial stuff we could win it because our goals-for was so good. But we just couldn't get anyone. They either weren't available or wanted a lot of money, and with Liverpool being out of it, we couldn't tempt them any more. Everyone wanted to go to Manchester United, and for less money, because there was the chance of being successful. The lad we really tried to get was Blanc, but in the end he wouldn't come and instead went to Italy. I'm convinced that had he joined us we would have gone on to win the League.'

At least Evans had identified a central defender who would undoubtedly have made a huge impact and might well have been the catalyst for success. It was true that in the mid-1990s there generally seemed to be a dearth of available and capable central defenders in Europe, and money wasn't the problem. At the time Liverpool could match most clubs in terms of finances, but those who were worth looking at either didn't fancy a move to the Premiership or were simply not for sale.

In 1994/95 Liverpool continued to leak goals at an alarming rate. The ever-changing back four did not operate as a unit, looking alarmed every time the ball was lobbed in their direction. David James didn't help either. The tall, athletic-looking keeper rarely looked confident when crosses came over, and his nervousness spread to the rest of the team. On his line, James was excellent, as good as any keeper in the top flight, but when it came to corners and crosses there were huge question marks over his ability. Instead of barging his way out of goal to take charge of the situation, he stood frozen to the spot. 'He might be six foot four inches, but he just isn't brave enough,' snapped the former Liverpool keeper Tommy Lawrence. Nobody seemed sure of who should be doing what in the defence, to the extent that every time there was a corner or a cross into the box, there was visible panic. The vast majority of goals conceded came from crossed balls.

But things improved, and Liverpool finished the season in fourth spot; they'd even challenged briefly at the top of the table. Some players were sold, and others, especially centre-back Neil Ruddock, looked rejuvenated; the signing of Phil Babb after an outstanding World Cup had added some steel to the defence. There was success, too, when Evans led the team out at Wembley for the Coca-Cola Cup final against Bolton Wanderers, won inspiringly by Liverpool's pencil-thin young winger Steve McManaman. Other talents also emerged from the youth ranks, such as Robbie Fowler, and young signing Jamie Redknapp was called into the England squad.

By the summer of 1995 it seemed that Liverpool had finally shrugged off the trauma and instability of the Souness years, and when a record £8.5 million was paid for the services of Stan Collymore, there was considerable optimism around Anfield. Sadly, it was not to be fully realised. Come the end of the 1995/96 Premiership campaign they were in third place, showing huge improvement but still some way short of the standards set by Manchester United. There was a chance for revenge on 11 May when they faced United in the FA Cup final at Wembley in front of 79,000 fans, but United proved marginally superior, Eric Cantona's goal securing them a famous double in one of the dourest games Wembley has ever staged. Liverpool left the pitch to empty terraces and a distinct feeling that the players had watched rather than participated in a cup final. It was no surprise to see a number of Liverpool scarves hurled at the players as they sloped shamefully down the tunnel.

The problem was that while the team could pass the ball every bit as well as Liverpool teams of the past, they seemed at the same time unable to progress. The ball would wend its way from one side of the pitch to the other, then back again, before ending up with the keeper. Then it would be repeated. They could hold possession for as long as they willed, and often the opposition was happy to sit back and let them pass the ball to death, but they could never advance far into the final third of the pitch, and rarely into the penalty area. They seemed bereft of ideas, lacking inspiration and showing no aptitude for taking a gamble. Players were incapable of taking the ball into the thick of a defence, of taking on players. And this despite having skilled wingers such as Steve McManaman and John Barnes. At times McManaman was the worst offender as he dribbled from one side of the pitch to the other, while Barnes, once the scourge of the Maracana, had taken up a role as sweeper operating behind the midfield but in front of the back four. Most of the time he played with his back to the opposition's goal and simply passed back to his own defenders.

'We didn't try to change much,' Evans said. 'We had a back three at one stage which with the personnel we had I thought would work. It did for a couple of seasons, but when it didn't work we got highly criticised and we were almost forced to go back to four.' In the business it was sometimes known as the Christmas Tree formation: goalkeeper, three centre-backs, Barnes ahead of them, then two wing-backs and two central midfielders, and finally two up front. At the time it was relatively popular, but it did require a couple of wing-backs who were capable of breaking down the opposition. Unfortunately, Liverpool did not really have two natural wing-backs anywhere near capable of performing at that level. All the opposition had to do was swamp the midfield and cut off the supply route to the front two, and with Liverpool employing only two in the centre of the midfield, this was not too difficult. The result was despairing, crablike football that won few friends and few matches.

But there's always next season. Unfortunately, record signing Stan Collymore proved to be a key disappointment. His early appearances promised much, his pace and shooting ability as good as any in the Premiership, but it wasn't long before he began to look overwhelmed by his task. 'At the time my form was quite good,' he reflected, 'and then I was asked to play in the reserves, and it was just a point of principle really that I refused to play in the game . . . I should have just got on and played the game and used that as a way of making my protest by sticking a couple of goals in.' But he didn't, and resentment towards him began to grow around Anfield. There was a feeling that he wasn't being treated the same as everybody else. Others were expected to toe the line, but Collymore was an independent spirit who could do as he wished.

You could almost see the confidence draining from Collymore's body as the months went by. By spring 1997 he was a mere shadow of the player he had been. At the root of it there were personal problems involving illness at home and a reluctance to move to Merseyside. That much was understandable, and Evans generously made as many concessions as he could to alleviate the situation, but he perhaps made one too many and Collymore began to skip training, often without informing the club. 'The discipline was reasonable,' Evans recalled. 'He and Robbie [Fowler] as a partnership were good. Had there not been the problems off the pitch they would have been as good as anything around. The discipline with Stan was because he wouldn't move and he didn't turn up for training on numerous occasions. Then the rest of the lads said, "Well, he's not here, what are we doing?"

It set us back a good twelve months or eighteen months. The lads were all at an age when they were still young and impressionable. The younger lads lost a bit of team spirit through that, unfortunately, and that's one thing we always had at the club.'

One of Evans's greatest strengths was his loyalty, and in his early days as manager it was indeed vital. He was not one to publicly criticise players, nor was he one to drop them. If a player was going through a bad spell Evans would stick resolutely by him and continue to select him. And so it was with Collymore. Stories leaked out of Anfield that all was not well, that Collymore was getting favourable treatment, and as time progressed and the side failed to make significant headway it became clear that changes were needed. Sadly, Evans failed to make them. He was also loath to introduce substitutes, preferring instead to let his starting eleven battle on regardless. There were times when games were crying out for fresh legs or different tactics, but they were never forthcoming. It all became too predictable.

Jan Molby thought Evans's foremost failure was in the transfer market. 'When he went and spent big money, he was umming and aahing a little bit. I think he got it wrong with a lot of the signings he made. Babb and [John] Scales were his first two signings. He spent £8 million on those two centre-backs. It was not particularly good business. Then Collymore and [Oyvind] Leonhardsen arrived, people who proved to be disappointments when he needed them to be spot on. He was great working with the players that were there. He got the maximum out of the players. But when he had to go and buy two players to maybe make us champions, that's when he failed.'

Throughout the 1996/97 season Collymore was overshadowed by young Robbie Fowler who netted 29 goals in all competitions and became the second highest goal scorer in the Premiership. With a young side and a meaner defence, despite many lacklustre showings there was a discernible feeling that things could only get better. For all the problems and criticisms, Evans, it seemed, was beginning to turn things around. There might still be visible problems on the field and signs of slackness off it, but there was little doubt that Evans had improved matters since the dark days of Souness. There was certainly a warmer, happier atmosphere inside Anfield and around Melwood. One last push and Liverpool would surely return to their rightful place in English football.

But the murmurings continued to grow as the 1997/98 campaign progressed. At times it seemed that far too many Liverpool players were being played out of position. Jason McAteer, a midfielder, was being played at right-back; Phil Babb, a central defender, was appearing at left-back; winger John Barnes was starring as a sweeper; and Steve McManaman, another old-fashioned winger, was roaming undisciplined wherever he fancied. It was a justified criticism the manager would have to bear.

Around the boardroom, after almost every game, heads were being shaken. Everybody knew that really it was not working. Liverpool were admittedly winning games, but they were never in serious contention for the title. Gaining points was sometimes like wringing blood out of a stone. They might have finished in respectable positions in recent years, but the likes of Arsenal and Manchester United were in a different league. The youngsters promised much, but some of the players they had signed and moulded into the side seemed to fall short in key areas. The days when Liverpool represented the gold standard of English and European football were long gone. Manchester United were now the benchmark of Premiership football. They had floated on the stock exchange, sold more replica kits than any club in the world, could boast a lucrative souvenir market, and were making plans to enlarge their stadium to a 70,000 all-seater. They had executive boxes galore, rich sponsorship deals, and were attracting huge audiences and a healthy cash flow via appearances in the Champions League. Money was literally pouring into Old Trafford. In contrast, Liverpool were second best, competing in the less lucrative UEFA Cup, playing in a smaller stadium, and selling fewer souvenirs out of smaller outlets. Liverpool were still the corner shop when United had become a supermarket.

When the Liverpool board cast their eyes across at United it was with more than a glance of envy. The reshaping of the European Cup into the Champions League now meant that that competition was where it was at. It was clear that if you were not playing in the Champions League, you would not earn as much money. Less money meant less cash available for transfer fees and salaries, and not playing centre stage in Europe also meant that it was doubly difficult to attract the world's best players to Anfield. What was needed was not just changes on the pitch but a revolution, of sorts, off it. Liverpool needed to charge fully into the modern world if the club was to survive. 'It was time for fresh thoughts and ideas,' Brian Hall confirmed. 'We were slipping behind. Had we slipped much further it might have been unstoppable.'

Evans knew his position as manager was in question. The papers were full of it, especially the tabloids. The local press were more gracious and supportive, but they were still astute enough to recognise that Evans lacked that little extra to take the team to the top. But just as Evans had shown loyalty to his players, so the board stood by their manager, even when a tad more ruthlessness might have resolved matters earlier. For an honest, unvarnished view, you simply had to look at the fanzines. The most popular of them, *Through the Wind and Rain*, was scathing in a spring 1998 editorial: 'Frankly, I want it to end. There are another eight games to go, and I'm dreading all of them. We have spent the last two years kidding ourselves that there is any real greatness in this team . . . Almost every opportunity at gaining an advantage over our rivals has been squandered. If anything, things are worse than last season . . . The League place and similar problems at other clubs will be cited as evidence that Evans is still the right man, but in your heart of hearts, in your guts, do you honestly agree with that?'

Nobody wanted to sack Evans, least of all chairman David Moores, who had known him most of his life. It was Moores who had stood by Souness for an undue length of time, reluctant to sack him when many of those around him were thinking the opposite. It was to be much the same with Evans. The problem is that if you sack a manager you need to know who you're going to replace him with. When Souness was sacked his replacement was already on site, ready and willing to take over, but it was not the same now. If they dismissed Evans, who would replace him? There was talk of going outside Anfield, of finding someone with no previous connection to the club, someone who might bring in new ideas – mainly because inside Anfield the options were limited. Former manager Ronnie Moran, with only a short time left before retirement, was never a contender; nor, it seemed, was Doug Livermore, the official assistant manager, brought in by Evans. He was considered too low profile, more a number two than a number one. Steve Heighway, successfully managing the youngsters, was a possibility, but he had always indicated that he did not wish to become a manager and his experience was limited solely to bringing on the youth players. If he was to be considered he would first have to be more closely involved with the first team. Sammy Lee was also on the coaching staff, but he too was considered inexperienced. For once, an inside appointment was simply not an option.

But when you looked around the Premiership there were not too many obvious contenders for the post either. Martin O'Neill at Leicester City was one possibility, but he was still largely unproven, although what he was doing at Filbert Street was impressing many onlookers. Ruud Gullit was also in the frame. There were thoughts, too, about a return to Anfield for Kenny Dalglish, but after what had happened before some wondered if he might not find the strain too much again. The other two potential candidates were Kevin Keegan, whose exploits at Newcastle had excited so many, and, again, John Toshack, who at the time was managing on the continent. With Keegan, however, there was always a question mark over his emotional stability, and there seemed to be an antipathy to Toshack which went back many years.

In the event, nobody was prepared to do the decent thing and simply sack Evans. Moores and Robinson dithered, reluctant to plunge the knife into a man they genuinely liked, so the club was obliged to continue with Evans until another option presented itself.

3. A NO-WIN SITUATION

Robinson decided to put some feelers out, and gave Houllier a call. When Houllier took the call he assumed it was merely a case of Robinson ringing to congratulate him about Celtic. 'Well, you're being a little premature,' the Frenchman said. 'I haven't actually finalised anything yet, there's still a lot of talking to do. But yes, I need to sort something out for next season, and I am interested in Celtic. I've decided that once the World Cup is over I'll quit this job and return to club management.'

'Have you set your heart on Celtic?' asked Robinson.

'Not really,' Houllier replied. 'It's an interesting proposition, but there's a lot to think about.'

'But you'd be quite interested in managing abroad?' Robinson followed up, warming to his quest.

'Yes,' Houllier confirmed.

'Then there's only one club you can come to,' he suggested. 'Liverpool.'

As the 1997/98 season had dragged on, Peter Robinson had become increasingly convinced that Liverpool needed fresh input. The defence was looking more vulnerable than ever, and it was no longer a case of just United opening up the gulf in quality, as Arsenal had now come into the equation as well. Both sides were streets ahead of Liverpool. Evans's stewardship was being muttered about throughout Anfield; what was needed was not just a new face but someone with fresh ideas, someone who could take the club forward into the new millennium.

The team of the season was undoubtedly Arsenal, who clinched the title from United by just one point. Robinson had in particular been impressed with manager Arsène Wenger's approach at Highbury. Wenger had been appointed to the Arsenal job as recently as September 1996; within two years he had taken them to the top of the tree. He was a quiet, thoughtful man with no exceptional record as a player. As a manager in France he had taken Monaco to championship honours and into the Champions League, and he was now doing the same with Arsenal. He had introduced some Gallic flair and had coupled that with honest English endeavour to produce not only that season's champions but the FA Cup winners as well. It had been a remarkable double, inspired by a manager only twenty months into the job.

Equally impressive was Ruud Gullit at Chelsea. Since taking over at Stamford Bridge in 1996 the Dutchman had taken Chelsea into the higher reaches of the Premiership and had also won the FA Cup by playing fast, cultivated football. Like Wenger, he had bought well, signing Italian and French stars and providing a feast of international football for the Stamford Bridge faithful. Chelsea were now on a par with Liverpool, with many predicting that they too would go on to be champions within a season or two. Liverpool, for so long the nation's number one club, were now among the also-rans.

Robinson knew from talking to people at Highbury, however, that it had not always been easy for Wenger. In his early days he had had to overcome a considerable amount of traditionalist thinking, but the Frenchman had stuck to his job and in the end it had paid dividends. It had been a visionary decision by the Highbury board to bring him in, but an even braver one to support him when many were crying for his head. Wenger was just the kind of man Liverpool needed.

Robinson had remained friendly with Gérard Houllier. The two occasionally saw each other at European football conventions, or bumped into each other at various matches across the continent. Robinson would also call him from time to time, just to chat and see how he was. Reading his newspaper one morning, Robinson spotted that Celtic were in serious negotiations with Houllier, with a view to making him their new manager. Sheffield Wednesday were also supposed to have been considering him, but that possibility had now fallen through. The more likely destination for Houllier seemed to be Glasgow. It was clear from what he was reading that Houllier was now seriously considering his future and a return to club management. It was May 1998, and the World Cup finals were about to begin. Once they were over, Houllier would be a free agent.

In those same weeks the club had been discussing Ronnie Moran's impending retirement. It meant that Liverpool would be a man short on the coaching staff. Now, thought Robinson, was an ideal opportunity to introduce someone with new ideas, so he pencilled in Houllier's name alongside one or two others he had discussed with Roy Evans.

Robinson decided to put some feelers out, and gave Houllier a call. When Houllier took the call he assumed it was merely a case of Robinson ringing to congratulate him about Celtic. 'Well, you're being a little premature,' the Frenchman said. 'I haven't actually finalised anything yet, there's still a lot of talking to do. But yes, I need to sort something out for next season, and I am interested in

Celtic. I've decided that once the World Cup is over I'll quit this job and return to club management.'

'Have you set your heart on Celtic?' asked Robinson.

'Not really,' Houllier replied. 'It's an interesting proposition, but there's a lot to think about.'

'But you'd be quite interested in managing abroad?' Robinson followed up, warming to his quest.

'Yes,' Houllier confirmed.

'Then there's only one club you can come to,' he suggested. 'Liverpool.'

Houllier was slightly taken aback by this. It was the last thing he had expected. Still, he asked for a few more details, and Robinson began to explain the situation.

'So,' he concluded, 'would you be interested in coming to Anfield to work alongside Roy Evans, maybe in the same role you have with Aimé Jacquet in France?'

'I certainly would,' Houllier replied.

'Look, this is not a formal approach. I'd have to talk to others at Anfield and they might take some convincing, but if you can stall Celtic, I'll come back to you, hopefully with a formal offer, in a day or so.'

Robinson now had his work cut out, even though Houllier was no newcomer to Liverpool. He'd been there before, several times. One Liverpool-based football journalist remembered bumping into him in 1986. 'I recognised him in the corridors at Anfield one matchday. He had come with another man [Arsène Wenger] to visit his friend Peter Robinson and to appreciate a team that was always close to his heart. Houllier had just led Paris St Germain to their first championship, and given that I was only a few days away from starting my first job in the sports office of the *Liverpool Echo*, my reporting instincts told me that the story of the former schoolteacher would be a good way to kick off my new job.' Rick Parry also knew Houllier well. When Parry had been at the Premier League he'd become quite friendly with him. They, too, met from time to time at European conventions, and Houllier had offered Parry considerable help when Liverpool had decided to start up their own academy. The Frenchman had even shown him round the French academy at Clairefontaine.

Robinson now set about convincing everyone at Anfield that Houllier could do a job for them, but he had two problems. The first was that he was suggesting bringing in not just an Anfield outsider but a Frenchman as well. Talking the board around to that idea would be tricky enough, let alone the players. The second problem was his job title. It was clear that the mood of the board was firmly against getting rid of Evans. He had to be given more time, and although he had his critics, everyone appreciated his loyalty and decency. He had bravely stepped into the spotlight following the chaos of the Souness years and had reintroduced many of the traditional qualities associated with Liverpool. Although there had at one point been an appetite to sack him, the mood had now changed.

So in what capacity would Houllier best serve the club? Why not just make him a coach, suggested one boardroom insider; give him Ronnie Moran's old job. No, Robinson told them, that would not be right. Houllier had to have some authority, and anyhow, he was one of the world's top coaches. Director of football, then? That way he could make all the necessary changes without interfering in team decisions. On paper that looked fine, but, Robinson argued, it simply would not work. Houllier was a coach and had to be allowed access to the players. Working with players was what he was best at. There was also a big question mark over whether Roy Evans would accept anyone coming in at a higher level. Someone even suggested reversing the roles, making Evans director of football and Houllier manager in charge of the team. That might have been a more realistic possibility, but nobody favoured the idea. It was clear that if Evans was staying Houllier would have to come in as his equivalent. They would have to be joint managers.

A four-man delegation from Anfield quickly jetted off to Paris to meet up with Houllier. They were impressed. Houllier had an encyclopaedic knowledge of European football, he spoke several languages, and he seemed to know everyone. He knew the French, Spanish and Italian leagues inside out. There was no doubting that he talked a good game, but the question was, could he translate that on to the pitch?

Even if he could, the board members still had their doubts, foremost among them was how the players and fans would react.

After all, Gérard Houllier was hardly a name that tripped off the tongue. Wenger might be doing a magnificent job at Arsenal, but foreign coaches didn't always work. What about Christian Gross at Tottenham? Spurs had finished up in the relegation zone after his one year in charge, and the splendidly named Dr Jozef Venglos at Villa had been an unmitigated disaster. Houllier might be involved with France, but he was working behind the scenes and nobody was quite sure what his role or influence was. This could be one of the most crucial decisions in the club's history, said chairman David Moores, and we have to get it right. If we fail, we could find ourselves sliding headlong down the League and into oblivion. Just look at Everton, he joked.

'If you want someone with European experience, why not appoint a person who also has a Liverpool connection?' another director suggested. 'Such as John Toshack.' The former Liverpool striker did indeed have the ideal pedigree. He'd made his name at Anfield and had proved himself as a manager, taking Swansea City from the Fourth Division to the top of the old First Division. He had then managed Real Madrid, as well as a number of other Spanish and Portuguese clubs. Toshack's name had cropped up in connection with a job at Anfield numerous times in the past. 'It would certainly be more acceptable than a Frenchman who nobody has ever heard of,' he argued.

But Peter Robinson was totally opposed to the notion. Toshack's success at Swansea was more than fifteen years ago, he warned them. 'To appoint Toshack either as manager, joint manager or whatever would be a backwards step. We need to be looking forward. Remember that Houllier will have Evans beside him. That at least guarantees that nothing will change overnight. It's not as if we are actually sacking Evans and replacing him with Houllier. It's a neat compromise that should satisfy everyone.' The idea of joint managers might be an uncomfortable one, but one they could live with. His argument won the day.

Fortunately, by the time the Liverpool board were close to giving the go-ahead for a formal approach, France had lifted the World Cup with more than a little flair. Houllier's part in their triumph had not gone unnoticed and was being more than emphasised by Peter Robinson. All they had to do now was discuss it with Roy Evans.

Evans, understandably, was hardly delirious, but he was happy to go along with it. Yes, a man like Houllier might freshen things up, he agreed, and we do need someone like him. His main concern was Houllier's job title, but given that he was himself at the time sitting on a knife edge, he was hardly in a position to argue too heatedly. A meeting was set up so that the two men could discuss the idea.

The announcement of Houllier's appointment on Thursday, 16 July 1998 came as something of a surprise. Nobody had anticipated it, and when the news first broke there was an immediate assumption that Evans was on his way. It had been a difficult couple of years for the manager and nobody would have been too shocked had he resigned, or been dismissed. But no, far from it, Evans was staying. At the press conference at Anfield to announce their new partnership Evans put on a brave face, smiled, and announced that although it was the chairman's idea, he was fully behind it. 'I have not been demoted,' he said. 'There is no question of that at all, and I'm very upbeat about my position here. If I had felt the club wanted someone else to be manager I would have said, "Fine, I'll walk away." But it wasn't like that at all.' Both Houllier's vast experience in Europe and his wide knowledge of players would be of invaluable help in the campaign to win the League title, he told the throng of journalists who had gathered half-expecting a dramatic change of management. 'The board,' he continued, 'has involved me in all discussions and I assured them I thought it was a good idea that could benefit the club. Things will continue as they were, we'll just have someone else throwing in ideas.' He even revealed that he'd had a couple of meetings with Houllier, and that there was no doubt in his mind that they 'shared the same philosophy'.

But when it came to the inevitable questions about who would make the final decision in team selection and so forth, both men were more than coy. Houllier sat alongside Evans and David Moores looking slightly embarrassed, clearly not certain as to how the partnership would work out in this respect, though he certainly wasn't going to admit it. He peered through his glasses, then spoke in perfect English. 'The reason Liverpool asked me to come was because aspects of their preparation needed changing.

When the game changes, as football has in the last few years, your preparation has to change too. In football you are never sure to succeed, but I am absolutely convinced you will fail if you do not do the right things.' He then tried to douse the flames by saying, 'I told Roy I wanted to come but only as long as he worked alongside me,' but plenty of sceptics remained.

The following morning's newspapers led the questioning. Who was going to be the real boss? Who would choose the team? Who would decide tactics? Who would make substitutions? Who would make transfer decisions? Who would take training? And surely, wondered one leading football writer, 'isn't Gérard Houllier far too intelligent to ever work as a joint manager? He is his own man.' Football columnist Des Kelly said pretty much the same thing, though maybe a little more forcefully, in the *Daily Mirror*: 'Abraham Lincoln's prospects were brighter when he went to collect his theatre tickets. And he was assassinated before he finished his popcorn. How anyone thinks that two men can assume joint control of a football club like Liverpool beggars belief. The split might not come in a week, perhaps not in a month. But it will come.'

Despite all the suggestions and explanations, the reason why Houllier ever accepted the role of joint manager in the first place remains puzzling. For a man who has written so eloquently about leadership and management, he must surely have realised it was a role that would never work. Houllier believes strongly that the manager is like a general leading his troops, yet here was the same man taking on a task against all his principles. Two generals leading the same army, and each with opposing views. It might have been Liverpool, a club dear to him, he was coming to, but it remains inexplicable that he should have accepted such working conditions. Not for Jan Molby, though. 'I think it was the only way he could get his hands on the job. He wanted to be manager of Liverpool, of that I'm sure, but the initial terms of the job were that he had to be joint manager. So he was prepared to come as joint manager knowing full well what would happen.' Of course, it is possible that he might have foreseen such a scenario and assumed that the crown would eventually be handed to him, but that seems too far-fetched a theory. The partnership might work, but just as likely were bad or indifferent times and a players' revolt against the outsider. Could it have been Peter Robinson who'd privately mapped out the scenario outlined by Molby: we'll give Evans six months, and if it hasn't worked he'll be gone and you'll take over? Again, it seems unlikely, and it would be reckless and hopeful to say the least for anyone to accept a job on such a basis.

All the evidence suggests that partnerships in management do not work. The best-known example in defence of the proposition is Brian Clough and Peter Taylor, but in the end they had argued and gone their separate ways; even during their years of success there was never any doubting whose was the most influential voice. Liverpool-born multi-millionaire businessman Steve Morgan, one of the largest shareholders in Liverpool Football Club, felt all along that Liverpool had made the wrong decision. 'Having two bosses like Evans and Houllier is an absolute disaster. You cannot ever have two bosses, whatever business you're in. It was just a dumb, stupid decision to bring two people in. There can only be one boss. You can work as a team, you can have two people working side by side, but there has to be one person with overall responsibility. You can have split responsibilities, but there has to be one man in charge, otherwise you get people playing off one against the other.' Molby, who hadn't long left the playing staff at Anfield, was equally critical. He knew Evans well, and perhaps spoke with more insight than anyone. 'I'm convinced that when it comes down to it there will have to be one of them with the final say.' He then added, with some intuition, 'I can see it being Houllier.' Molby had read the signs and clearly knew that Evans's days were numbered.

But there was another argument. The Liverpool bootroom had always been a democratic body where everyone was encouraged to throw their twopenn'orth in to any discussion, whether it was about players, team selection, tactics, injuries, new signings or whatever. In essence, Liverpool had evolved a system of joint managership long before anyone else, and the Evans–Houllier axis would be no different.

But, of course, it was. The truth was that Roy Evans was sceptical as well. In public he put on a brave face and told the cameras that they would get along fine, that Houllier was a world-class coach who would bring new ideas to the club, but privately he wondered how such a partnership was going to operate. None of the essential details questioned by the press had really been worked out. Even if they had been, it was all very well saying that this person would do this and that person would do that, but in reality the situation was fraught with dilemmas. Evans had let Moores and Robinson talk him into it, perhaps against his better judgement.

Although he had met Houllier on a couple of occasions, Evans barely knew the man. That in itself was not a good starting point for a partnership. Although Evans had gone along with the idea, Houllier was in effect being foisted upon him; there's no guessing as to what would have happened had Evans categorically vetoed Houllier's appointment. He didn't really want Houllier, even though he admitted that the Frenchman might be able to bring some new ideas. When Evans had been appointed in 1994 he had himself brought in an outsider in Doug Livermore, who had coached under Terry Venables at Spurs. But at least Livermore had once been at Liverpool as a player. Nobody on the playing staff at Anfield knew anything about Houllier. He was a mystery man. Houllier as a coach, he reckoned, might have been a possibility, but as an equal it was only ever going to cause confusion. But that's what the board wanted, so they simply had to get on with it.

What's more, Houllier had also managed to secure the board's agreement to the introduction of a new French coach. That man was an old friend of his, Patrice Bergues. 'Just after the World Cup, Gérard Houllier asked me if I would go with him to Liverpool,' Bergues said. 'At that time I wasn't considering a new job because I had only been with the French FA for a short time and had given no thought to looking for a different role in football.' However, the chance to move abroad and coach at Liverpool was simply too good an offer for Bergues to turn down. He had fond memories of the short time he had spent in the city in September 1969 when he had visited Houllier. The two men had even stood together on the Kop when Liverpool destroyed Dundalk 10–0 in the UEFA Cup. Now he had an opportunity to be alongside his old friend in the dugout at Anfield. It was uncanny how the two had become almost inseparable. Not only had they known each other from an early age, they had also followed each other around, first to Noeux-les-Mines, then to Lens, and then to the French FA. Houllier was sure that Bergues could introduce some new training techniques to Anfield as well as work effectively with Sammy Lee on the technical and fitness side of matters.

Evans, however, had never heard of Bergues. What were his areas of expertise? What were his abilities? What was going to be his role? Wasn't the whole idea to bring Houllier in to fill the coaching gap left by Ronnie Moran? Now they were suddenly increasing the coaching staff. Even more worryingly, he'd heard that Bergues wasn't anywhere near as fluent in English as Houllier. How was Bergues going to fit into the set-up, and what would the players think? Fortunately for Evans, the Bergues appointment was not announced until the following day, and then very quietly, by which time the press had moved on to something else.

The situation was just as difficult for Houllier. He liked Evans; he found him friendly, decent, a typical scouser. He knew that superficially he could get on with him, even though they were very different personalities. But of course there were drawbacks. The biggest question was how the players were going to respond to his appointment. Who would *they* regard as the boss? Given that Evans was the incumbent, it was inevitable that he would be the one they would consider as the man really in charge. That was natural. But there was another fear, that the players would attempt to drive a wedge between them. It would be difficult to maintain a united front; there were bound to be occasions when one manager differed with the other. The players would see that and would take advantage. They would soon suss out who was the stronger of the two, who was the most likely to accept their excuses for turning up late or for training poorly. They'd soon work out who to go to.

There were yet more problems which at the time Houllier had not entertained. The Frenchman was an outsider, the first real outsider ever to enter Anfield's inner sanctum in almost 40 years. Houllier had never been a Liverpool player, and nor had Bergues. Their only knowledge of Liverpool was from the occasional visit, or from the newspapers, and there were 40,000 people out there just as qualified, if not more so. In time, that and other problems connected with his being a 'foreigner' would cause numerous difficulties.

'It quickly became clear that it wouldn't work,' Molby said. 'Evans knew what was going to happen. He knew you couldn't have two managers running one club. Houllier has to do things his way. He is his own man. He knows what he wants.'

Certainly, not only had Houllier arranged for his new sidekick Bergues to be brought in, he had also persuaded the board to sign Norwegian defender Vegard Heggem from Rosenborg for £3.5 million. Houllier had told Evans and the board that Heggem could do a good job for Liverpool. Evans knew nothing about him, but Houllier was flavour of the month and had little trouble in having his way.

The Frenchman was making an impact almost before he had unpacked his bags. He was by his own admission a workaholic, but no one had quite anticipated the level of dedication they were to see. He was soon drawing up lists of possible signings. He was on the phone every five minutes talking one language, then another. Evans barely knew what was going on; it was impossible for him to keep track of things. Top of Houllier's list was a new goalkeeper – at least Evans was in agreement with him on that. David James's days were numbered. He had already been dropped by Evans the previous season, but his replacement, Brad Friedel, had fared only marginally better. Liverpool had to have a top-class goalkeeper if they were to win anything, so Houllier promptly set about signing Fabien Barthez from Monaco, but the French keeper fancied another season in France and it seemed he would be far too expensive anyway. Next on the list was the Paraguayan keeper José Luis Chilavert; Liverpool made a bid, but their valuation of him fell far short of that of his club. Securing the services of a new keeper would take the two men far longer than they had imagined.

Still, the partnership began well. On 16 August, the opening day of the 1998/99 season, Michael Owen, now the hottest property in European football following his famous World Cup goal against Argentina, was the focus of attention as he inspired Liverpool to a 2–1 at The Dell. That was followed by a creditable goalless draw with champions Arsenal at Anfield before Liverpool destroyed Newcastle United at St James's Park, taking a four-goal lead by half-time. Expectations were suddenly high. Owen was going to inspire Liverpool to glory, with Robbie Fowler still to return from a cruciate ligament injury. Once Fowler was back and partnering Owen, Liverpool would be unstoppable. It hardly mattered if they leaked a few goals as they would have more than enough power up front to compensate. It was a view strengthened by yet another victory on 9 September, this time against Coventry at Anfield.

Then, just as quickly, the rot set in. At Upton Park on 12 September the defensive pairing of Phil Babb and Steve Staunton did little to bolster any belief that Liverpool's problems in that area had in any way been solved, and West Ham won 2–1. Behind the scenes there were more difficulties. Although Norwegian defender Vegard Heggem had been signed, largely on the insistence of Houllier, there now seemed to be a dispute over what his best position was, at full-back or in the midfield. One man thought one thing, the other thought another. Fowler returned for the next game, against newly promoted Charlton at Anfield, but although he scored twice Liverpool could do no better than draw 3–3. Four days later at Old Trafford, all the expectations were laughably exposed as United put Liverpool in their place and cruised to a comfortable 2–0 victory. It was the beginning of the end for the Evans–Houllier partnership.

At Melwood, there was confusion. Houllier would later admit that 'it was difficult for the players in the long run. The players like to be able to refer to one manager. The concept was obviously extremely difficult for them.' As for Evans, he was in a no-win situation. If Liverpool did well then everyone would claim it was Houllier's input that had helped turn things round; if they lost, it would be his fault in tandem with Houllier. Rifts began to appear. 'There were all sorts of tales of player disruption,' Steve Morgan recalled. 'If only half the tales that came out were true then it was the proof of the pudding that appointing the two as joint managers was a bad, bad decision.' Houllier, it turned out, was not particularly popular. Evans had given him a free hand when it came to introducing new training methods; letting him free at Melwood, he reckoned, would make him feel more involved, and out there he was less trouble.

But Evans was growing increasingly weary of Houllier. 'The Professor', as he had become known, could be irritating. In a UEFA Cup game at Valencia on 3 November Liverpool produced a quality performance. They led 2–1 until four minutes from the end, when McManaman was dismissed along with Carboni after the Valencia man had appeared to whack McManaman in the face. It was a mite unfair on McManaman, but what followed was unforgivable for a senior professional: Paul Ince took his revenge by pushing one of the Valencia players full in the face. Ince was promptly red-carded too, and Liverpool were down to nine men. That in itself angered Houllier, especially as the hot-headed Ince had virtually gone in search of trouble, but then Valencia scored from the resulting free-kick to snatch a draw, although it was not enough to take them into the next round.

After the game Evans was, as ever, non-committal, seeking no doubt to protect his players. 'I didn't see an awful lot,' he claimed. 'But nothing much seemed to happen. There was some pushing, but no punches landed.' Still, the two men now had to serve a ban and would miss the next UEFA Cup games, and the incidents would surely make the next day's headlines when the newspapers ought to have been reporting a fine result for Liverpool.

Back in the dressing room, Evans caught Houllier rummaging around in a pile of Liverpool shirts that had been thrown on to the floor as the players changed. Houllier was picking out some of them and draping them over his arm.

'What are you doing ?' Evans asked irritably.

'I'm picking out some shirts,' replied Houllier.

'Why?' asked Evans.

'Well, I've just been into the Valencia dressing room and they've asked if they could have some Liverpool shirts as souvenirs.'

'Like fuck they're having any,' Evans snapped. 'They've just got one of our men sent off.'

In Evans's eyes, this story was a slur on Houllier who was demonstrating a lack of loyalty to his players and failing to understand the traditions and history of Liverpool FC. But what it really showed was that Houllier was proud of the club and not petty-minded enough to allow a red-card incident to interfere with relations between the two clubs. It also showed, as Houllier realised, that other clubs and players were in awe of the Liverpool legend. If anyone needed berating, it was Ince.

Houllier could see the state of indiscipline within the club. The players were running things, but as long as Roy Evans was there the discipline would not improve. Steve Morgan agreed that a firmer hand was needed. 'Running businesses is like running a football club,' he argued, 'and being Mr Nice Guy is seldom the right attribute to head a successful organisation, whether it's a football club, a hotel or a house-building company. To my mind, Roy Evans was an absolutely perfect number two, but not a number one. I understand the reasons behind appointing Roy, getting back to basics, getting back to the old-fashioned values which had gone by the wayside in the Souness era, and had Roy been used like an assistant manager or head coach or whatever with somebody else doing the driving, I think it could have been an inspired decision. But I think it was a mistake to make Roy manager.'

Evans was certainly regarded as one of the nicest men in football. He was always co-operative with the media, and made himself available to the fans. No one in football has a bad word to say about him. Chairman David Moores was his biggest fan. Jan Molby, however, reckons Evans has to take some of the blame for what had happened at Liverpool. 'Everyone blames Graeme Souness, but Souness realised that things needed to be changed and began that process. When it didn't work immediately, they all pointed the finger at him and he was out. Roy simply took it back to what it was before, when really he should have been taking it on. The result was that four or five years later Liverpool were in an even worse state.'

Although there had been some impressive results at the beginning of the season, it was not long before Liverpool were back to their old confusing and frustrating ways. On the last day of October they lost 1–0 at Leicester; a week later lowly Derby County came to Anfield and walked away with a 2–1 win. As the team left the pitch, the boos rang out. Liverpool had now crashed into the lower half of the table and the fans, once Evans's staunchest supporters, turned on him. The clock was ticking. Three days later, in a Worthington Cup clash at Anfield, Tottenham Hotspur stormed into a three-goal lead. Even the Kop were jeering now. It was clear that this was no championship-winning side, and now they were out of the Worthington Cup. That didn't leave much else to play for.

Evans had had enough. He simply could not continue. Even the *Liverpool Echo*, as sure a barometer of local opinion as any, had turned against him. Nobody had said much in the boardroom after the Spurs game. There wasn't much to say. You could hardly make excuses. He knew he had been in a no-win situation. In some ways he blamed the players, but he could understand the confusion they felt. He found Houllier likeable and decent, but they were totally different personalities. Evans was a players' manager. He understood their foibles, their way of life; above all, he understood English players. He didn't mind them having a drink and a laugh. It was bonding. He'd been a player himself and had got up to some legendary antics. He'd spent the best part of 30 years at Anfield and had worked with some of the greatest managers in the game. He was not convinced that a foreign manager was the answer. After all, United hadn't needed to go abroad to find success.

In his office late that night, surrounded by a few close friends, Evans suggested the unthinkable. He was going to go. One friend, Alan Brown, recalled trying to change his mind. 'I tried to persuade him to stay but he had it in his mind that he wanted to go, he'd had enough. It wasn't working between the two of them.' Others also tried to convince him to give it more time, but the cracks were too wide to be plastered over. It wasn't that the two managers had fallen out, it was just that they were miles apart to begin with. More importantly, as far as Evans was concerned, all the fun had disappeared. One director remembered spotting him after the Valencia game. 'He was walking just under the balcony where we were standing, and although we'd got a reasonable result that night and were through to the next round, Roy just looked so tired and fed up. He looked then like he'd had enough.'

Evans no longer ruled the roost, no longer had total control; on the coaching staff there was no Ronnie Moran, no John Bennison, and Tom Saunders wasn't around any more either. For him, the laughter and camaraderie had gone out of football. Now, it was all desperately serious.

Evans was virtually the last man out of Anfield that November night. It was cold, and beginning to rain again. He wearily stepped into his car, turned on the heater and drove home through the dark streets of Anfield knowing full well that his Liverpool career was over. He didn't even bother to turn on the radio. Radio City or Radio Merseyside would no doubt be berating him and the side. It didn't bear thinking about. He just wanted some peace and quiet. The closer he drove towards his home the more convinced he became that he was making the right decision. He knew others would try to convince him to stay, but he couldn't see a way out. Even a good night's sleep wouldn't change his mind. In the morning he would have to face up to the facts. It would not be easy to throw it all aside: the club had been his life, and at 50 he had no idea what he would do when he left. He had gone from young apprentice to manager, something no other man had ever done at Anfield, and along the way he had helped lift countless League titles, FA Cups and European trophies. He might not have been on the field when all those honours came Liverpool's way, but he had been behind the scenes, planning, guiding, making sure that all the small details had been worked out, which could be just as important as putting the ball in the back of the net. He had been there at almost every celebration, in Rome and Paris, at Wembley and Anfield. He left knowing that somewhere along the line he had played a vital part in the club's enormous success.

4. LA BELLE FRANCE

In France he'd always kept a watchful eye on the progress of Liverpool Football Club. Liverpool were among the top clubs in Europe; he'd seen them on television and read about them in the French sports daily *L'Equipe* and other French magazines. 'I was a fan of Liverpool before coming here. My heart was always Liverpool. I deliberately chose to come here because of the football.'

Anyone who has ever driven south towards Paris from the Channel ports of Calais or Boulogne will have been struck by the unyielding flatness of northern France. Only the occasional copse, war cemetery and village break up mile after mile of lowland, treeless, undulating and offering extraordinary vistas towards La Manche. When you look at the sparse geography of this region it's little wonder that in the First World War the armies of France, Britain and Germany became bogged down in a stalemate of trench warfare. On these unforgiving plains more than a million men gave their lives in a futile struggle for a handful of hectares of land around the Somme as northern France was ripped apart by tanks, artillery and trenches. The front line moved just a few metres one way one month, then a few metres back the next. In all, it never shifted more than a couple of miles from where it had started. Twenty-five years later, during the Second World War, it was again the principal theatre of resistance to the German onslaught, particularly after the D-Day landings of 1944. Yet again buildings, farms, forests and homes were rent apart as bombs, tanks and men exploded across the terrain. Northern France suffered appallingly in the last century, but in the twenty-first century there are few traces of its agony. It's green and pleasant today, though still depressingly flat, and only the odd scar of its past can be spotted. It's restored to what it once was, but it still carries painful memories of what happened here between 1914 and 1945.

The small Pays de Calais town of Thérouanne, where Gérard Houllier was born, lies some 25 miles from Calais itself and just a few kilometres off exit four of the dual carriageway autoroute that every year carries thousands of British tourists from the

Channel ports south to Paris, the Loire, Dordogne and beyond. Few, if any, notice the exit that leads you to Thérouanne. It's not the kind of place at which you stop off as you hurry towards your southerly destination. If you are visiting the war memorials or the trenches, you're more likely to halt your journey a few miles further down the road, closer to Péronne or Bapaume.

Thérouanne, like so many French towns, is almost ghostlike. You can drive through it at any time, night or day, and barely see a soul. It's a largely unimpressive place, slightly to the south of what was once an important medieval town of the same name that was destroyed by the Spanish emperor Charles V in 1553 in an act of revenge after the French garrison had given him repeated trouble. In those days it was an important cathedral town with a substantial diocese stretching from Ypres in the north to the Somme in the south.

The town is typically northern French, full of small, terraced, red-brick houses, mostly just one storey. There are few *maisons bourgeoises* here. Although surrounded by fields and agriculture, it nevertheless has an industrial feel to it; it was once inhabited by miners or steel workers. There are no hotels, a few bars, a cemetery, a church, and some basic shops. A simple war monument, typical of so many paid for by public subscription in France, lists some 23 local men who lost their lives in the bitter conflict of the First World War. Further names have been added for those who died in the Second World War. It's certainly not the kind of place prospective English house buyers turn up at.

The France Houllier was born into was a sad reflection of what had existed in the pre-war period. The trauma of the First World War, the uneasy peace of the twenties and thirties, the German occupation of the Second World War and the final conflict of 1944 left northern France a sad shadow of its former tranquil self. The war might finally have ended when Houllier was born into a close family on 3 September 1947, but it had left in its wake dereliction, chaos and poverty. At least there was hope. For the first time in two generations there was an opportunity to make peace work.

He was the eldest of three brothers. His father, Francis, was a keen football fan and Houllier is the first to admit that it was his influence that determined the course of his life. 'I used to go with my dad when he played football,' he said, 'and then he became director of a small local club. He never played professionally but he gave me the bug for the game. When you're young you play football. At the time I didn't have much choice. It was either that or athletics.' After school Houllier would play out in the fields around his village, often with one or more of his brothers or some of his school pals.

He was sixteen when he began his friendship with Patrice Bergues, then his school friend, which has lasted through to this day. 'Gérard was always passionate about Liverpool,' said Bergues, who's just five months younger than Houllier. 'We were always playing football together and talking about the game. Even then he was very knowledgeable.' For a brief time their friendship was disrupted when Bergues went on to train to become a PE teacher while Houllier decided to study English at Lille University – a time when, despite his overwhelming love for the game, it seemed that Houllier was lost to football. He had always wanted to be a professional footballer but family circumstances stopped him. 'My father refused to allow me to become a professional, so I stayed a top amateur. And then he fell ill, so I had to get a job to pay for my studies.'

Houllier plumped for the teaching profession, and after Lille his first job was as a primary school teacher. But there was always an itch, a determination to do better and go one step further, so he decided to take a postgraduate course. This required writing a dissertation. He recalled that the chance to study abroad was available only to those who had done particularly well at university and obtained a good degree, and fortunately he had. What he wanted to do was make a study of inner-city deprivation, and he chose as his subject Liverpool. Why Liverpool? 'For the life and the football. I'd heard so much about the place. I've always been an Anglophile. I've always liked the English people and the English traditions and I wanted to improve my English.' In France he'd always kept a watchful eye on the progress of Liverpool Football Club. Liverpool were among the top clubs in Europe; he'd seen them on television and read about them in the French sports daily *L'Equipe* and other French magazines. 'I was a fan of Liverpool before coming here. My heart was always Liverpool. I deliberately chose to come here because of the football.'

In 1969, when Houllier arrived, the city of Liverpool was facing its gravest crisis since the Second World War, when Luftwaffe bombs had rained down on the docks and its hinterland. Unemployment was steadily rising. The docks, for so long the nerve centre of the city and its biggest employer, were beginning to experience the hardships of a changing economy. Sea transport was no longer the principal means of importing and exporting the nation's goods, nor was America the principal supplier; Europe and air transport were the new driving forces of the economy. Liverpool faced westwards, towards America, stuck out on a limb of Britain. Although efforts were being made to introduce new industries into the area, the lack of skilled labour and Liverpool's geographical position made it difficult to attract prospective employers. What's more, Liverpool had an unenviable reputation: it was said to be prone to strikes, its industries ruled by trade union militants. Its local politics were also confusing and chaotic. The days of the 1960s when Liverpool ruled the world with its music had almost disappeared. The promise and hopes of that era had slowly evaporated. The Beatles, and all the other Merseybeat groups, had taken the rich gravy train to London and elsewhere, and the traditional industries of the area were also moving out or dying off, leaving behind empty shops, factories and warehouses, mounting unemployment and severe social hardship.

So it was not a particularly appealing city Gérard Houllier came to live in, though Toxteth, where he lived and carried out his research, was a prime area for his dissertation. Everywhere you looked you could see signs of the encroaching social deprivation. Within the space of a couple of years unemployment would rise to staggering levels, rivalling the days of the 1930s. In Liverpool alone almost twenty per cent were without work, and in some parts of the city one in every two men was unemployed. The consequences were devastating, but the one saving grace through-out these torrid years was football. Both Liverpool and Everton held their heads high, winning championships and FA Cups throughout the sixties and into the seventies.

He retains fond memories of his days on Merseyside as a student. 'I came to Liverpool as *un assistant*,' he explained, 'working at a school in 1969/70. The main part of my work consisted of teaching in a comprehensive school, and I wanted to write a thesis; my research dealt with the social aspects of Liverpool. I wrote a paper whose title was "Growing Up in a Deprived Area". My time was shared between teaching and research, and I spent a lot of time in the difficult areas of Liverpool, Liverpool 8 [Toxteth] mainly. I was there for one year.' It is not surprising to learn that one of his first ports of call was Anfield, which he visited whenever he could. Alsop High School, where Houllier taught, was on Queens Drive, not far from Goodison, and some nights he would work late then trek across Stanley Park towards Anfield to watch a match. 'My first experiences as a fan also date back to that time. I think the first European game I went to see was when Liverpool won 10–0 against Dundalk in a UEFA Cup tie [on 15 September 1969]. It's funny, because my friend Patrice Bergues was there with me; he had come over to visit and we went together. But apart from that I went to see as many other games as I could when I was not playing myself. I was playing for the Old Boys team at the school, which I enjoyed very much. So I went to the game whenever I could. I stood mainly in the Kop. At that time when you were in the Kop it was swaying and colourful. It was an experience.' What impressed him most was the desire not just to win but to keep going until the final whistle. 'It was a completely different culture to what I had been used to in France. In England the game is never over until the final whistle, no matter what the score is. After seeing what I saw, it didn't surprise me that England began to dominate European football not long after that.'

Alsop High School was a typical inner-city Liverpool comprehensive. It had been a grammar school but had switched to being a comprehensive a few years earlier. Graham White, who was head of economics at the school, remembers Houllier well. 'He was a French assistant, and we became quite friendly. He would come round to my house for a meal with myself and my wife. He had a small Renault 4 car and I remember he took me in it to an interview I had for a new job. He must have been lucky because I got the job.' The Alsop School Old Boys played in the Zingari League, and White played for them alongside Houllier. 'He was a centre-forward. We had about four Old Boys teams and he played usually for the first team, but sometimes for the second eleven. In those days we always thought continental players never made centre-forwards because they weren't tough enough, but I can assure you that Gérard was as hard as they come. He was what you might call vigorous and enthusiastic. I remember he came into school one Monday with a bad cut on his forehead after taking a knock on the Saturday that required stitches. He was such a nice young man, very nice, and very intelligent. He really loved the city of Liverpool.'

Once he had completed his year's teaching and finished his dissertation he returned to his classroom in France, and continued to play football as an amateur. His return did not spell the end of his love affair with Liverpool FC, as Bergues explained. 'He was always looking out for Liverpool results. Years later, Gérard told me that he was returning to Liverpool, especially for the 1977 game against St Etienne.' Houllier taught at primary, secondary and grammar school level before becoming a lecturer in a school of commerce, and when he wasn't teaching in the classroom he'd be outside teaching on the soccer pitch. During these years he played amateur football initially with Hucqueliers, and then in 1973 with Le Touquet until the sport's appeal finally forced him to quit teaching. He had already been doing some coaching with Le Touquet and had enjoyed it so much that when he spotted a job advertisement for the position of coach of a local team at Noeux-les-Mines, just a few miles away from Thérouanne, he decided to go for it.

Back in the seventies, Noeux-les-Mines was a major coalmining centre; today, the old pit head has been turned into a dry ski-slope. Noeux-les-Mines hardly boasted much of a side when Houllier arrived in 1976, initially as head coach and later as manager, but he set about changing their fortunes. Also playing for Noeux-les-Mines was Patrice Bergues. In his six years there Houllier took them from the French Third Division to the Second Division and into a challenging position for promotion, and notched up a number of youth cup wins. It was the equivalent of, say, taking Ellesmere Port into the heart of the Football League. That astonishing rise for so minor a team was enough to bring him to the attention of the well-known French clubs, and in 1982

Houllier was offered the job as manager of French First Division side Lens. He was now in the big time.

Lens is a small town of just 35,000 people in north-east France. Surrounded by slag heaps and war cemeteries, it was once, like Noeux-les-Mines, a thriving coalmining area. Its ground, the Stade Felix Bollaert, one of the most English-style stadia in the country, was built by unemployed miners during the 1929 Great Depression between Seam One and Seam Nine just outside the town centre. The club had long been the standard bearers for the mining community; indeed, it's not that long ago that the cry '*à la mine!*' ('to the mine!') would be yelled at any player not giving one hundred per cent. It was just the kind of community Houllier liked: industrial, hard working, and not without its problems.

In his first season at the club Lens rocketed to the top of the division, finally finishing fourth and qualifying for Europe – another astonishing achievement. The following season, 1983/84, Houllier had his first taste of European football as Lens launched into the UEFA Cup. In the first round they overcame AA Gent, in the second round, Royal Antwerp. That put them into the last sixteen and a tie with another Belgian club, RSC Anderlecht. It was a tight game, and after a draw in Lens they lost 1–0 in Anderlecht, but this was no disgrace as the Belgian side went on to reach the final, losing it (to Spurs) only on penalties. Lens's commitments in Europe clearly had a bearing on their League performance, however, and that season they wound up in thirteenth place, but at least they had consolidated their position in the top flight. In 1984/85 they were high flying again, this time winding up in seventh spot. Such had been their success that in 1984 the stadium underwent a major reconstruction. Ambition was high, but it should hardly have been surprising to anyone at the club that this kind of success would bring the richer clubs rushing to Lens, and in 1985 Paris St Germain turned up looking for Houllier. PSG were the biggest club in France, playing in the capital, and they had much more money to spend than Lens. They made Houllier an offer he could not refuse.

A year later PSG were champions of France, their first ever title. Paris was ecstatic, and Houllier was the toast of the capital. One man who played under Houllier in Paris was the Argentinian striker Omar Da Fonseca, who won the French championship with him in 1986 and then went on to win the championship two years later under Arsène Wenger at Monaco. He sees a huge similarity between the two men. 'The other coaches I've known have tended to be ex-players who were passionate about football. They lived and breathed the game and nothing else. Arsène and Gérard are also very passionate, but I found they had a much more futuristic approach than these coaches. Houllier, through having been a teacher, was very good with the psychology. Also, he was prepared to go to other countries to see how they worked. He is an intelligent man with an open mind. I think it's been helpful to Gérard that he's experienced another profession before moving into coaching. When it came to media relations he always knew how to express himself well and to handle that side of things. Because of his background and his language ability he is able to communicate with a cross-section of players, too. That's very important.'

But the glory in Paris didn't last. The following season PSG crashed out of the European Cup in the first round, beaten by the unknown Czech side Vitkovice. Houllier remained in Paris throughout that season, but in July 1988 took a post with the French Football Federation as a coach. Then, in 1989, he became technical director of French football before joining Michel Platini as his number two and coach of the French national side for the European Championship of 1992. In that competition France became the first team ever to win all their qualifying games. The omens looked good, but in Denmark they could only manage two draws and one defeat and failed to reach the semi-final. After the finals, Platini stepped aside and handed over the reins to Houllier. It was a move that would bring him to the attention of high-profile managers across Europe.

One manager to benefit from Houllier's advice was, ironically, Alex Ferguson. Houllier bumped into Ferguson one afternoon in September 1992 while watching Manchester United beat Leeds United 2–0. After the game Houllier chatted with the Scotsman and waxed lyrically to him about how good a player Eric Cantona, then wearing a Leeds shirt, was and how highly he rated him. 'He had a very high opinion of his abilities,' Ferguson recalled, and it was enough to alert the United boss to the possibility of signing the Frenchman. Houllier was also able to put Ferguson's mind at ease over the media image of Cantona. 'He's not the devil in disguise the media likes to make out,' said Houllier. 'He likes to train and he trains hard.' Ferguson remembered that when others at Old Trafford were hesitating over signing him, and it convinced him that Cantona was the man for United. Houllier would probably prefer to forget that piece of advice today, but it does illustrate the growing respect for the Frenchman throughout the game and his uncanny ability to spot the potential in a player.

Houllier's main priority at this time was the 1994 World Cup finals in the United States and France's qualification for it. Houllier approached the pre-tournament games with not undue confidence. France had been drawn alongside Austria, Sweden, Bulgaria, Finland and Israel; compared to England's group of Holland, Poland, Norway, Turkey and San Marino, the French looked to have a fairly comfortable passage through. Sweden and possibly Bulgaria looked to be the only sides likely to cause them some problems.

France's first game, however, away to Bulgaria, alerted Houllier to the fact that this was going to be a far from easy passage. France lost 2–0 in Sofia, but in Paris in October 1992 they regained the initiative with a 2–0 win over Austria. The following month Jean-Pierre Papin and Eric Cantona gave them a 2–1 win over Finland, and France's World Cup campaign was well under way. In February 1993 they travelled to Israel and comfortably won 4–0, and in March they took the away points by beating the Austrians by a single goal. A month later they overcame Sweden 2–1 in Paris.

France Football was beaming with confidence and already predicting that France would be through to the US finals. Houllier was doing a good job, they claimed, and had either introduced or was developing some talented young players, among them Eric Cantona, Jean-Pierre Papin, Bixente Lizarazu, Laurent Blanc, Didier Deschamps, Christian Karembeu and a certain David Ginola. So far, so good. France was lying second in the group, on equal points with Sweden but a point ahead of Bulgaria who had played a game more. More importantly, they were six points ahead of Austria in fourth spot. There were clearly only three countries in it, vying for the two qualification spots.

By October 1993, with just two games to go, France was in pole position: all they required was one point from their remaining two fixtures, both at home, against Israel and Bulgaria. Bulgaria might again be a tricky proposition, but Israel in Paris had to be a walkover. First up were Israel, bottom of the heap and with a bagful of goals conceded. Paris celebrated when Ginola put France ahead, but then in an astonishing turnaround they ended up losing 3–2. It was a catastrophe. The situation could still be rectified against the Bulgarians, but from a position of comfort, France was now in a state of panic. The Bulgarians, after all, had already taken the points in Sofia.

Ginola's outstanding performances for Paris St Germain and France had made him a favourite with the French press who were now campaigning for his inclusion in the side to face Bulgaria. Houllier, however, remained unconvinced, especially as he did not want to break up the Cantona–Papin partnership up front. But in an unusual about-turn, the French manager did decide to pick Ginola. It was to be one of the biggest mistakes of his career; even then, Houllier was but one minute away from success. After 89 minutes of the match on 17 November France had the point they needed to qualify, but in that dramatic final minute Ginola gave away possession with a loose pass. Bulgaria intercepted, and five passes later Emil Kostadinov fired the ball into the back of the French net. France were out of the World Cup.

It was inevitable that the French press would seek out a scapegoat, and Ginola was their number one target. Number two was Houllier. The French manager was furious; two years' work had gone up in smoke. On television the next day he berated Ginola. 'David Ginola is a criminal! I repeat, he is a criminal!' It was unusual, to say the least, for Houllier to be so damning of a player, especially in public, even though most French people probably agreed with him. Yet the loss was not entirely Ginola's fault. There are eleven players in a side, and the defeat at home by Israel was almost certainly the blow that really killed off France. That was the game that should never have been lost.

The public condemnation of Ginola would not be forgotten, especially by Ginola himself. Four days later, playing for Paris St Germain, he was booed as he came on to the pitch. Every time he touched the ball the jeers went up again, and on every pitch in France on which he played for the remainder of that season the same booing and jeering followed him. In effect, it marked the end of his career at PSG. A year later he moved, sick and tired of the hostility that surrounded him. For Ginola, the whole episode, unsurprisingly, left a nasty taste. A couple of years later in his autobiography, he wrote, 'I haven't seen Gérard Houllier since then. I have never spoken to him since and I never will.' Still, Ginola was picked for the next international game, away to Italy, a game France won 1–0. But it wasn't Houllier who picked him. By then he had quit and a new French manager, Aimé Jacquet, was in charge. Despite this, his international career was virtually over. Jacquet was no fan either, and he was left out of the Euro 96 qualifiers and the final squad.

Houllier was, naturally enough, deeply disappointed by France's failure to qualify. 'Yes, that was a difficult moment from a human point of view,' Houllier later admitted. 'But as far as sport was concerned I knew that what had been done was right. I'd given Youri Djorkaeff and Marcel Desailly their chance in the national team. Had we gone to the World Cup I'd already decided that I'd bring Zinedine Zidane into the squad.' But it was not to be, and with the French press howling for Houllier's scalp he quietly stepped aside and handed over to Aimé Jacquet.

Although he was discarded as manager of the national side, he was asked to take over the running of France's national youth sides. Initially he worked for a couple of years with the under-18s, then spent a year with the under-20s. It was a role that gave him the opportunity to begin a total reorganisation of the game at youth level. He encouraged the development of academy systems at club level, and at national level began to bring together the best young players in France on a regular basis. Many of those coming under his tutelage had already spent some years developing through the national youth system at Clairefontaine, but others were added as they improved. Houllier was soon boasting a squad as good as any other collection of young footballers in the world. It was an impressive roll-call that included David Trezeguet, Nicolas Anelka, Mikael Silvestre, William Gallas and Thierry Henry. Within five years those players alone would be worth £100 million or more in the European transfer market, but it wasn't until 1996, when the under-18 French side won the European Championship by beating Spain 1–0 in the final, that people realised the importance of the work Houllier was doing

Ludovic Roy, the French goalkeeper with the under-20s side, remembers Houllier at the time as a calm, considered character, but he does recall one occasion when Houllier totally lost his temper. 'Lots of managers shout and lose their tempers, but I can honestly say I've only heard Gérard swear once – before an Oporto tournament match with Portugal when he stormed into the dressing room in a rage and said, "Come on, we've got to beat these bastards!" Why he was so wound up I'll never know, but it had the desired effect as we won 3–2. Still, he had a right go at me at half-time for coming out of a fifty-fifty with their striker and losing the goal as he booted my chest. Houllier was pointing his finger at me, shouting, "What the bloody hell happened with that goal? You chickened out of it." I just lifted my top to show a massive hole where the striker's stud had caught me, and replied, "This happened." To his credit, he said sorry.'

Working with the youngsters also brought about a reunion with his old friend Patrice Bergues, whose career was uncannily paralleling that of Houllier. After playing with Noeux-les-Mines, Béthune and St Omer, Bergues had become coach at Béthune, then youth coach at Lens after Houllier left. He had eventually become manager of Lens between 1992 and 1996, in which year Houllier took him on board as a national coach to help with the French World Cup campaign. Along with Aimé Jacquet, Michel Platini and a young French coach-cum-psychologist by the name of Jacques Crevoisier, they set out to bring the World Cup to France. Many of the young players Houllier had worked with in the under-20s were drafted into the squad, and during the finals they would come of age. Houllier undoubtedly played a major role in putting French football on the world map. Indeed, Jacquet insisted that Houllier be awarded a special World Cup winners' medal for his contribution to the campaign.

5. CULTURE SHOCK

Finally, he was an intellectual. He was thoughtful, well read, had a university degree or two and spoke a couple of languages. He was a different breed to your normal footballer. He didn't drink much, and when he did it was usually wine. He didn't throw tea cups and he didn't swear at the players. This made him an even larger figure of fun. The more polite members of the squad dubbed him 'The Professor', the less polite simply stuck with 'The Frog'.

When in November 1998 Roy Evans told vice-chairman Peter Robinson that he was definitely quitting, it was no more than PBR had expected. Nevertheless, chairman David Moores once again pleaded with him not to go. 'Give it more time,' he insisted. 'Things will get better.' Moores had always been a Roy Evans supporter and genuinely did not want him to leave. After all, he had known Evans, it seemed, most of his life. Moores had also been a supporter of Souness, and had similarly given him longer than he'd ever warranted. Loyalty has long been one of the most virtuous characteristics of scousers; true to the type, Moores stood by those he had helped to appoint. He appreciated Evans's steadfastness and integrity, and the fact that he had steered the club through a difficult time following the sacking of Souness. 'It was a very emotional and difficult time for all those concerned,' remembers one club insider.

Evans, however, was adamant. He'd had enough. It wasn't working, he said. Although there had been no major argument or dispute with Houllier, and discussions between the two had always been polite and civilised, Evans knew that the two-bosses arrangement was causing confusion and could not continue as it was. One of them had to go, and he knew full well that the club was not going to sack Houllier. There was only one person who would get the sack. Better to go now before that happens, he thought. He also felt he'd taken Liverpool as far as he could. The fans had turned against him, and that, more than anything else, hurt him. He'd taken the club to third spot in the table on a couple of occasions, but no matter how hard he tried, he didn't seem to be able to get past that final hurdle.

The formalities for Evans's resignation were quickly settled and the board agreed that Houllier should assume responsibilities as manager. Houllier was hardly surprised either. Recent results had been poor, and there was no real rapport between the two men, yet he felt a sadness to see Evans leaving a club where he had spent his adult life.

In 1998, there was probably no harder task in football than for a foreign manager to take charge of an English football team. Overseas footballers might have been a part of the English football scene for a few years, but overseas managers were quite a different matter. With their xenophobic attitudes, less than committed lifestyles and narrow horizons, English footballers at that time seemed little different from many of the hooligan fans who followed them around the world. They looked on foreigners with suspicion and superiority. Playing alongside a foreigner was one thing, but having one as your boss was quite another.

English football has long regarded itself as somewhat superior, an attitude founded on history. After all, was it not the English who invented and perfected the game? For so long English football ruled unchallenged. There were blips in the past, of course. In November 1934 the Italian world champions (though not recognised by England as such) gave England a run for their money at Highbury, losing only narrowly, 3–2. Then, at the 1950 World Cup finals, the USA caused what was arguably the greatest footballing sensation up to that time when they defeated England 1–0 in Belo Horizonte to help knock us out of the tournament. But that, argued the footballing authorities, probably had more to do with an appalling pitch, the blistering heat and the fact that it was many miles from our shores. Then came 1953 and the visit of the Magic Magyars to Wembley. Hungary, in one of football's finest ever displays, whipped England 6–3 on a murky late November afternoon, and just to prove that it wasn't a fluke they emulated the trouncing six months later by winning 7–1 in the sunshine of Budapest – a result now largely forgotten.

Those matches against Hungary should have been the wake-up call for English football, but they weren't. Things continued in much the same vein. True, England began to export a few players. John Charles swanned off to Juventus and was soon followed by others, such as Denis Law and Joe Baker. Italy, Spain, even Germany, were regularly importing players from abroad, but not England. It was rare to see a Spanish, Italian or German player displaying his skills in English football. Sadly, wage levels meant that it was one-way traffic: England lost its best players to the super-rich clubs of Europe with their mega stadiums, sky-high salaries and huge support.

Scottish, even Irish players might have been signed, but it wasn't until the seventies that England experienced its first genuine influx of foreign players. There might have been one or two oddities beforehand, such as Eddie Firmani at Charlton and a host of white South Africans, but generally it wasn't until the likes of Arnold Muhren at Ipswich and Allan Simonsen at Charlton arrived that English clubs woke up to the possibility of signing foreign players. At first they were mostly Scandinavians – usually cheaper and, of course, a lot less trouble. Then in the 1990s Chelsea, under their innovative Dutch manager Ruud Gullit, began seriously to change things with the signing of a number of top Italian players such as Gianluca Vialli, Gianfranco Zola and Roberto Di Matteo. By then, of course, domestic salaries had dramatically increased and the chances of attracting top players had similarly improved. England might not have been able to compete with continental weather and lifestyles, but suddenly we were able to compete with Italian and Spanish wages.

Oddly enough, Liverpool was among the first British clubs to welcome foreign players. Indeed, the first ever Liverpool side, back in 1892, contained not a single English player. They were known as the 'Team of the All Macs' simply because all eleven players were Scottish. They might not have been overseas players, but at least it demonstrated that the club set its horizons beyond Liverpool. From the thirties into the fifties there was always a South African or two at Anfield, some of them very successful, as well as one American, but it wasn't until the late seventies that the non-English-speaking players arrived. First in was the Israeli defender Avi Cohen, who was signed in 1979, but he made little impact at Anfield, making only sixteen appearances. Still, he didn't really rank as a top-flight foreigner. He was a player coming from a nation with no footballing reputation.

Typically, most of the early recruits were safe Scandinavians who knew our ways, weren't too pricey and shared the same miserable, damp climate. Many of them even spoke English. Jan Molby, who joined Liverpool from Ajax in 1984 for a bargain £200,000, was probably the first genuine foreign player to join the Anfield ranks. Molby was a huge success with his range of accurate cross-field passes, and once he had adopted a scouse accent he further endeared himself to all Liverpudlians. Molby was followed by others, some of them, such as Torben Piechnik and Istvan Kozma, best forgotten, but some were comparatively successful, such as the Swedish defender Glenn Hysen. Generally they fitted in well. All they needed to do was, like Jan Molby, perfect the vernacular.

By then the old First Division was becoming awash with foreign players, but there were still few foreign managers. In 1990 Aston Villa hired the first ever European coach in English football when they appointed the Czech Dr Jozef Venglos as their manager. It was a total failure. Although Venglos was a highly respected manager he was barely given any time to begin his task. A year later, he was gone. It was undoubtedly the appointment of Ruud Gullit as manager of Chelsea in 1996 that really began the change of culture in English football. Gullit had been at Chelsea as a player for some years before being appointed manager. That at least made him a fairly safe appointment. The gifted Dutch midfielder was popular, fluent in English, a player of proven ability, and he knew the Premiership inside out. He was to be an enormous success. Under him, a cosmopolitan Chelsea side won the FA Cup, the European Cup-Winners' Cup and the League Cup.

That same year, 1996, Arsenal surprised everyone by appointing the then unknown Arsène Wenger as their manager. Although Wenger had taken Monaco to a French championship and been successful in Japan's J-League, it hardly constituted much in the way of credentials for managing a big club in one of Europe's toughest leagues. What's more, Wenger had never really enjoyed much of a career as a player. He was not the man many Arsenal fans had in mind at the time. Nevertheless, Wenger was to prove one of the most inspired appointments since Herbert Chapman had walked up the marble corridors of Highbury.

Wenger no doubt warned Houllier about the troubles he would face managing an English club, particularly one so steeped in tradition as Liverpool. He'd been through it all himself, and even now, a couple of years after his appointment and after such success, he sometimes felt he was still on probation. Tom Saunders had also foreseen that there might be a problem. Saunders, a director of the club, was a long-standing servant of Liverpool. A former headmaster, he'd given up teaching to take up a coaching position at Melwood and had spent many of his years trekking around Europe looking at opponents. Saunders was one of the most trusted and respected men at Anfield. Whatever Saunders said made sense. Now in retirement, he nevertheless continued to visit Melwood every morning and did a little light training with John Bennison. His ear was still close to the ground. He knew the whispers and gossip, and how the players reacted to Houllier behind his back. He could sense the resentment towards the Frenchman, and with Evans set to go there was no doubt that Houllier would get the blame, irrespective of whether or not he was to blame. Evans had been popular with the players, and while they might not have won trophies under him, they certainly led a comfortable existence. They regarded him as a close colleague, even though at times Saunders reckoned they had let the club, and Evans, down.

At the time of Evans's departure, Saunders became convinced that Houllier needed someone to work alongside him. He decided to sound out Peter Robinson. 'What if we were to give Houllier an assistant, someone steeped in Liverpool colours, someone who knew the English game and the Liverpool ways?' he wondered.

Robinson looked at him. He, too, had recognised the potential problem. 'Yes,' he agreed. 'But who?'

Saunders had already given some consideration to that question. 'Phil Thompson,' he replied.

It was precisely the name Robinson had been chewing over. Thompson had been a popular player with Liverpool and had already had a stint as a coach under Kenny Dalglish. That appointment, however, had ended in acrimony when Graeme Souness sacked him. Thompson was furious and had threatened to take the club to an industrial tribunal, but the hearing never took place because the two sides came to an out-of-court settlement.

Phil Thompson had been a fan of Liverpool Football Club long before he ever signed up. His love affair with the club had begun as a a ten-year-old, the day his mother took him to watch Liverpool play Inter Milan in the semi-final of the European Cup. As he sat in the Kemlyn Road stand that evening, he knew where his destiny lay. Seven years later, he signed professional forms for Liverpool and at the age of 18 made his debut during the 1973/74 season. He was to remain a regular in the side until 1983 when the emergence of Alan Hansen and Mark Lawrenson left him on the sidelines. His finest moment was when he lifted the European Cup and the following evening memorably took it back to his local pub in Kirby where it sat all night on the shelf above the bar while everyone, as Thompson admits, got 'very pissed'.

Thompson was the ideal man: one of the most decorated men in English football, a former captain of the side, an England international and someone who had been around Anfield since the days of Shankly. He had also already demonstrated his loyalty to the club by refusing numerous financial incentives from Fleet Street after he had been sacked to spill the dirt on Souness's stewardship. Instead of taking the money, Thompson had quietly retreated to his do-it-yourself business in Kirby and done some media work with Sky Television. And this journalist, for one, can confirm that Thompson has repeatedly refused to say anything about the incident despite being asked on several occasions.

'It would be something of a climbdown for us if we were to take him back,' Robinson pointed out.

'So what?' said Saunders. 'It doesn't matter. It was Souness's argument, not ours.'

When the suggestion was put to Houllier, he was more than delighted. 'That's precisely what I wanted,' he said. 'I know there will be problems with some of the players and I could do with his help. I don't know him, but I'm more than happy to give it a try as long as the understanding is that I am the manager, the man in charge. I don't care what title you give to him, but I'm in charge.'

There were still a few raised eyebrows the next day when it was publicly announced that Gérard Houllier would be the new manager and Phil Thompson would be his assistant. One or two pundits wondered if Thompson had been installed as the heir apparent, ready to jump into Houllier's shoes as soon as the Frenchman failed. Others simply wondered how on earth these two men would get on. Houllier and Thompson were chalk and cheese: one a well-educated Frenchman with impeccable qualifications, fluent in a number of languages and with extensive contacts in European football, but with no playing experience; the other a former player with a bagful of honours but with only a short stint as a coach with Liverpool, a Kirby lad with little formal education and no experience of European football administration apart from having captained the finest side in Europe. When you look at it like that, it was little wonder a few questions were being asked. But in the minds of Robinson and Saunders, Thompson was the right choice. Saunders, for one, had spotted something in Thompson. He liked the passion he showed and knew that this would compliment the more quiet and thoughtful Houllier. If he could somehow convey that passion and desire to win to the players, then they would be in good hands. And Brian Hall, the club's public relations and community development officer, was convinced Houllier was the right man at the right time. 'It needed a strong character,' he said, 'a really strong character to cope with the history of this club and to deal with some of the characters in the dressing room. In Gérard Houllier I felt that they had found such a man.'

When Houllier took sole charge of Liverpool, he faced a number of problems. First, he was a foreigner, the first ever to hold a position of authority within the club. Liverpool is an insular city, proud of its own kind but always suspicious of outsiders. Arsène Wenger might have been a crusader performing miracles at Highbury and Ruud Gullit might have been doing similar things at Stamford Bridge, but they were almost alone in the Premiership, and anyhow, London clubs were far more cosmopolitan. What's more, Houllier was French, and that made him an easy target. To some players he was known as 'The Frog'. Had he been Italian, Dutch or even German there might have been more respect.

Second, in an official capacity he had no previous connection whatsoever with Liverpool Football Club. For 40 years, every

Liverpool manager had had such an association with the club. Paisley had been both a player and a coach at Anfield; Fagan had also been a coach; Dalglish and Souness had been players; and Roy Evans had been a player and a coach as well. Even many of the backroom staff over the years had played for the club, including Geoff Twentyman, Ronnie Moran, Steve Heighway and Sammy Lee. All these men were steeped in the history and traditions of Liverpool Football Club. They knew the club and its employees inside out. But Houllier had no connections apart from the occasional visit to see his friend Peter Robinson and a handful of trips to the ground as a fan. He was an outsider. How could anyone come in from the blue like that and expect to understand the club?

Third, Houllier had never played professional football. He was an unknown name. A Platini or a Gullit stepping in as the new boss could at least have commanded some respect for his pedigree. But who was this man? He had only ever played football as an amateur, and that was in France with a club nobody outside of northern France would ever have heard of. When it came to slamming the medals on the table, Houllier's pockets were empty. He could barely kick the ball or demonstrate what he wanted his players to do.

Fourth, Houllier's pedigree as a manager was also limited. What had he actually won? Not much, was the answer. He'd taken Lens into Europe. So what? He'd then won Le Championnat with Paris St Germain. OK, that was impressive. Then he'd managed France but had failed to take them through a comparatively easy group to the World Cup finals. He'd also managed various under-20 and under-18 French sides, highly successfully, but that didn't really count. And when France were finally successful in the summer of 1998, Houllier had been employed in some kind of backroom/upstairs job.

Fifth, he had originally arrived as joint manager. Now he was in charge after ousting the players' favourite, Roy Evans. The players would remember that.

Finally, he was an intellectual. He was thoughtful, well read, had a university degree or two and spoke a couple of languages. He was a different breed to your normal footballer. He didn't drink much, and when he did it was usually wine. He didn't throw tea cups and he didn't swear at the players. This made him an even larger figure of fun. The more polite members of the squad dubbed him 'The Professor', the less polite simply stuck with 'The Frog'.

There was no doubt that the English players at the club did not want Houllier as manager. They had been running the show under Evans, and Houllier's appointment was only going to upset that state of affairs. Things had been comfortable around Anfield, but it was clear that Houllier was not going to allow that atmosphere to continue any longer. Anfield was going to be about changes, big changes. If players were not prepared to give one hundred per cent, they could leave. There would be no ill feelings. It was quite simple: take it or leave it. Some of them decided on the latter.

Houllier was undoubtedly taking on a huge task, one that was impossible fully to understand at the time, but he was at least fortunate in having a number of supporters at the club. Houllier did not really know Thompson, but he could trust in the judgement of Robinson, and there was always Patrice to turn to. Over the next three years the balding Bergues with his Gallic mannerisms would prove to be an immensely popular character around Melwood and Anfield. For the players he was an ideal go-between, always ready to listen and advise or iron out any problems before Houllier got to hear of them. In many ways he fitted perfectly into the role Ronnie Moran had performed so magnificently. Bergues always had a smile and a laugh for the players, and when he decided to leave and return to Lens in France his departure was greeted with enormous disappointment.

Yet for all his popularity he always maintained a low profile, firmly believing that it was not his role to feature on the back pages. He rarely gave interviews and rarely made any public statements. Many wondered what he did, but there was little doubt that he was picking up on everything that was going on. Bergues knew Houllier's ways and style. He was his eyes and ears around the place; he sussed out the troublemakers, listened to the gossip and gauged opinion. He also helped to persuade others that Houllier was hugely respected on the continent and that they would do well to heed his advice. It was always said that Bob

Paisley, particularly on cold days, liked to stand in front of the radiator at Melwood, watching the players from the warmth of his room. Indeed, it was something of a joke among the players. But Paisley was watching every move of every player, judging whether or not they were putting one hundred per cent effort into training. Bergues did much the same from the touchline.

The Liverpool board were more than happy to allow Houllier the luxury of Bergues, especially as Doug Livermore had also taken his leave, although Phil Thompson must have wondered exactly how he was going to fit into this scenario. Bergues might, to some extent, have been seen as a spy in the camp, but the more obvious candidate was rumoured to be a player. One of Houllier's first signings was the French midfielder Jean Michel Ferri, who was signed from Turkish club Istanbulspor within a month of Houllier taking over. Ferri was immediately suspected by the other players of being a spy brought in to inform on what was happening in the dressing room. They were very suspicious of him, although whether he ever really revealed much to Houllier is debatable, as is the notion that Houllier ever brought him in for that purpose. Nevertheless, what was important was that this was how he was perceived by some players.

In many ways, Houllier taking over at Liverpool was probably as much a culture shock for Houllier as it was for everyone else, but at least the Frenchman was mentally equipped to deal with it. When he first arrived at Anfield he had been horrified at the amount of drinking, the lack of dedication, and the poor training methods. It was hardly difficult to identify the problems. If he was ever going to sort them out, he needed to stamp his authority on the club before it was too late. Of course, there was always a danger that it might backfire as players revolted and tried to ease him out, but as long as Houllier had Robinson and Saunders backing him in the boardroom and Bergues supporting him in the dressing room, he had a fighting chance.

In those last months of 1998 when Houllier took over as manager, there is little doubt that a clique of players ruled the roost. And to a man they were all English. For whatever reason, none of them fancied the idea of Houllier as their new manager. Paul Ince had already gone on record to say that he did not want a manager to come in who might disrupt things. What he wanted was a continuation of the status quo where his own power remained intact. The big question inside Anfield was how Ince would react to Houllier's taking sole charge. Houllier rated Ince highly as a player, and there was no doubting his leadership qualities. If Ince was prepared to knuckle down, train hard and give one hundred per cent commitment to the job, then there would be no problems. But, of course, it was never going to be that easy. Even Alex Ferguson had experienced some local difficulties with Ince and had been glad to see the back of him.

One of Houllier's first edicts was to stop the post-match drink in the players' lounge. From now on, no alcohol would be allowed after the game, certainly not at Anfield at any rate. The announcement was greeted with disbelief and stony silence, but Houllier had realised that he had to stamp his authority on Anfield immediately. 'From now on,' he told the players, 'everyone turns up for training at ten a.m., not at one minute past ten.' Houllier also decided to introduce Sunday training. Football at Anfield was from now on going to be a seven-days-a-week job.

For the rest of the 1998/99 season Houllier was prepared to give every player the benefit of the doubt. He would certainly introduce a few off-the-pitch changes, but he was not going to be rushed or bullied into doing anything too dramatic on the pitch. Only at the end of the season would he make decisions based on how they had performed. To have immediately started swapping and changing things around would have left him wide open to criticism. It was also pointless casting players aside if he did not have replacements. The fact that the season was already four months old and was effectively over so far as Liverpool were concerned, in terms of chasing trophies, did at least give him some breathing space. Nevertheless, it was to be a busy six months as Houllier combined the task of reorganising the playing staff and taking long, hard looks at what was happening with the players off the pitch and at Melwood with endless scouting trips, both in the UK and abroad, to bring in new players. It was time to start planning for the future.

One of the more obvious signs that things were changing at Anfield was that when the fans arrived at the ground they discovered the players were already out, warming up and being put through various routines by coach Sammy Lee, long before kick-off time. There were cones on the pitch and portable goals, and most of the players and substitutes were sprinting around in some sort of ordered fashion with Lee shouting at them, while Patrice Bergues stood on the sidelines and watched carefully. Even the keepers were being put through their paces by goalkeeping coach Joe Corrigan. Houllier's attitude was that footballers were athletes, and as such had to both warm up before games and warm down after games. You couldn't just go out cold; muscles had to be loosened, players had to be up to speed. That way you might have an advantage over the opposition, by catching them out early. It was not an uncommon practice on the continent, and at some Italian grounds space had been created beneath the stands for players to warm up. But in England it was unheard of. It was a Houllier innovation, designed to get his players ready from the moment the whistle went. Within a few months every player in the Premiership would soon be out on the pitch a good 45 minutes before the game started.

Not every player took to the idea, however. One notable absentee from these sessions was Paul Ince, a fact that did not go unnoticed by either the fans or Houllier. Ince maintained that he was superstitious and did not like to go out on to the pitch before a match. He preferred to be the last man out, and to be pulling his shirt on as he ran out. If he participated in the warm-up he would be breaking his long-held tradition. Houllier shrugged his shoulders and made a mental note.

Brian Hall remembers being impressed from the beginning. 'I used to go down to Melwood regularly. I always knew everyone, so I could just pop in and get done whatever business needed to be done – a football autographed, or whatever. There was never any problem, it was all very informal, but once Houllier was in charge we had to decide boundaries. He was very good with me. His first priority was the players and preparing them for the game. Nothing could interfere with that. So we negotiated what I could and couldn't do. I found that really helpful. If he didn't want something doing he'd tell me and also give me a reason. We evolved the boundaries. I admired that, rather than me going down and upsetting people.' Jan Molby, too, admired Houllier's determination in what was 'as big a job as when Bill Shankly came. So much needed to be done. People didn't realise just how far behind [the continent] we had fallen.'

A sign had also gone up at Melwood, a framed message designed to enforce the Houllier philosophy and to emphasise what was expected of every member of Liverpool Football Club. It read: 'Respect. Be a winner. Always think team first. Be a top pro.' At first there was amusement – another one of the nutty professor's quirks. Players giggled and gossiped about it. What next? they wondered. At least someone like German international Karl-Heinz Riedle could figure out what Houllier was trying to do. Riedle had not always been a fan of the Frenchman but at least he appreciated what he was trying to achieve. 'He's a typical manager from abroad. He is bringing a lot of things that are standard in Europe, particularly in Italy. He likes us to be disciplined and to do the right thing.' Another overseas player, Vegard Heggem, understood as well. 'Things have changed,' he admitted at the time. 'The manager and his team make us concentrate intensely. They are constantly demanding more from us, on and off the field.' Houllier wanted his players to perform in training. He did not like shirkers. If you can't give one hundred per cent in training, then you won't give one hundred per cent in a game. You can't just go through the motions in training, he told them. It's not about what you do, it's about how you do it. The game is the gloss on the week's work. Former player Mark Lawrenson was also quick to notice the changes. 'Gérard Houllier is the best thing to happen to Liverpool in many, many years. He is not a tub-thumper, nor is he demonstrative, but he has moved the club forward very swiftly. There is light at the end of the tunnel.'

Peter Robinson had told Houllier that there would be ample funds available for rebuilding the side, but he insisted that did not mean he had an unlimited treasure chest. Domestically, that presented a problem for the new manager. He could look around the Premiership and pinpoint a few players, but the fees being asked were astronomical. 'We looked closely at Ipswich's Kieron Dyer,' said Phil Thompson, 'and were quoted a staggering £4 million.' Back in 1999, that was a considerable amount of money for an unproven player. Although Liverpool might have been able to afford it, it would have restricted their buying ability elsewhere. In the end, Dyer signed for Newcastle United and was successful there, but at the time he was an expensive gamble. The picture was the same wherever Houllier looked in English football. A whole host of players were scouted and approached, from Sol Campbell to Rio Ferdinand, but the asking prices were too high. The only realistic option was to look abroad.

To do that, Liverpool needed more scouts in Europe, so Alex Miller, the former Scottish international, was brought in to spearhead the overseas campaign. Ron Yeats remained in charge of scouting, but suddenly it had become one of the busiest and most important jobs at Anfield. The less than glamorous days when scouts drove 50 miles to watch a player at Bramall Lane or the County Ground on a wet Wednesday were disappearing; they were now more likely to be jetting off to Milan, Barcelona or Oslo.

Another change was the pre-season tour. Formerly it had been a holiday-camp affair, little more than a series of half-hearted friendlies against mediocre opposition. Players regarded it as fun, as an excuse for some late-night drinking, card games and maybe even a bit of womanising. One fan recalled the old days, a Roy Evans pre-season tour during which Liverpool played in a triangular tournament with some other top-notch European clubs. 'I happened to be staying in the same hotel as AC Milan,' he said. 'I came back to the hotel after a night out and there was total silence in the hotel, nobody about at all. So I decided to go to the Liverpool hotel just up the road. You could hear the noise from halfway down the road. Players, fans, even a senior club official were rather the worse for wear, singing, dancing and so forth. It did make a sharp contrast to AC Milan's attitude.' All that changed under Houllier. He took them to a training camp where they could concentrate on getting their fitness to a peak. 'How you perform during the pre-season games will be important,' he told them. 'If you don't perform to the maximum, you'll not be included in my early plans.' It was blunt talking.

The remainder of the 1998/99 season brought little obvious comfort to most Liverpool fans. Within a month or so of Houllier taking over Liverpool had lost a couple more Premiership games and had been knocked out of the UEFA Cup by Celta Vigo. The new year did not bring much improvement, with a further seven losses including successive home defeats at the hands of Aston Villa and Leicester. If anything, things were going from bad to worse. The club finished in seventh place, having lost fourteen games and conceded 49 goals. The only consolation was that seventh place was just enough for them to have another shot at the UEFA Cup.

Perhaps the most dispiriting defeat of the season came on 24 January in the fourth round of the FA Cup at Old Trafford. With a minute remaining, Liverpool led 1–0, Owen having put them into the lead with a headed goal after just a couple of minutes. It looked as if Liverpool were about to record their first win at Old Trafford in years and send United reeling out of the cup, but then, in the 89th minute, the unthinkable happened. United equalised, and they struck again deep into injury time. Four months later United would do something similar in the European Cup final. For Liverpool it was a bitter blow. Paul Ince had retreated from the fray with ten minutes remaining, complaining of exhaustion. His replacement, Jason McAteer, had then run around like a headless chicken in the midfield. Neither man would be forgiven.

Inside Anfield there were also discipline problems. Although Houllier was beginning to lay down the law, the 1998 Christmas party possibly came a little too early for players to realise just how serious he was. The traditional bash, held in the basement of a bar in the city centre, not only descended into unruliness, it also hit the front pages of the Sunday newspapers. A stripper had been organised and her antics clearly aroused some of the younger players a little too much. The result was that Jamie Carragher, who had arrived dressed as the Hunchback of Notre Dame, made something of a fool of himself as he cavorted with her, half naked himself. The incident could well have been something of a set-up by the *News of the World*; still, Carragher and company had fallen headlong into the trap. It did not make for pretty reading. The morning after publication, Carragher was read the riot act. He was young, he was told, and therefore was allowed one mistake. 'But,' Houllier emphasised, 'do anything like that again and no matter how good you are you'll be out of this club.' It was a rude, and perhaps necessary, awakening for Carragher. 'The problem here,' confessed Houllier, 'is that players think they can drink and drink. Drinking alcohol is as silly as putting diesel in a racing car.'

Robbie Fowler was another to fall foul of the new disciplinary ethos at the club when his suggestive gesture to Graeme Le Saux was replayed time and again on *Match of the Day*. But Fowler did not learn from the lesson, and a couple of weeks later he was at it again. After converting a penalty against Everton, he celebrated by pretending to snort a line of coke, represented by the white touchline. Rumours had been circulating in the city that Fowler was a 'smackhead', and his performance in front of the Goodison Park faithful was his answer to such a ridiculous suggestion. In a way it was quite a humorous riposte, but the FA predictably did not see it that way. Fowler was banned for four matches and fined £34,000 for his misdemeanours. He was sailing close to the wind.

All the time Houllier was taking stock, watching the antics of his players, examining their commitment to training and playing, and keeping his ear close to the ground. It was clearly going to be a busy year of buying and selling. There were a number of departures in addition to the higher-profile exits of the so-called 'Spice Boys' Jason McAteer, Steve McManaman and David James, dealt with in the next chapter. Jean Michel Ferri also left, returning to French Second Division club Sochaux for £1.5 million, having either fulfilled or failed in whatever role Houllier had wanted him to play. He had made just two appearances. Sean Dundee was off that summer as well, a £1.5 million signing for German club Stuttgart. Also leaving that summer were Oyvind Leonhardsen, recruited by Tottenham for £3.75 million; Karl-Heinz Riedle, who joined Fulham for £200,000; and Bjorn Tore Kvarme, who went to St Etienne for £750,000. It was the biggest clear-out Anfield had seen since the early days of Bill Shankly, even bigger than Souness's clear-out. Houllier was determined to get rid of any player he felt did not match up to his standards, whether in terms of commitment, discipline or ability.

Still, although most fans had written off Liverpool's season early, criticism remained rife, fuelled by a feeling that nothing much had changed in the months since Evans's departure. Goals were still being leaked at an unacceptable rate, Houllier didn't seem to know his best team, and there were precious few signs of any serious buying activity in the transfer market. Liverpool were being linked to plenty of players, but new signings were few and far between, and if Jean Michel Ferri was an example of Houllier's ability in the transfer market it did not augur well for the future.

At least Houllier found comfort among his allies inside Anfield. Phil Thompson was proving to be an outstanding student. He might not always have agreed with Houllier, but he was prepared to listen and learn, and Houllier was beginning to appreciate the kind of support he was showing. There were also his old friends Peter Robinson and Tom Saunders. Saunders was to prove a crucial ally. He had total and implicit faith in Houllier. Manager after manager had spoken glowingly of Saunders' value to the set-up. During Dalglish's early years he was an ever-present ear. Robinson once said that he had influenced Liverpool Football Club more than any other man. 'This club owes a great debt to him,' he added. 'I don't know how he can ever be repaid.' When Houllier was being critically examined in his early days, Saunders told one journalist 'make no mistake, this man will make Liverpool great again'. Coming from Saunders, it was the kind of remark that was listened to with some respect. He would prove to be spot on with his prediction, too, although sadly he did not live to see it fully realised.

6. THE SPICE BOYS

'Who would you rather have a night out with, the Spice Boys or the Manchester United back four?' asked one female television presenter. Well, she had a point. Liverpool did look a great deal more interesting. Yet in time United would become considerably more flashy than those Armani suits as David Beckham, under the careful tutelage of Posh Spice, upped the fashion stakes. Maybe United simply took a leaf out of Liverpool's book and decided to inject a little fashion sense and image into themselves. It was soon all tattoos, fancy women and movie premieres. But at least United had won the right to be flashy. Liverpool hadn't.

Those cream Armani suits were to be an abiding memory for Liverpool fans, one that will always be associated with the Liverpool side of the mid-1990s. Quite where the nickname Spice Boys came from, or when it became attached to Liverpool, is a matter of some conjecture, but one thing is for certain: it was there by the time of the 1996 FA Cup final. And it stuck.

In truth, the suits were rather flattering. Fashionable Italian haute couture, red roses pinned to their lapels. Stylish, but not outlandish. They looked very smart. True, they might have been more suitable for a wedding, but as soon as Liverpool walked out on to the luscious Wembley turf sporting their new attire, you had a feeling that this was not going to be their day. The suits seemed to represent arrogance, poseurs rather than hard workers.

You see, it wasn't so much the suits themselves as the image they presented. You could hardly fail to be taken aback or even impressed as they strolled on to the pitch for the traditional pre-match walkabout. They strutted around the national stadium like peacocks, full of self-assurance, waving to their fans. There was a cockiness about their approach. They looked a cut above United, who meandered on to the playing surface in dreary grey flannel trousers and blazers. But that afternoon, Liverpool proved to be far from the best.

Had Liverpool won the cup, perhaps nobody would ever have reminded them about the suits. Indeed, the suits would have been appropriate – style outdoing endeavour. It was the manner of Liverpool's defeat that really turned the suits into a *cause célèbre*. The FA Cup was lost with as lukewarm a display as has ever been seen at Wembley. They were supposed to be up for the occasion against their greatest rivals; instead, they strolled carefree around Wembley as if they were still conducting their pre-match walkabout. There was no urgency, no self-respect, no spirit, no battle to Liverpool's performance that day. Not that Manchester United were much better, far from it; they looked just as insipid and uninventive, and only a speculative volley from outside the area, which nine times out of ten would either have struck another player or soared into the upper terraces, won the day and the double for United. Liverpool were the Spice Boys, all show and no substance; United were less flashy, more fulfilling.

'Who would you rather have a night out with, the Spice Boys or the Manchester United back four?' asked one female television presenter. Well, she had a point. Liverpool did look a great deal more interesting. Yet in time United would become considerably more flashy than those Armani suits as David Beckham, under the careful tutelage of Posh Spice, upped the fashion stakes. Maybe United simply took a leaf out of Liverpool's book and decided to inject a little fashion sense and image into themselves. It was soon all tattoos, fancy women and movie premieres. But at least United had won the right to be flashy. Liverpool hadn't.

The Spice Boys image stuck. Liverpool players were having a wonderful time off the pitch, but not on it. It irked the fans, who expected their players to pursue the philosophy of Shankly: a fair day's work for a fair day's pay. 'They would never have got away with it in Shankly's day,' ran the most common complaint. 'He would have jumped on them like a ton of bricks.' That was undoubtedly true, but times had changed. Player power had increased, and the poor old manager was left trying to instil some discipline into an increasingly anarchic dressing room. The old boundaries and rules were being re-drawn wherever you looked. Shankly would have cringed and probably would have wanted no part of it any more. When he was once told that a certain Chelsea player had bought a house with a tennis court, Shankly's response was predictable and cutting. 'But the lad's never even won an international cap!' he exclaimed.

'The Spice Boys tag was created by the media,' insisted Stan Collymore. 'It never really existed. All you had was a group of young, good-looking players who were playing for a big club.' The tag was particularly attached to Paul Ince, Jason McAteer, Steve

McManaman, Robbie Fowler, David James and Phil Babb. Others, such as Jamie Carragher and David Thompson, were on the fringes. They were the good-time boys, a bunch of exceptional young lads, mostly single, who enjoyed a night out clubbing and drinking, spending the money they had earned. They were hardly unusual. Young men with plenty of money to spend, fast cars, and time on their hands featured at most Premiership clubs. The culture of athleticism hadn't quite arrived yet. Perhaps in the end there were not enough older and wiser heads in the dressing room to calm down youthful spirits. These lads were simply following in the traditional footsteps of most footballers, Liverpool players included, who enjoyed a night out and a few drinks. Successful Liverpool players in the past had got into trouble for excessive drinking. Terry McDermott, Jimmy Case and even Ian Rush were fond of a few drinks.

In his book *Entraîneur: Compétence et Passion*, written with Jacques Crevoisier – the ebullient, Ph.D.-laden sports psychologist whom Houllier brought to Anfield in the summer of 2001 after the departure of Patrice Bergues – Houllier talks about players being like big kids. 'Above all they like playing games – for example, lots of them like playing cards. They like the chance. Consequently, they tend to live for the moment. A manager has to acknowledge the different priorities players have according to their age.' So it wasn't necessarily a bad thing, and the Spice Boys tag was probably a little unfair. As Steve McManaman has pointed out, the Liverpool lads usually frequented the same clubs, wore the same fashionable clothes and drank the same amount as their Manchester counterparts. But once you've been tagged, it tends to stick, and the ignominious defeat at Wembley ensured that the tag stuck with the fans.

No matter how much truth or not there was to it, the image persisted, and it began to do irreparable damage to the club. It soon became a catchphrase in the media for Liverpool and was generally regarded as the reason why the club had not achieved anything of note for years. 'Players would never have got away with that kind of behaviour at Old Trafford' was the view of many. That, too, might or might not have been true, but still it was a problem that needed to be addressed by the new manager. Indeed, it was to be the number one item on Houllier's agenda. The Liverpool players were undoubtedly not as dedicated to the cause as they should have been. They did not show enough professionalism, and by doing so were sitting targets for any criticism.

At the centre of the web was one Paul Ince, formerly of West Ham, Manchester United and Inter Milan. Ince's capture in the 1997 close season for a fee of £4.9 million was regarded as a major coup for Liverpool. He was seen by many as the missing link in the side, the unflinching midfielder they had been searching for since Steve McMahon's departure, a man who would fill the boots of Souness, Case and Hughes. He had helped inspire United to the title before joining Inter Milan for £7 million. Ince's signing was greeted with overwhelming enthusiasm. At Old Trafford he had been dubbed 'The Guvnor' because of his authority on and off the pitch. It was just what Liverpool needed.

In Old Trafford circles, however, it was known that the United manager Alex Ferguson had become increasingly disillusioned with Ince and his attitude, a fact that was later aired publicly in Ferguson's autobiography. 'His attitude and his performance had altered to a degree that I could not tolerate,' he wrote, adding that 'his insistence on trying to assume a role in the team for which he was not equipped diminished his usefulness'. Nobody at Anfield, of course, had access to Ferguson's innermost concerns. Had they, they might have had second thoughts about signing Ince. Then again, Ince was such a high-profile player that any such doubts would probably have been brushed aside. After all, this was Liverpool, not Manchester United. At the time, Ince was regarded by anyone associated with Liverpool as their saviour, the man who would bring them the League title. How differently it all turned out. Ince enjoyed a bright first season but faded along with the team's fortunes. He was not a bad player, but rarely, in his entire time at Anfield, did he reproduce the authority he had shown on the field at Old Trafford.

Off the field, however, he ruled supreme, and this naturally gave Roy Evans a few headaches. The pendulum of footballing power had swung firmly in the direction of the players. Roy Evans found himself in a changing world. Football was in the throes of a revolution, with television money beginning to pour into the clubs. A game that had declined in popularity, status and image since the Heysel disaster was suddenly undergoing a big change. Hillsborough had been one of the catalysts. After the Taylor Report the decrepit terraces were pulled down to be replaced by all-seater stands. It meant that more women and more families were beginning to attend games, the new facilities offering congenial eating areas and comfort. In most grounds alcohol was banned from public areas. The turnstile queuing and crushing that had accompanied every visit to a football ground suddenly disappeared as games became ticket-only. Of course, there were drawbacks. Spontaneity became a thing of the past; you had to plan your visit to a game, and the pushing and shoving that was a part of the atmosphere went with it. Suddenly, it was acceptable to be a fan. Nick Hornby wrote a book about it, and the chattering classes gradually discovered football. Indeed, it soon became quite fashionable. And then came Sky Television with its live coverage and mega bucks. Wages exploded, transfer fees soared, agents proliferated and all kinds of sticky fingers were being plunged into the jam pot.

Roy Evans had always been liked by the players. A former player himself and a fixture in the bootroom for decades, he enjoyed a good night out and was considered one of the lads. Although he did not condone some of the antics his players got up to, he knew very well that he had done precisely the same at their age. In other words, he was understanding, if not sympathetic. There was always a feeling that he would turn a blind eye, especially if players could still produce the goods on the pitch. No doubt punishments were occasionally dished out, but under Evans life at Melwood was comparatively easy, certainly easier than it was to become. At times, the line between management and players could become blurred. The players would claim that they respected Evans, and to some extent that was true. They undoubtedly liked him, but whether they genuinely committed to him is another matter. Certainly when change came in the form of Houllier many found it alien and uncomfortable.

During the days of shared management, Evans, as the senior partner, would conduct his team talk and then hand over to Houllier. As Houllier began to speak, others in the background would be hovering, making gestures behind his back, while the watching players would sit there and snigger. 'There is no doubt,' recalled Jan Molby, who was still close enough to Anfield at the time to know what was going on, 'that the discipline was lax. They always treated players here like adults and didn't have to impose too many disciplinary rules and measures, but there is no doubt that some people were taking advantage. The old disciplines and values had gone.'

One of the first of the Spice Boys to disappear was Steve McManaman, although ironically he was the one player Houllier would have liked to hang on to. McManaman was always set apart from the others. Good-looking, fashionable, chirpy, even intelligent, he was a close friend of Robbie Fowler. The two of them had been at Anfield for years, having come through the ranks of junior and youth football together. But whereas Robbie was very much the home-loving, Toxteth-rooted lad, McManaman always had wider horizons. He was ambitious, enthusiastic, thoughtful, and knew that his game would improve if he went abroad.

McManaman was one of the most exciting players of his generation. The Liverpool-born youngster had made the breakthrough into the Liverpool side at the beginning of the 1991/92 season, taking over from the injured John Barnes, and had already been capped at England under-21 level. He was an instant hit as he terrorised defences with his direct running and precocious footwork. He had been given his chance by Souness, and throughout the Evans years he continued to be one of Liverpool's most important players. By the end of his first season he was an FA Cup winner, having turned the Sunderland defence inside out to inspire a Liverpool victory. Although his game went into brief decline in 1992/93 as defences began to suss out his trickery, he eventually learnt how to be more subtle and soon became the talk of the Premiership. A League Cup winners' medal came his way, as well as a full England debut. At times, though, he could be frustrating, his runs more horizontal and less direct. He was also given free rein, switching between the right and left as the fancy took him, demanding the ball yet doing little with it when he got it. In some respects he was a luxury; nevertheless, he remained popular with the Liverpool training staff, if not always with the fans, and was much sought after on the continent. At one stage Barcelona made an £11 million bid, and although McManaman voiced some interest, he decided to stay at Liverpool a little longer.

In the summer of 1998, Liverpool faced a dilemma. McManaman was talking openly about the possibility of moving abroad. Numerous clubs were interested in him, but McManaman, although interested himself, remained hesitant. He genuinely did not know what to do. On the one hand, he loved Liverpool, the club, the city and his many friends. He was a Liverpool lad born and bred, and Liverpool lads don't leave Liverpool without a great deal of heart searching. On the other hand, the club was not doing well. Manchester United had supplanted them at the top of the tree and Liverpool's fortunes had continued to fester.

With just twelve months remaining on his contract, McManaman knew that he had to make a decision. Liverpool, too, knew a decision had to be made, or else under the new Bosman ruling he would become a free agent. They talked at length, but still McManaman dithered. One week he was going to stay, the next there were rumours of his leaving. Liverpool simply hoped that he would eventually sign a new deal, that thoughts of playing in Spain or Italy would be forgotten.

Towards the end of the 1998/99 season McManaman's mother was taken ill and many assumed that her illness, and subsequent death, would tie McManaman to Liverpool for another contract. But as the summer approached, McManaman finally made a decision: he was leaving Anfield and going to join Real Madrid, who had offered him a lucrative deal, and according to the new UEFA legislation that allowed a player at the end of a contract freedom to go wherever he chose, Liverpool would receive not a single penny out of the move. Behind the scenes at Anfield there was fury, directed both at McManaman for not making a decision at least a year earlier and at themselves for not having taken a tougher line during the negotiations. Had they done so, they could have sold him for at least £10 million. Now, not only were they out of pocket, they would have to replace him. In effect, the failure to secure any transfer fee for McManaman probably cost Liverpool in excess of £15 million.

McManaman had been something of a test case. At that time the Bosman ruling was largely untested; he was the first high-profile player in Britain, possibly in Europe, to have left a club according to its terms. It left Liverpool's treasure chest sorely depleted at a time when they desperately needed money to make new signings. The ramifications, as much Liverpool's fault as McManaman's, would be felt for some years to come – a period when few, if any, other English clubs, having benefited from Liverpool's example, would be making the same error.

In truth, Liverpool had been far too considerate. Rather than dictate the terms themselves, they had allowed McManaman's hesitation to rule them. It was clear that Liverpool should have been far more brutal, should have initiated contract negotiations much sooner and demanded some indications of his leanings. It was an appalling and costly lesson for the club, and Houllier would never allow it to happen again. A couple of years later, when there was dithering over Robbie Fowler's new contract, he issued a stern warning to all his players. 'I won't be soft,' he insisted. 'I will not be held to ransom. Either the player stays or you sell. I am not going to have another Steve McManaman situation otherwise you let the players rule the club.' Houllier's attitude was that any hesitation led only to unease within the dressing room. 'I don't want players sitting on two chairs. They are either with us and want to commit to us, or they're not. If they're not, then they will leave . . . The length of time a player is contracted to a club will affect their team spirit, so a player who only has one year in a club will be concerned with finding another club rather than thinking about objectives for the following season,' he claimed in his book *Entraîneur: Compétence et Passion.*

Of course, the one lesson he did learn from the McManaman episode was that good players could be picked up under the Bosman ruling free of charge, and over the next couple of years he would take full advantage of this by signing Markus Babbel, Gary McAllister and Pegguy Arphexad, all on Bosmans. In a way, it was some sort of compensation.

Jason McAteer was another local lad, born and bred over the Mersey in Birkenhead. He came from a well-known family of local boxers, so it was surprising that he escaped the clutches of

Liverpool and Everton scouts during his youth. Instead, he found his way to Bolton where, alongside another Merseyside lad Alan Stubbs, he began to win glowing reports. There was soon talk of both of them leaving Bolton to return to one of the big Merseyside clubs. During 1994/95, impressive performances by McAteer against Liverpool in the FA Cup and the Coca-Cola Cup made it inevitable that he would soon join his favourite club. Liverpool, however, decided to take a rain check on Stubbs, although judging by the rate at which their defence was conceding goals Stubbs, in the end, might have been the better choice. McAteer finally joined Liverpool in September 1995 for the not inconsiderable fee of £4.5 million.

It seemed like a match made in heaven, but rather than play him in his natural position in midfield, the position in which he had shone at Bolton, Roy Evans decided to convert him into a right wing-back. From the outset McAteer looked uncomfortable, and although he gradually adjusted, there was always a feeling that he was being played out of position and that he would be far better off playing alongside Paul Ince. Unfortunately, that spot was already assigned to Jamie Redknapp. McAteer always lacked the pace to become a genuine attacking full-back while at the same time he lacked the guile to become a natural full-back. Even Republic of Ireland manager Jack Charlton, as astute a manager as you'll ever find, saw McAteer's natural position in midfield. McAteer was a battler and would always relish the man-to-man combat of the midfield. It wasn't that he was a failure as a wing-back, it was simply that he always looked hesitant and uncomfortable. He was not helped either by an appalling injury sustained when he fell awkwardly against Blackburn Rovers during the 1997/98 season. He broke his leg and was sidelined for the rest of the season.

It was inevitable that McAteer would be regarded as one of the Spice Boys. He was young, wealthy, local, single and enjoyed a good time. Houllier tolerated him briefly, but the end came during that FA Cup tie in January 1999 with Manchester United. McAteer came on in place of an exhausted Ince with instructions to hold his position, keep the shape of the side and remain disciplined but, typically, McAteer began to chase the ball and Liverpool lost their shape. The result was two late goals for United. Houllier was furious. Liverpool had thrown away a one-goal lead against their biggest rivals, a lead they ought to have been able to conserve. McAteer's career at Anfield was over; shortly afterwards Houllier offloaded him to Blackburn Rovers for £4 million.

Goalkeeper David James had been signed by Graeme Souness from Watford for £1.3 million in June 1992. At the time he was the most expensive goalkeeper in the country, yet, for all his potential, James had never looked the part. Tall and strong, he was as good on his line as any keeper in the Premiership, but when he ventured off it he looked vulnerable. Former Liverpool goalkeeper Tommy Lawrence called him a coward. 'He won't go where it hurts,' he said, and there was certainly some truth in the allegation.

There was no doubt that James was a problem. He didn't seem to communicate with his defenders, and where there should have been confidence in his ability there was instead uncertainty. Houllier was concerned, and he told James that he needed to mend his ways. What concerned Houllier most was James's lack of concentration; Houllier was sure that it was down to his off-the-field activities. James had a contract to model clothes, drove a flashy sports car and fully took advantage of the life that goes with being a highly paid single footballer. He was into computer games and mobile phones, too. There were suggestions that he was playing on his Gameboy too much, though it was difficult to take them seriously. Still, it became a joke among staff at Anfield who were sick of seeing him either on the phone or playing games. It was his obsession. When Houllier finally decided to ban mobile phones from Melwood, it was James who led the protests. He led other protests, too. 'You have to get your priorities right,' Houllier told him. 'First and foremost you are a professional footballer, and you have to concentrate on that. All the modelling, clubbing, drinking and flashy cars can come later. It's time for you to start a new challenge.' It was a message he would have to repeat to a number of players at Anfield. Many heeded the advice immediately, others did not, including James.

James readily confesses that he was a negative influence at Liverpool, a clubber who was also inclined to bury himself in the pub when things didn't go right. 'I used to dwell on my mistakes, and I used to think that all the stick I got was unique to me. In the past, the first thing I'd have done was go round the nearest pub and not come out for a week.' He also remembers how Houllier had asked him to shake Brad Friedel's hand before a game. Friedel had just ousted James from the goalkeeping slot and James wasn't too pleased at the suggestion. 'I thought he was mad, but I did it, and realised it wasn't me, David James, but me as part of Liverpool Football Club who was encouraging the side to win. Now I go around before a game and shake everybody's hand.' It was all part of Houllier's philosophy that the team comes first and that every player must be pulling for the team, not just for themselves.

James says that he has friends in Liverpool who hate Houllier for what he did to him, but James bears no grudges. Today, he can see the sense in Houllier's thinking and is happy to thank him for helping him realise his priorities. 'Houllier was a major influence on my career. He stopped me having a self-centred attitude,' he says. But the realisation didn't come quickly enough, and in the summer of 1999 Houllier sold James to Aston Villa for £2 million.

Stan Collymore had been another thorn in Liverpool's flesh. Collymore was signed by Roy Evans in the summer of 1995 from Nottingham Forest for what was then a British record transfer fee of £8.5 million. He had been a prolific goal scorer with Forest, having joined them two years earlier from Southend United for £2.2 million. But Collymore was a man known to have had problems along the way. He had begun his career at Stafford Rangers and had then moved on to Crystal Palace, where difficulties had seemed to home in on him. Life at Palace was not easy, and two years after joining, and having played only a handful of games, he dropped down a division to link up with Southend, where his career began to blossom. Fifty goals in two seasons at Forest made him not only one of the country's top scorers but also one of the hottest talents in the game. It was hardly surprising that Liverpool should have outbid a number of other clubs for his signature.

Initially, there weren't any problems. Collymore was a highly talented striker and he soon found the net in the most dramatic of ways. The crowd took to him and much was expected of him, but then the devil seemed to get into him. It wasn't that Collymore was a hellbuster or anything like that; he was simply moody, distracted, depressed. The main problem centred on getting him to move to Merseyside, which he seemed reluctant to do. Admittedly, Collymore's mother had been ill and this influenced, for a time, his decision not to move to Merseyside, but his continuing reluctance to move north undoubtedly caused friction among his fellow players. There was talk that Collymore was being made an exception to the rule, that Collymore could skip training but if they did they got fined, and so on. You could understand the players' complaints, and it did little to help team morale. It might have been just about tolerable had Collymore's skills on the field also not gone into decline. As the season wore on he scored fewer and fewer goals. He seemed disinclined to chase lost balls, his shoulders dropped, and his spirit vanished. It was a sad sight, for Collymore was a natural talent, and an exciting one at that. At his best he was as good as any striker in the top flight, but at his worst he was a waste of space.

Although he could never really be counted among the Spice Boys, Collymore's lack of effort on and off the field only added to the problems that were circumnavigating Evans. His mere presence was undermining any chance of discipline. Fortunately, it was not a problem Houllier had to deal with directly, though he would have to sort out its ramifications, for in the summer of 1997 Collymore was sold to Aston Villa for £7 million. In view of his continuing problems, Liverpool could count themselves lucky to have recouped most of the fee they had paid for him. Had they waited another year, they almost certainly would have taken a very hefty loss.

Danny Murphy was another player labelled as a Spice Boy who almost lost out but who, by good fortune, was lucky enough not to be thrown out of Anfield. Chester-born Murphy had been signed by Roy Evans in the summer of 1997 from Crewe Alexandra for £3 million after a series of impressive performances with the then Second Division club. The twenty-year-old was given an early opportunity at Anfield, but despite performing decently he soon made way for older, more experienced players.

He returned to the first team towards the end of the 1997/98 season but still could not hold down a permanent spot.

It was hardly surprising, given his age, that he should soon be labelled as one of the Spice Boys, and indeed there was probably more fact than fiction to the allegation. Houllier was not happy with him, and although he gave him some early opportunities, the new manager decided that Murphy was surplus to requirements and placed him on the transfer list. Surprisingly, there were few enquiries and no offers. The only interest came from Crewe manager Dario Gradi, who told Houllier that he'd be happy to take him back to Crewe on loan. Houllier readily agreed, and towards the end of the 1998/99 season Murphy returned to the lower divisions. It was to be a turning point for Murphy, who later returned to Anfield determined to prove that he had the ability to hold his own at Liverpool. Much of this new-found commitment was undeniably thanks to Gradi, as shrewd a manager as any, who always seemed to get the best out of his players. 'He'd had problems at Liverpool because of his behaviour off the pitch,' Gradi said, 'which although not outrageous had not been highly professional either. I think he went back to Anfield with an increased determination to succeed.'

When Murphy returned to Liverpool most of the Spice Boys had departed and a new culture was settling on the club as the foreign players brought with them a fresh set of values and professionalism. Houllier scrutinised him carefully and was impressed by his enthusiasm and determination, particularly in training. As a result, he decided to offer him a further opportunity. Murphy, to his credit, grabbed it, and during the treble-winning season was to become a regular member of the squad, winning high praise from his manager. In August 2001 his play had improved to such an extent that he was awarded an England cap. Murphy was more than grateful. 'I can't thank the manager enough,' he said, 'firstly for being honest with me and then for sticking to his promise of giving me a chance if I put in the right kind of application. I did what he asked, and now I'm reaping the rewards.'

Murphy was lucky enough not to end up walking the streets of Liverpool, but another youngster repeatedly blotted his copy book. His name was David Thompson. The young midfielder was a local lad who'd been given his debut against Arsenal on 19 August 1996 at the age of eighteen. A wide player with pace and a ferocious shot, he was expected to become a regular, but it was not to be. After being red-carded in a reserve match, Thompson was lambasted by Houllier in the dressing room. He was told that he should never have reacted, that he was letting his team-mates and his club down, and that he had to mend his ways. But instead of taking the criticism on the chin, Thompson answered back. Players froze as they listened; Thompson had gone too far. Within days Thompson found himself banished to the Youth Academy in Kirby, sometimes known around Melwood as Liverpool's punishment cell, for a couple of weeks. 'I thought that might be it,' he later confessed, but when he returned Houllier made all the right noises about giving him another chance. Thompson did make further appearances – in all, he played 56 games for Liverpool and scored five goals – but Houllier was clearly still not impressed enough to make him a permanent fixture in the side.

By the summer of 2000, Thompson had decided that things were not working out at Liverpool and that if he ever wanted regular first-team football he would have to leave. Still Houllier asked him to stay, but Thompson was adamant and he was sold to Coventry City for £2.5 million. Although he did enjoy first-team football at Coventry, it was not with huge success. Coventry were relegated in 2001, and during the late summer of 2002 Thompson was transferred to Blackburn Rovers where he finally began to show his potential. He was rewarded with a call-up into the England squad in October 2002.

Steven Gerrard had his run-ins with Houllier too, and was in danger of also becoming a Spice Boy. The young Liverpool player was, like many of the other Spice Boys, and unsurprisingly for someone of his age, fond of a good night out and a few drinks. Houllier had to warn him. Football was no longer a hobby; he was a full-time professional athlete and as such he had to look after himself and behave in an appropriate manner. And that did not involve going out drinking or clubbing. 'He has to live for the job,' Houllier argued. 'If his mates want to go to a nightclub, let them. By the time he has finished, he can buy one of his own.' But until then he had to try to steer clear. That was enough to frighten the youngster, who swiftly began to mend his ways. 'He's shown everybody that if you're not working hard for the good of the team, he'll get rid of you, whoever you are,' Gerrard said of his boss, and towards the back end of 2002 the midfielder was given a further reminder of his duties after some lacklustre performances in a red shirt.

Of the other so-called Spice Boys, Phil Babb, who had never fully realised his potential following his signing after the 1994 World Cup finals, departed for Sporting Lisbon on a Bosman free transfer. This time Houllier was more than happy to let a player go for nothing. He knew he would never have received more than a pittance by way of a transfer fee, and anyhow, he felt the club would be better off without his wage bill. In his final years at Liverpool Babb had been dogged by injury and loss of form and his move out of Anfield was both predictable and welcome. Paul Ince, too, was always going to be on his way out, even though Houllier had been prepared to give him every chance. Ince did not take the opportunity. He'd had to be substituted against Manchester United when he claimed to be 'tired', and this was to have dire consequences. Ince had also been indisciplined, and had been sent off in the final minute in the UEFA Cup against Valencia, the Spaniards then hitting an equaliser. In the summer of 1999 he joined Middlesbrough for £1 million. He later spilt a few stories to the papers.

Houllier's philosophy is simple: you have to give one hundred per cent commitment to the team. That means your private life will always impinge on your public performance on the pitch, so if you drink or abuse your body in any way, you will let your team-mates down, and that is simply unacceptable. Footballers are athletes, and as such have to maintain a level of fitness. You would not expect to see Linford Christie out drinking the night before a race, or legless three days before an Olympic event. Footballers should not think they are any different.

Phil Thompson likens Houllier to Joe Fagan. 'He's strong and hard. If there is discipline to be handed out, they don't come harder than Gérard Houllier. He's like Joe Fagan. He quietly goes about his business, but you never, ever cross him.'

7. A CHRISTMAS TALE

'Sami who?' was the question every Liverpool fan was asking. While other clubs were spending millions bolstering their defences with world-class signings, Houllier had apparently plumped for an unknown Finn to be the new heart of the Liverpool defence. It raised more than a few eyebrows. What's more, he was only costing £2.6 million from a small Dutch team with an uninspiring name. 'If he was any good,' sniped Liverpool fans, 'why is he not playing for a big club, and why aren't Real, Barcelona, United and the rest queuing up for his signature?'

Anfield, Christmas Eve 1998. Gérard Houllier was only a month or so into his new job. The festive celebrations had begun much earlier that day as staff members congregated for their annual drinks and food bash. Some of the players turned up, and of course club officials were also present. Houllier, Phil Thompson, Sammy Lee, Joe Corrigan and all the others from the coaching staff were mingling with other employees, enjoying a drink and a good laugh. But while the celebrations continued in the trophy room area at Anfield, Houllier, Thompson and club chief executive Peter Robinson walked off down the corridor for a meeting that would prove to be one of the most important in the club's history.

Houllier and Robinson had not had much of a chance to get together and chat over the last few weeks. Too much had been going on. But over mince pies the two men had begun an exchange about future plans. As the conversation became more intense, Robinson suggested retreating to the quiet of the boardroom. 'Let's bring Phil in,' suggested Houllier. 'He's got a few ideas as well.' And so the three men, grabbing some plates of food, retired to the calm of the boardroom leaving the laughter and jollity of the party behind.

Houllier pulled out a sheet of paper, and between them the three men started to make a list of players who would be shown the door. They then began to compile a list of players they would like to bring in. They reckoned that they probably needed seven new players for the following season, 1999/2000. It was the beginning of a massive rebuilding programme. As each name was put down, they decided just how serious they were about him. Was he really good enough? Would he fit in? Would he be genuinely committed to the Liverpool cause? They then had to estimate the likely chances of signing them.

Having finalised their list, all three men pulled out their mobile phones and began to make a series of calls across Europe enquiring about the availability of certain players. Houllier made most of the foreign calls, Thompson called the English clubs, while Robinson used his extensive contacts to call those agents and chief executives he knew best. As it was Christmas Eve it was not easy to track people down, but the three persevered and found those they wanted to speak to in offices, bars, homes, even on motorways.

Top of the list were a number of English players, one central defender in particular. Houllier was keen to have a substantial English contingent in his side, but the stumbling block was sure to be the price. Rio Ferdinand and Sol Campbell headed the wanted list. 'We tried desperately to recruit English players,' Robinson recalled. 'We asked about a centre-half we were interested in, and we were told that the figure he might leave for, only *might*, was £15 million.' No way could Liverpool afford that. Even if they could, they knew it would be ill advised. It was out of the question and would eat too far into their cash reserves, restricting the number of other players they would be able to sign. The more they looked and the more phone calls they made, the more obvious it became that they would have to go abroad for the bulk, if not all, of their new recruits.

The meeting continued well into the evening. Everybody else had left the ground, making their way back to their homes to prepare for the following morning, but Houllier, Robinson and Thompson had become so caught up in their phone calls, so excited by some of the responses, that they had not realised the time and had forgotten what day it was. With Christmas Day only a few hours away the three men decided that enough was enough. It was becoming more and more difficult to track down agents and chairmen anyway, most of whom were now busily getting ready for Christmas morning, and the three of them had already made major inroads into their rebuilding process. Some players had been struck off the list as too expensive, others had shifted from one category to another, while some had been heavily pencilled in as potential signings. Robinson later reckoned that if he had not called it a day Houllier would still have been there in the morning. 'I look back and smile now,' he said, 'that while people were enjoying the start of the festive period, we were sitting in the boardroom and coming to conclusions about selling players and bringing seven new players in.' Although none of them probably realised it at the time, that meeting laid the foundations for future success at the club.

It wasn't long before Houllier's backroom team began the lengthy process of watching each player on numerous occasions and compiling a dossier of their strengths and weaknesses. One by one they went down the list. Some were struck off, reckoned not to be quite as exciting as they had originally supposed, while others they had not initially regarded too highly became firmer possibilities. Slowly, a final hit list emerged of players who might be available at the right price who possessed the qualities Houllier demanded.

What Houllier wanted above all from any new player was total commitment to the cause. He wanted hunger, dedication and professionalism. He was after players who wanted to win but who were also prepared to be team players. He needed players to gel with his new culture. Once the player had been identified it was over to Rick Parry and Peter Robinson to begin the process of negotiations. These took some time to complete, right through into the spring of 2000, and the dividends did not begin to appear until the summer of that year.

But early in the new year of 1999 they had their first recruit, the Cameroon international defender Rigobert Song, who arrived from Italian club Salernitana for £2.6 million. Song, an outstanding header of the ball, was equally adept at full-back or in the centre of defence. He could also run at defences, and he quickly became a Kop favourite, always remembered for 'One Song, we've only got one Song!'

That summer, Sami Hyypia arrived. One of the oddities about Hyypia's signing was that the initial interest in him came not from Houllier, Thompson, Robinson or any of the scouts at the club. Instead, it came from one of the most unexpected of sources – a television cameraman. 'It was midway through the 1998/99 season,' Robinson recalled, 'when there was a knock on the door of my office at Anfield.' Outside was a young man who asked if he could have a word. Robinson ushered him into the room and told him to sit down. 'I had never met the chap before. He came in and introduced himself as a cameraman who covered football in Europe. He knew we were looking for a strong defender and recommended us to take a look at Sami, who was then playing for Willem, one of the smaller Dutch clubs.' Hyypia was a Finnish international, he said, a tall lad who was as solid as a rock. He reckoned he would be perfect for Liverpool. Robinson smiled and politely thanked the man, thinking that there was probably nothing in it. After all, Robinson and others at Anfield get a dozen such recommendations from members of the public each week. Robinson, however, decided to pass the message on to Houllier, and over the next few months Liverpool had him watched on several occasions in Holland.

'We knew that Sunderland were also interested in him,' Robinson added, 'but there was a general perception that because of his size he might be a bit too slow for English football.' That might have been the view in Sunderland and among other Premiership clubs, 'but that was not the opinion formed by our backroom staff. Ron Yeats, Phil Thompson, Tom Saunders and Patrice Bergues all thought he was just the player we were looking for, and when Gérard confirmed that, we opened talks to bring him to Anfield.' Hyypia took little persuading, and in the summer of 1999 he left Willem II of Tilburg to join Liverpool in a £2.6 million deal.

'Sami who?' was the question every Liverpool fan was asking. While other clubs were spending millions bolstering their defences with world-class signings, Houllier had apparently plumped for an unknown Finn to be the new heart of the Liverpool defence. It raised more than a few eyebrows. What's more, he was only costing £2.6 million from a small Dutch team with an uninspiring name. 'If he was any good,' sniped Liverpool fans, 'why is he not playing for a big club, and why aren't Real, Barcelona, United and the rest queuing up for his signature?' They were difficult questions to answer, although one website correspondent who knew a thing or two about French, Dutch and

German football emailed in to say that Sami Hyypia was outstanding and would be a revelation at Anfield.

So six-foot-four-inch Sami Hyypia arrived at Anfield. Had Shankly been the manager, he would have invited the press corps to walk around Hyypia, as he once did with Ron Yeats. 'Look,' he'd have told them, 'he's as tall as Liverpool Cathedral!' Although nobody realised it at the time, Hyypia was to become another Yeats, one of the new manager's first signings and one of his most significant and successful. He was a man around whom a team could be built, and who in time would become club captain. There was much that was similar between Yeats and Hyypia. Both were dominant in the air, both marshalled their defences in a similar way, both got on with the job without any fuss, both were calm in a crisis and both provided quiet but inspiring leadership.

That same summer Houllier signed a second central defender who turned out to be equally inspiring. Stéphane Henchoz had been playing with Blackburn Rovers, who had just been relegated to the First Division, but given the number of goals Blackburn had conceded, any interest in Henchoz looked to be ill conceived. Still, the Swiss international had previously played with Hamburg and Neuchatel and clearly had plenty of experience. Both Houllier and Bergues watched him play for his national side and were convinced that he had the class to play at the top end of the Premiership. Blackburn's relegation opened a window of opportunity both for Liverpool and Henchoz; £3 million brought him to Anfield. With that central pairing in place Houllier felt a far happier man, even though nobody outside Anfield had much faith in the largely unproven pair.

After the two central defenders, the next priority was a goalkeeper to replace the increasingly sidetracked David James. Fabien Barthez was a possibility, but he wanted to remain in France; the Dutch number one keeper Edwin Van der Saar was also considered but Juventus demanded more than Liverpool were prepared to pay, Houllier looked elsewhere, and finally settled on Van der Saar's Dutch deputy Sander Westerveld of Vitesse Arnhem, who at £4 million was as cheap as you were likely to find anywhere on the international quality-goalkeeper market.

The backbone of the team was now taking shape, but to complete it another striker was needed. Houllier's search again took him to Holland, and with not much money to play with he signed Eric Meijer on a free Bosman transfer from Leverkusen. A trio of midfielders were also snapped up. Vladimir Smicer, a Czech international, was playing with Houllier's old club Lens at the time. Nobody knew much about him, but Bergues and Houllier had enough contacts within Lens to persuade them that at £3.75 million Smicer was not only reasonably priced but a man to open up defences. Titi Camara, a powerful goal-scoring midfielder, also came to Anfield from France, this time from Marseille for £2.5 million. Finally, there was Dietmar Hamann, a strong defensive midfielder who had just enjoyed a successful season with Newcastle United. At £8 million Hamann was Houllier's most expensive signing, almost a club record. That price tag dictated many of Houllier's other deals.

When Houllier officially unveiled his new players to the media there were some quizzical looks. 'Henchoz we knew from his time at Blackburn, and Hamann we knew as well,' remembered one local journalist, 'but as for the rest, nobody had ever heard of them.' This was not Liverpool's style. Normally they would be trading at the top end of the market, signing players with the biggest reputations, yet here was the virtually unknown Houllier signing half a dozen players nobody in English football or the media had ever heard of. It did not bode well. 'Trust me,' Houllier urged when local journalists asked a few pertinent questions. But that was asking an awful lot, especially when other top Premiership clubs were raiding the European market and returning with big-name signings. It felt like Liverpool were the poor relations, forever doomed to buy in the bargain basement while the likes of United spent lavishly in the sixth-floor salons. Still, in all, Houllier had spent almost £25 million on half a dozen new players and at the same time recouped some £10 million in sales. It wasn't bad business, and he was far from finished.

The 1999/2000 season kicked off with a sense of excitement and trepidation: excitement because there were so many new faces, trepidation because they were, generally speaking, unknown quantities. The pre-season friendlies had brought mixed fortunes, but on 7 August, the opening day of the season, Liverpool made an encouraging start with a 2–1 win at Sheffield Wednesday.

Newcomer Titi Camara scored a goal, but on the downside Dietmar Hamann picked up a serious injury and was to miss much of the autumn. A week later, they lost disappointingly at home to Watford. A couple of impressive wins followed over Leeds and Arsenal, but any encouragement that might have come from those results was dissipated at Anfield on 11 September when Manchester United beat them 3–2, although on another day the result could just as easily have gone Liverpool's way. At the end of the month came another home defeat, this time to Everton.

As the final Christmas of the twentieth century came and went, Liverpool could draw a measure of comfort from the first half of their season. So far they could boast a dozen wins and four draws – not bad at all for a side undergoing such dramatic change. They stood fourth in the League, four points behind leaders Leeds United. Nevertheless, there was still plenty of criticism from the fans, the chief complaint being that they did not look convincing and that half the time they seemed to rely on good fortune rather than skill. Results were being ground out. The most dramatic improvement was undoubtedly in defence, where Hyypia and Henchoz were beginning to put together an effective partnership, while between the sticks Westerveld looked much better than James and Friedel. Only twenty goals had been conceded. The team might not have been firing on all cylinders, but you could hardly fault the defence. Part of the problem was injuries. Hamann had missed a bagful of games, and Smicer, who had begun the season promisingly, had also been injured, prompting one fanzine to describe him as 'a delicate version of Pat Nevin'. Redknapp, as ever, was on the treatment bench.

Into the new millennium, and Liverpool kicked off with a defeat at the hands of Tottenham. Hardly a good omen, especially as it was followed by a 1–0 loss at home to Blackburn Rovers in the fourth round of the FA Cup. They were already out of the Worthington Cup as well, beaten by Southampton, so once again it was looking as if Liverpool's season was effectively over in January. Nobody had expected them to win the League, but there had been hopes that they might enjoy a decent run in both cup competitions.

Then, an injection of £40 million into Liverpool Football Club by Granada Television early in 2000 gave Houllier a rare opportunity of matching the purses of Arsenal and Manchester United in the transfer market. Top of his list was a new striker. There was no doubt that Liverpool were still short up front. Robbie Fowler was not as effective as he had been, while Michael Owen, still only nineteen years old, needed careful nurturing if he was to maintain his astonishing progress. Dutchman Eric Meijer had proved to be a laughable buy, his goal instinct never matching his enthusiasm.

The name at the top of Houllier's list was Emile Heskey, the powerful Leicester City front man. Houllier confessed to having spotted Heskey years earlier when he was still working in France, and he'd kept a watchful eye on the youngster's progress via Sky Television. Heskey was still young, only 21, already an England international and with plenty of experience of playing alongside Michael Owen at national under-21 level. He was the kind of player who could hold up the ball, force his way past players, and even put the ball into the back of the net himself. He was the ideal foil for the more goal-minded Owen and Fowler. Of course, Leicester City's manager Martin O'Neill didn't want to lose Heskey, but he was intelligent enough to realise that the striker was ambitious and needed a bigger club to fulfil his personal ambitions. Behind closed doors, a £9 million deal was struck to bring Heskey to Anfield in the summer, but when a Champions League place began to look possible Houllier enquired if Heskey might be available immediately, especially as Leicester had just won the League Cup and were not seriously in contention elsewhere. It was possible, came the reply, but it would cost Liverpool an extra £2 million. The final total of £11 million smashed Liverpool's transfer record by some margin.

Heskey stepped straight into the side and made a huge impact as Liverpool put together a run of eleven games without defeat which took them into a challenging spot for a place in the Champions League. But then, as the season reached its crucial climax, they lost three of their final five games and drew the other two, and any hope of a Champions League place disappeared over the horizon. At least they had done enough to earn themselves a crack at the UEFA Cup. It was a start, and although they might have hoped for better, the expensive signing of Heskey had paid dividends. Admittedly, the UEFA Cup was not anywhere near as lucrative as the Champions League, but it did put Liverpool on the European stage and, as every Liverpool fan knew, that was where they belonged.

If the first team offered only limited success, the reserves' was unqualified: they topped their division for the first time in years. 'For me, the reserve team is not a reserve team, it's a Liverpool team,' insisted Houllier. 'When they wear the Liverpool shirt, people should give the best account of themselves.' The reserves had struggled in recent years to maintain their top-flight status, but as the new millennium dawned they were crowned champions of their league, despite the fact that a number of seasoned professionals had refused to turn out for them, deeming it beneath themselves. It would not be long before these players failed to turn out for the Liverpool first team, too, this time rejected by Houllier. The manager was outraged that any player could regard himself above playing for the second string. It's a squad game, he insisted, and people have to play for the reserve side now and again. The names of those who made it known that they did not fancy a game on cold Tuesday evenings at Haig Avenue were carefully noted in Houllier's little black book.

Throughout 1999/2000, Houllier continued to strengthen his grip on team affairs and discipline. Even though he did not fully accept the validity of the Spice Boys tag, he knew there was more than an element of truth in it. It was a tag Liverpool had to get rid of, and they had to be publicly seen to be changing the culture of the club. Players needed to focus. There were far too many distractions in the form of modelling assignments, guest appearances, media interviews, sponsorship commitments and so forth. It had to end.

Mobile telephones were going off all the time. As one Melwood insider remembers it, 'wherever you went players would be on their mobiles, either taking calls or playing games on them. Phones were going off with those hideous ringing tones all the time. They seemed to be competing with each other for the worst ringing tone.' There used to be a time when players were almost incommunicado at Anfield, impossible to get hold of, because of the lack of telephones. There were just one or two pay phones, and that was it. When players came to Anfield in those days, they came to train, but then the age of the mobile phone dawned and the little devices soon began to dictate players' lives. When they started going off in team meetings, Houllier decided he had had enough, and he banned them. This new edict certainly did not endear him to those players whose lives had become so centred around the mobile that life without it was almost unthinkable. They grumbled, but in reality their days were already numbered.

Houllier was also taking a close look at diet. Back in the early 1990s, Graeme Souness had been the first to consider imposing a more rigorous diet on the players. Souness, who had played in Italy, had experienced the continental approach to diets where energy-packed foods had replaced fatty foods such as chips, pies and sausages, but his plan had not gone down well at the time, Ian Rush pointing out that he had broken all kinds of goal-scoring records even though his diet before a game consisted of chips and steak and kidney pie. But at least Souness had begun the revolution. It continued under Evans, though not with the same commitment. Players were known to sneak in chocolate bars, and when they left Melwood it was accepted that there was little that could be done if they suddenly went off to McDonald's for a burger and chips. The worst culprits were undoubtedly the British players, many of whom had largely been brought up on what is now termed junk food. Gary McAllister recalled that when he was at Motherwell they always ate gammon, steak and eggs for lunch on a Saturday. The foreign players were far more careful with their diets, tending to eat more fruit and pasta. It was part of their culture.

Houllier was determined that all players would from now on adhere to a strict eating code. All fatty foods disappeared from the canteen menu, and in came low-fat, energy-rich foods such as pasta, jacket potatoes, rice, chicken, tuna, fruit, vegetables and salads. The biggest hit, according to one of the chefs, was fruit salad. Dieticians were even brought in to explain to the players in simple language the benefits of wholesome food. Players' weights were also monitored more regularly to make sure that no one was sneaking off home to a plateful of fish and chips. When Houllier caught David Thompson munching on a chocolate bar after training one day, all hell broke loose. It was yet another nail in the young player's coffin.

What Houllier was trying to instil into his players was his own philosophy that the team is more important than the individual. Whatever individual actions players decide on, they will inevitably have a bearing on the team's performance. If a player gets drunk the night before a game, it will have an effect on the way the team functions. The team will operate at its highest potential only if every constituent part of it is fulfilling its personal obligations. Although football needs individuals, and individual skills, it is essentially a team game; if any player is not performing to his full potential, the sum of the team also falls below its full potential. It was a simple philosophy, but in many ways it ran counter to what most footballers had been thinking for decades, and to the belief that one moment of magic from a gifted player can win a game. It also begs the question of how players such as George Best and Paul Gascoigne would have fared under Houllier. The guess is, not very well.

At the end of the season Houllier could reflect on a promising start in terms of regime change and signings. Hyypia and Henchoz had brought a new resolution to the defence. Sander Westerveld in goal also looked assured, while Dietmar Hamann, although making a listless start to his Anfield career, was undoubtedly a player of some quality. The young players too had continued to make impressive progress, the precociously talented Steven Gerrard in particular beginning to look as if he might be a star of the future. Alan Hansen described him as his 'highlight of the season', and thought he was 'going to be a dominant figure for Liverpool over the next five or six years. The future is very bright for him and for Liverpool.' Michael Owen's progress had been hampered by injury, but the promise was still there and Houllier knew that once his problems were behind him Owen would score many more goals in the Premiership.

Yet the carping continued. Hamann was himself the focus of some of it, but the majority was levelled at Houllier. Some people on the terraces and inside the corridors of Anfield were still suspicious of his ways and wondered if he really knew what he was doing. And among the legion of former players, many were quick to criticise. They could not understand why so many foreign players were being drafted in, why local lads could not be given more of a chance. Their attitude was that Liverpool should stick to the old ways which in the past had been so successful, not to go swallowing the continental approach. Paul Ince, by then at Middlesbrough, had a pop at Houllier in the tabloids. 'I can't even believe he's managed a team before because he certainly doesn't seem to know how to,' Ince claimed, before spitting some venom in Phil Thompson's direction. 'All Thommo does is shout his mouth off, he doesn't coach.' He then added that 'Liverpool are the kind of club who deserve success, but they have a management that will just drag the place down.' This piece did not win him any friends on Merseyside, most of whom reckoned he ought to have examined his own contribution to the Liverpool demise.

As for the fans, it was difficult for them to spot much in the way of improvement. Sure, new players had been introduced and the defence looked more solid, but in the midfield Liverpool looked as cumbersome and slow as ever. There was much chuntering on the Kop; Liverpool were not convincing and wouldn't win anything with this side. Houllier was under pressure, but all he asked for was time and patience. It won't happen overnight, he told fans, it will take maybe four or five years. We are still some way behind Manchester United, but we are beginning to catch them. 'And mark my words,' he stressed. 'We *will* catch them.'

Houllier was even having to defend himself against those who should have known better – some of the Anfield old boys. Ian St John had been a legend at Anfield during the Shankly years. Indeed, he had been one of Shankly's most important signings and had helped instigate the Scottish manager's revolution at the club. Since retiring as a player St John had briefly worked himself as a manager, largely unsuccessfully, and then as a television pundit where he was highly successful fronting an ITV Saturday lunchtime programme with former England international Jimmy Greaves. Since the demise of that programme he had continued to work in the media. In 1998 he began to host a radio phone-in programme on Liverpool's independent radio station Radio City. The programme went out on a Saturday evening immediately after the match and typically involved fans calling in with their comments, to which St John would respond. In the early months of Houllier's reign his responses were not always positive.

In some ways you could not blame St John. After all, he had now swapped coats and was a pundit rather than a supporter; it was now incumbent upon him to be analytical and critical, whether positively or negatively. At the same time, however, he was also only echoing what many of the callers thought. After a defeat or an uninspiring draw, caller after caller would voice their concern that Houllier was not resolving the problem. More often than not St John would agree with them, but at times he was too critical and too flippant, failing to understand or acknowledge the mammoth problem Houllier was facing. St John seemed to think it was easy when in fact the situation was far more complicated.

It was well known that St John was a good friend of Roy Evans, and his line was that if Evans had to go, why not Houllier as well when they were supposed to be joint managers? You can't blame one without the other. There was a certain logic to that argument, but it totally ignored the fact that Evans left of his own accord. An interview with St John in one matchday programme, while not critical of the club and management, quietly angered Houllier who felt that space should not be given to him. When it came to revamping the programme for the following season, Houllier insisted that there should be less emphasis on the legends and more on the current side.

For St John was not alone. There were other well-known former Liverpool players who at times were just as scathing. The television and radio networks were full of ex-Liverpool players either hosting programmes, acting as pundits or simply all too eager to voice their opinions. They included Alan Hansen, Mark Lawrenson, Barry Venison, Jim Beglin, Tommy Smith and David Fairclough. Alan Hansen, however, always carefully crafted his words so that they did not come over as too critical. He was wise enough to appreciate the size of the task facing Houllier, and the way he was going about trying to manage it. But it was not always so with Mark Lawrenson, who was usually more forthright. Tommy Smith was even more outspoken. He'd been the principal thorn in Graeme Souness's flesh whenever the Scotsman was facing difficulties at Anfield.

At least Houllier could always depend on his allies inside Anfield, and after his first full season in charge he was winning over many of the players. Perhaps not all, but captain Jamie Redknapp was certainly one of them, and when he drew a comparison between Houllier and other managers he'd worked with, it made for interesting reading. 'He is such a hands-on boss at the club, more than any other manager I've known, and everything we do he decides,' he claimed. 'He has such a massive input into the club.' It was a fascinating description given that Redknapp had served under such Anfield legends as Kenny Dalglish, Graeme Souness and Roy Evans, as well as more than one England manager. 'The training is great,' he added. 'You really enjoy yourself. He sets the right example for players. He is a real perfectionist. He doesn't suffer fools. If he doesn't think you're pulling your weight or giving your best for the club, he'll blank you. He ain't got no time for that . . . he has a real aura about him.'

8. THE BOARDROOM COUP

In a briefing paper to the board, Rick Parry argued that a flotation on the stock market was not the way forward. It was not Liverpool's style. But he did state that Liverpool would need a cash injection of some £20 million every year over the next three years. That amount of money would enable them to get into the Champions League. 'That's where we have to be,' he emphasised. 'If we don't make the Champions League in three years, we could go crashing down the League and become a very ordinary club.'

The success of Manchester United irked everyone involved with Liverpool Football Club. It wasn't just that United had left them behind when it came to the football; off the pitch, as well, United had now become a mega-million-pound business that had far outpaced the two Merseyside clubs put together.

United had always been well off. With some justification they called themselves the country's best-supported club, and they'd always been able to more than match Liverpool in the transfer market. Even when United were relegated in 1974, they still took a vast army of supporters around the country with them every other Saturday. It was United who had blessed the game with the Busby Babes, it was United who were the first English club to win the European Cup, it was United who had boasted Best, Law and Charlton, it was United who had what was probably the best ground in the country. United had arrogance, power and prestige. Mention the word Manchester anywhere in the world and the reply was always 'Manchester United'. A journalist once compared United to Sainsbury's – big, brash, busy, rich, but a little overpowering – while Liverpool were the local corner Co-op: small, friendly, not as well stocked, no car park but at the same time no pushing trolleys. It might have annoyed a few Liverpool fans, but you could understand what he was getting at. Liverpool might have enjoyed unparalleled success throughout the seventies and eighties, but people still talked of United as the 'nation's side'; the gap might only have been marginal then, but it was there. By the mid-nineties, however, that gap was in danger of becoming a chasm.

What had changed it all was that in 1991 United became a public company and floated on the stock exchange. They were not the first football club to go public, that dubious honour had fallen to Tottenham Hotspur, but Spurs had never been able to capitalise on any market success because they had failed to match it on the pitch. It was the latter which was to prove crucial at Old Trafford. United chairman Martin Edwards might have been derided by the fans for taking United down a far too commercial avenue, but there was no doubt that his foresight and business acumen, as well as his continuing faith in new manager Alex Ferguson, had helped to turn United into one of the richest football clubs in Europe. Indeed, they had become so wealthy and so attractive a sporting business proposition by 1998 that in September of that year Rupert Murdoch's Sky Television agreed a £575 million takeover deal with Edwards. The headline deal eventually floundered, though only after the Monopolies and Mergers Commission had ruled it unacceptable.

As far as United fans were concerned, that was yet another indication that Edwards was really only interested in making as much money as he could. His heart, they claimed, lay in United's commercial activities, not on the pitch in the Theatre of Dreams where theirs were. Yet it was Edwards who laid the foundations for the commercial success that eventually supplied the cash for the on-the-pitch success. The two went hand in hand. Plans were laid for the stadium to be developed. It grew from a 45,000 all-seater to 55,000, then to 60,000; today it's topping 67,000. At one point United were valued on the stock exchange at £1 billion. The increased gate receipts, merchandising revenue plus television money from successes at home and in Europe meant that Ferguson had a vast treasure chest he could plunder for the finest talents in world football. In the summer of 2001 he was able to spend a mighty £50 million on just two players, and he followed that up twelve months later by spending £30 million on Rio Ferdinand alone. It was the kind of money other managers could only dream of. Such sums made the Liverpool faithful wonder if they could ever compete with United again.

Much of United's success came from exploiting the merchandising side of their business. United was a world brand name with an unrealised potential. Edward Freedman, who had been successfully branding Tottenham Hotspur, was brought in to carry

st a couple of months into the job as joint manager with Roy Evans, and Gérard
ullier surveys the size of the task ahead. (© Popperfoto)

Above Press conference
Anfield, November 199
Gérard Houllier takes
over as manager of
Liverpool. Phil
Thompson, his new
assistant, looks on in th
background.
(© Popperfoto)

Left 'Mon dieu! Surely
that was a mile offside re
(© Popperfoto)

ıst for once the normally articulate Gérard Houllier is tongue tied. Must be
ıother Robbie Fowler misdemeanour. (© Popperfoto)

Above Another Liverpool/Manchester United clash, May 1999. Honours are even but Si Alex demands a further ten minutes of injury time. (© Popperfoto)

Left Houllier and Thompson look distinctl unhappy. But there was nothing to fear as Liverpool beat Huddersfield Town in the third round of the FA Cup. (© Popperfoto)

ne-two, one-two-three. A unique treble for Houllier and Liverpool as the Reds
in the UEFA Cup to make it three cups in a season. The rest of us needed a good
down. (© Popperfoto)

Left Oh happy days! Gérard and his best pal Robbie Fowler. But you just knew it wouldn't last. Before long the two had parted company. (© Popperfoto)

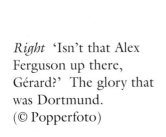

Right 'Isn't that Alex Ferguson up there, Gérard?' The glory that was Dortmund. (© Popperfoto)

Above 'Give it to Owen!'
Houllier screams at
Patrik Berger to wellie
the ball upfield to Owen
on a sweltering hot day
in Cardiff's Millennium
Stadium as Liverpool beat
Arsenal 2–1 to win the
FA Cup. (© Popperfoto)

Right The pressure's on.
Nail-biting times for
Houllier as Liverpool
throw away a four-point
lead at the top of the
table. (© Popperfoto)

The rot sets in. Liverpool about to exit the Champions League at the hands of Swiss club Basle. (© Popperfoto)

out a similar operation at United, and he was to prove one of the club's best signings. He literally overhauled United's marketing activities. In particular the merchandising was expanded. United dreamt up new products, had them produced to their own standards, then sold them through their outlets. New shops, not just at the ground, were opened, as well as a website. There was a café, a movie, even a television channel, owned by Granada TV, Sky and United, which transmitted for six hours every day of the year. United were soon making more money from such operations than through the turnstiles. That, coupled with a sudden surge of interest in football in the nineties, highly lucrative television deals and on-the-pitch success, saw the company's profits and share price go through the ceiling. One international survey claimed that United were far and away the richest club in Europe.

Of course, United were fortunate in many respects. Had they not enjoyed such overwhelming success on the pitch, who knows what might have happened to them commercially. They might well have over-extended themselves and crashed into debt with a stadium half-empty every Saturday, but umpteen Premier League triumphs, a second European Cup and continuing representation in the Champions League guaranteed them a healthy cash flow, sky-high profits and the wherewithal to sustain a high expenditure rate in the transfer market.

Liverpool had always been a big-spending club and on numerous occasions had smashed the British transfer record. Tony Hateley, Alun Evans, Kenny Dalglish and Dean Saunders were signings made at the highest end of the market. Back in the seventies and eighties, and even into the nineties, Liverpool had always been able to compete with United in the transfer market. Money was never a problem. But all that changed as the twentieth century drew to a close. Suddenly, with the influx of television money, transfer fees were spiralling out of control. Liverpool might have been able to compete with most Premiership clubs, but they could not fork out £20 or £30 million for a single player.

The club had always been run like the metaphorical friendly corner shop. Peter Robinson acted as storekeeper and stockman, creeping away after a day of serving customers to keep the books. There was nothing pretentious or arrogant about Liverpool. It had been run this way for years, highly successfully, and there seemed little reason to change things. Even the minutes of board meetings had never been recorded. But during the early nineties Liverpool were forced to face up to a number of problems. The most immediate was the need to turn Anfield into an all-seater stadium, following the recommendations of the Taylor Report. It was set to be an expensive operation, costing at least £7 million, and if Liverpool were to continue dealing in the transfer market, extra cash had to be found. Players' salaries were escalating alongside transfer fees, and the building of the new all-seater Kop would reduce the capacity at Anfield, thereby reducing gate revenue.

Liverpool had never really had a rich benefactor. The Moores family, who owned the Littlewoods shopping empire, had long had an influence on Merseyside through their substantial shareholdings in both Liverpool and Everton. They had been more closely identified with the latter, too, and had donated generously to the Goodison Park coffers; their involvement at Anfield had generally been low key. Nevertheless, at times they had brought some influence to bear, particularly during the early days of Shankly when John Moores recommended one of his employees, Eric Sawyer, as a board member. Sawyer was appointed to bring some business acumen to the club as well as support for Shankly's transfer dealings, although there was never any evidence that the Moores family ever dug into their own pockets to fund the club or any of its dealings.

As the nineties dawned, insiders at Liverpool began to realise that a wealthy benefactor was vital if they were going to retain their position as the country's top club. On top of the need for a cash injection, there was also the problem of Sir John Moores' substantial shareholding falling into the wrong hands when he died. Already in his nineties, Sir John had effectively given up any active interest in football, although he could still occasionally be spotted in the directors' box at Goodison or Anfield. Nobody, of course, knew the contents of Sir John's will, or what might happen to his vast shareholdings, and at the time there were at least two multi-millionaire supporters keen to get a foothold in the club. It was the then vice-chairman Sydney Moss who pointed out that the solution was obvious. Sir John Moores' nephew David was a fanatical Liverpool follower, and when Liverpool travelled across Europe David could usually be spotted somewhere in the vicinity. He was rich (a substantial shareholder in the Littlewoods company), young, keen, related to Sir John, and a Liverpool supporter to boot.

So early in 1991 Moores was invited on to the board. Some months later a new share option was issued, to be underwritten by him. It came as no surprise that the vast majority of these shares were purchased by Moores, thereby giving him a major stake in the club. Now the majority shareholder, it was only a matter of time before Moores became chairman. For many Liverpool fans it was perhaps not the most democratic takeover, but given the death of Sir John Moores a short time later and the chaotic state in which neighbours Everton found themselves as a result, it was perhaps just as well that Liverpool had sorted out the problem before it bit them.

Unlike many other football club chairmen, Moores was never one to interfere; he was more than happy to leave the daily administration and decision-making to either Peter Robinson or Rick Parry. He had enormous respect for Robinson (always known as PBR), who had been around Anfield almost as long as anyone. He figured that they knew more about it than he did, and just as he had made a decision to take a back seat in the running of the Littlewoods empire, so he made a similar decision with Liverpool.

But with success eluding the club on the pitch, Liverpool could so easily have gone the way of other clubs such as Everton, Sheffield Wednesday, even Nottingham Forest, all of whom had spent heavily in an attempt to buy success but had merely finished up with crippling debts. Fortunately, in Rick Parry Liverpool had taken on board a man astute enough to understand how a balance ledger worked. Parry was born and bred in Liverpool and had been a Red all his life; he even claims to have had a goalkeeping trial with the club when he was a teenager. After university he became an accountant with leading firm Ernst Young, in their Manchester office. In 1985 he made his first venture into the sporting business world when he was seconded to work with Bob Scott on Manchester's first bid for the Olympic games. Although the bid was unsuccessful, it was enough to make Parry realise the business potential of major sporting events, and just as he was facing a decision as to whether he wanted to join Bob Scott for a second crack at bringing the Olympics to Manchester, he received a call from Graham Kelly. Would he be interested in joining a consortium to set up a new Premier League? Parry jumped at the opportunity and soon became a leading light behind its formation; it was hardly surprising that when the new league began in 1991 Parry was its first chief executive. Without the breakaway Premier League football would never have been able to reap the millions that were lying in wait. It was to Parry's credit that he realised this potential.

Five years later, with the second television deal agreed, Parry was being tempted by offers from a number of clubs. He was certainly interested, but before going down that road he wanted to make sure that the one club he really fancied did not want him. So he called PBR. To cut a long story short, PBR, who was then three years off retirement, saw in Parry an able and ideal successor. Parry was coming home.

Over the next few years Parry would gently revolutionise Liverpool, but he was vehemently set against carrying out the kind of revolution United had forced through, even of going down the United path at all. Above all, he did not want Liverpool to become a brash, overpowering, soulless institution whose main concern was making money. Still, he recognised that Liverpool had to change. In 1999, Parry outlined his business philosophy for the club. 'You cannot run football clubs like you did in the seventies,' he argued. 'That's gone, whether you like it or not. But my own view is that there is a business around football. I don't necessarily say football is a business because football to me is a game, but you have to be businesslike. My own view is that we can be very businesslike without losing the essence of what Liverpool is all about. I actually don't think we should lose touch with our roots or what is attractive about Liverpool. We don't have to be big and brash, or be what Manchester United are. What makes Liverpool attractive is the very essence of what Liverpool is all about. So I don't think you rush out and over-commercialise. You can still be very professional in a business sense without losing the heart of Liverpool. It's very attraction to the five million people worldwide who support Liverpool is that it is not brash and over-commercialised.'

It was an intelligent and well-formulated view that was spot on as far as most fans were concerned. In a nutshell, Liverpool needed to adopt a more businesslike approach but that did not mean they needed to be as rapacious as United.

'There is a paradox for United,' Parry continued, 'in that they are both the most loved and most hated club. Liverpool don't have that, and there's no reason why we should become over-commercialised. It's a challenge, but to me there is still a family feel about Liverpool, though I think we have maybe lost touch with supporters to an extent. I think that has drifted, but it is not irreconcilable. We and United are the two national clubs, indeed worldwide clubs. We are successful; people want to share in our success. You don't knock that. It's a success that came from that special relationship.'

In a briefing paper to the board, Rick Parry argued that a flotation on the stock market was not the way forward. It was not Liverpool's style. But he did state that Liverpool would need a cash injection of some £20 million every year over the next three years. That amount of money would enable them to get into the Champions League. 'That's where we have to be,' he emphasised. 'If we don't make the Champions League in three years, we could go crashing down the League and become a very ordinary club.'

Also concerned about the poor showing of Liverpool as a commercial enterprise was Steve Morgan, also Liverpool-born and also a life-long Red, having followed them across the country in his younger days. Since then Morgan had gone on to establish the multi-million-pound building company Redrow. Morgan himself was a multi-millionaire and the second largest individual shareholder in the club. He was particularly critical of the way in which the club had failed to grasp its full commercial potential. He could foresee a financial crisis. Salaries had escalated and transfer deals were spiralling out of control, but revenue was not rising to sustain these increases. The club, he claimed, was not being run properly. He complained, too, about the fact that minutes of board meetings were not being taken. Liverpool, in a word, had to get its act together if it wanted to survive in the twenty-first century.

His criticisms were aimed not at any manager, but at the board, chairman David Moores in particular. Nor was Morgan afraid to tell Moores or anyone else of his views. In 1999, Morgan even made an audacious takeover bid for the club, offering £50 milllion for a 30 per cent stake; his one stipulation was that Moores should step down as chairman and hand over the reins. Not surprisingly, Moores turned him down, but at least Morgan's actions alerted the board to the fact that others in high places and with considerable business acumen and resources could spot that Liverpool were not realising their full commercial potential.

It was Rupert Murdoch's £575 million attempted takeover of Manchester United that alerted television companies to the business prospects of becoming involved in football. Live football coverage produced healthy viewing figures and it was little wonder that television companies were keen to put more football on their screens. Football was also advertising-friendly, and was certain to attract a wide range of products from alcohol to cars and sportswear. It was a lucrative end of the market. Sky, who had won the first live coverage contract, had fully demonstrated the importance of football to its channel, having attracted not only advertisers but subscribers as well.

Every four years the price of live coverage to the television companies rose in spectacular leaps. It did not take much of a commercial mind to realise that if television companies became involved in football clubs, they could thereby influence future coverage of the game as well as contracts. In other words, their involvement would ensure that live coverage continued on television, hopefully on satellite and cable channels as well as terrestrial channels. Therefore a number of television operators began to move into the football industry by buying up stakes in clubs, although the ruling of the Competition Commission in April 1999 had been that the maximum stake allowable was 9.9 per cent. Although Sky had not been able to fulfil its wish to take over United, it continued to hold a 9.9 per cent stake. The cable operator ntl purchased a 6.3 per cent stake in Newcastle United, and other clubs, including Leeds United, also became the subject of media involvement.

Liverpool had always had a close relationship with the Manchester-based ITV provider Granada Television. Over the years

Granada had covered, usually as edited highlights, many games at Anfield, and it was not unusual to spot Granada personnel at the ground on matchdays. Granada had operated a studio and newsroom base in Liverpool, initially at Exchange Flags and later in the Albert Dock complex. With Sky so heavily involved at Old Trafford, the Manchester-based Granada was effectively barred from extensive involvement with its closer neighbour, so instead Granada decided to turn its attention elsewhere.

What nobody has ever known is that back in the early nineties, some years before Sky's aborted takeover, Granada themselves had come close to making a formal bid for United. Granada's then chief executive, Steve Morrison, had argued forcefully that Granada should consider buying the club. At that stage Granada could probably have bought United for as little as £20 million. Indeed, when Robert Maxwell sniffed around United in 1984 a £10 million price tag had been attached to the club. Five years later, Michael Knighton had looked set to buy the club for £20 million, only to discover that the banks would not lend him the cash. One or two bank executives must today feel that they were rather short-sighted, although given Knighton's later antics United fans must feel relieved that the banks were so reluctant to stump up the readies. Morrison's line was that being a Manchester-based company involved in televising football, Granada was the club's obvious parent. What's more, Granada had money to spare and was looking for business opportunities. The debate inside Granada reached a serious level, but in the end the board decided that they did not want to manage a football club. It was far too complicated a business for them; they wanted to stick to areas they knew about.

By 1999, Granada had effectively become the largest company in the ITV network. A takeover of London Weekend Television and Yorkshire Tyne Tees Television left them with the largest share of the independent sector. The ITV network was also keen to win the chase for the next live football contract, so the idea of becoming involved with a football club was once again mooted. It was a natural commercial development for Granada to consider taking some kind of stake in one or more leading football clubs. The possibility of taking over a club, however, was no longer feasible following the decision by the Competition Commission to stonewall Sky's bid to take over United, but there were other avenues of opportunity, chief among which was to take a stake in a football club. This had an obvious appeal for Granada. For a start, the stipulated 9.9 per cent stake would be cheaper than a takeover; it would still give them a voice inside the world of football but, crucially, it would not commit them to the actual day-to-day running of a club. Given Sky's involvement at Old Trafford and the fact that Granada had already become involved in setting up Manchester United Television (MUTV) by taking a one-third interest, Liverpool was the obvious target.

More than anyone, Rick Parry understood the correlation between football and television. He also appreciated that Granada was a far different animal to Sky, and did not have the kind of predatory instincts that had made Sky so hugely successful but also so universally despised. Granada was always more likely to offer friendly advice and help rather than inflict any prescribed style of management on the club. Parry had known Steve Morrison and another leading executive, Jules Burns, for some years, and those relationships were to pave the way for a Granada involvement in Liverpool. The two sides talked for some nine months before finally announcing in July 1999 that they had reached an agreement, with Granada taking a 9.9 per cent equity stake in the club at a cost of £22 million. New shares would be created, with club chairman David Moores remaining as the majority share-holder with 51.4 per cent of the enlarged share capital. 'We have no intention of buying a club,' stressed Granada, 'but we are entering into a deal that will make us a partner in Liverpool's off-the-field activities.' Top of the joint agenda was the possibility of a Liverpool Football Club TV channel. It seemed a good deal, especially for the club, which would now be able to benefit from the commercial skills of Granada as well as use the £22 million in the transfer market. For Granada, too, it was something of a bargain.

The decision by Granada to move into Liverpool was generally greeted with enthusiasm by fans at the club. The majority could see the benefits. Granada, as the local ITV provider for over 40 years, was a trusted local company and the £22 million they were putting into the coffers of the club would help Gérard Houllier's rebuilding process. At the time you could buy quite a few players with £22 million. It was also obvious to anyone that for years Liverpool Football Club had failed to capitalise on its famous name. Commercial opportunities had gone almost unnoticed. Fans only had to glance down the East Lancs Road to spot how their closest rivals were growing fat on the burgeoning football industry. Everyone realised that Liverpool could do with a little more business acumen, even though it might have been anathema to the basic instincts of many fans. But if you had to jump into bed with a commercial giant, then Granada was as good as any.

What the Liverpool board did not generally know, however, was that while Granada were negotiating with Liverpool they were secretly making plans for another deal with Arsenal. Once the agreement with Liverpool had been signed and sealed, Granada officials quickly made their way to Highbury and put an offer to Arsenal. A couple of months later they surprised everyone by announcing a 4.99 per cent stake in Arsenal – bought for a cool £40 million. One or two directors at Liverpool were horrified. Although there had been talk that Granada might look elsewhere for a business involvement in football, it seemed outrageous to them that not only should they be jumping into bed with one of Liverpool's closest rivals, but also that they should be paying them much more money for the privilege. Admittedly the negotiations with Arsenal had not begun until the Liverpool deal had been fully settled, but while Granada were easing themselves into the Anfield boardroom they had at least already been thinking seriously about easing themselves into Highbury as well.

Granada's strategy had always been to buy into either another top-brand club or into a club local to one of the Granada franchise areas. There were only ever a few options. Of the bigger clubs, Manchester United were already out of the equation, Everton were no longer considered a top brand, and Manchester City were going through lean times. The truth was that there were only three major branded clubs in English football: United, Liverpool and Arsenal. If Granada wanted a stake in another top-brand club then Arsenal was the only viable route. As for buying into a local club, the only feasible possibility was Leeds United, but in hard commercial terms the likely returns from such a deal were small. Leeds were local in every sense of the word. In the end, Granada decided against pursuing a local club and decided to settle for Arsenal.

'I couldn't believe it,' was the reaction of one Liverpool board member, 'especially when I heard that Granada had paid Arsenal twice what they had paid us. It made their deal with us look like a huge bargain. It was a bit insulting really.' Even Parry was surprised at the amount Arsenal had raised. Jules Burns, who had been assigned as Granada's man on the board, had to appease them and explain that prices had shot up in the few months since their deal with Liverpool. They also had to understand that football was now big business and had to operate as such. These things happened.

For many fans the deal with Arsenal was also insulting and incomprehensible. It was rather like changing your allegiance, deciding to support another club for whatever reason while still wearing the colours of another. Former Tory minister Edwina Currie had once suggested to someone calling in on a radio phone-in programme to complain that the prices charged by his club were too high that he should go and find another, cheaper club. Anyone associated with football knows that such a suggestion is anathema to football fans. Support of a club has deep roots, often to do with family, childhood or geography. And once you have a club, you don't go jumping on a bandwagon or changing your allegiance to another club. However distressing it may be, you're stuck with your first-choice club for ever.

Businesses, however, work on different principles. When Liverpool fans welcomed Granada into the club, they felt privileged that the local ITV provider should wish to nail its colours to their mast, especially when the company was more identified with Manchester than Liverpool. But as one Granada insider remarked, 'Football has to learn that this is business, and different rules apply.' What, of course, they didn't tell anyone was that many years earlier they had seriously considered taking over Liverpool's biggest rivals United.

Although it made sense for Granada to take a stake in another major football club, they were taking something of a gamble on the reaction at Anfield. You could see the sense in the deal for Granada, but football sentiment does not operate in the same way. Who was to know what mysterious influences might be brought to bear in boardrooms at opposite ends of the country? As it happened, Granada's deal with Arsenal turned sour. Two years later relations between the two were said to be 'grim'. There was no Granada representative on the Arsenal board, and as Granada's financial problems mounted with the crash of ITV Digital, and with their share price, advertising revenue and profits falling, they were left wondering why they had ever paid £40 million for a stake in the club.

To some extent, Granada were later able to appease the doubters on Merseyside by announcing a second deal, a year later, to buy Liverpool's dot.com business for £20 million. This deal, however, was not driven by sentiment but by hard commercial business. Granada wanted to develop the Liverpool website on broadband and saw in it the potential to use any rights of games which might revert to them in future contracts with the Premiership. Still, the extra £20 million meant that Liverpool had now largely fulfilled Rick Parry's ambition to bring major investment into the club. Parry had planned for £60 million in three years; they had now managed £42 million in less than two, and with television viewing figures for live football matches at an all-time high, and with digital and pay-per-view channels coming online, it was proving to be a shrewd business move for other media companies to line themselves up alongside the major Premiership clubs, especially with a new contract in the offing with the Premiership for televised rights. All Liverpool had to do now was get into the Champions League ahead of schedule.

Naturally, for Parry the arrival of Granada at Anfield was like a breath of fresh air, and there is no doubt that their presence led to some radical changes. Part of the deal allowed for Granada to nominate a member to the board at Liverpool. Their initial nominee, Stacey Cartwright, however, barely served on the board as within a couple of weeks she had taken a new job. Quite how the male-dominated boardroom would have reacted to a female in their midst was, sadly, never to be discovered. In her place, Granada nominated Jules Burns, the executive who had largely been responsible for the deal in the first place, even though he was not a known football fan. Two years later Burns himself would leave Granada.

The new commercial drive also meant that minutes were now written up methodically, but the biggest shake-up focused on Peter Robinson, Liverpool's legendary chief executive. PBR had been at Liverpool since 1965 and was widely regarded as the most influential person inside Anfield. Every major decision taken at Liverpool over a period of 30 years, apart from team selection, had to have PBR's stamp of approval. Chairmen had come and gone, but PBR had remained as the controlling influence. He might have run Liverpool as a fiefdom, but he was hugely respected for his knowledge and professionalism. While some other clubs were run like second-hand car businesses, PBR had guided Liverpool through the muddy waters of agents, backhanders, transfer deals and other questionable deals with honesty and dignity. It was PBR who had been principally responsible for the inspired appointments of Bob Paisley and Kenny Dalglish as managers; it was PBR who had negotiated midnight transfer deals and ensured that Liverpool had the best hotels and facilities in their travels across Europe. In the world of football, PBR was as respected a figure as anyone, but by the turn of the century even his professionalism did not fit into the modern era of football. The game was now big business, and as such it required more commercial expertise and youthful energy. The board could no longer operate as the preserve of one individual, it had to operate on business principles.

By 1998 questions were being asked about just how much longer PBR would remain at Anfield. 'I'll retire in 2000,' he announced. It was, after all, PBR who had initiated the rule that all club employees should retire at the age of 60. More importantly, Parry had been hired and groomed as his successor, but after a couple of years at Anfield it seemed that Parry was getting no nearer to the number one job. Parry, unsurprisingly, was growing restless. There were offers from elsewhere, and while he was much involved in the important work at Anfield, nothing could ever be sanctioned without PBR's approval. What's more, there were always limitations on just how much initiative he could use. Parry, ever the accountant, recognised more than anyone that changes were needed and that Liverpool Football Club had to gear itself up to the challenge of a new century. He could see how Liverpool were slipping behind Manchester United and Arsenal. Changes were needed, sooner rather than later. It was little wonder that Parry had encouraged the Granada deal. Indeed, some might even say he instigated it. Parry needed support from outside, and Granada understood what he was saying.

With Granada on board, the succession became considerably easier. In Jules Burns, Parry had a sponsor. It was clear that the club was not being well run as a business. It was coping, but it was not being proactive in an industry that was becoming increasingly competitive. Unless it began to seize initiatives and take immediate advantage of its international brand name, then the chances were that the club would implode.

It was only a matter of months before events came to a head. Initially, PBR agreed to step down, but a short time later he changed his mind. Everyone appreciated PBR at Liverpool, especially David Moores and other members of the board. Parry also owed him a special debt. But the one person who owed PBR more than anyone was probably the manager. Houllier had known PBR for many years, and it was PBR who had been the driving force behind bringing him to Anfield. Pushing him aside was not going to be easy, but it had to be done if Liverpool were to grow as a commercial enterprise. For Moores and Houllier it was a particularly difficult time, especially as PBR continued to resist whatever gentle pressure was being applied. There were even fears that Houllier might fight a rearguard action on PBR's behalf, perhaps even threaten to resign. Eventually, the board had to be firm with PBR, and he left the club in June 2000, bitter at the way his long commitment to Anfield had ended. In his place, Parry was officially appointed chief executive. The revolution was now almost complete; the reformers were in charge. Houllier was running things on the field and Parry was in control of Liverpool's off-the-field activities.

Like most reforms at Liverpool, save perhaps the Souness era, it was no more than a quiet coup, but the changes were dramatic nonetheless. In Parry and Houllier Liverpool Football Club were fortunate to have two highly intelligent men, both smart enough to understand the changing business of football. Houllier could not have carried out the kind of reforms he wanted to make without the total support of the board and without Granada's money, but now he had to get it right. Football was becoming an increasingly costly business. Even the most mediocre of young English players now commanded fees of around £3 million; for anyone more experienced it was £5 million, and internationals were costing £7 million and more. In Houllier, Liverpool were fortunate to have a man whose contacts and ability in the global transfer market were second to none. As a result, over the years, he was able successfully to bring in, for example, Sami Hyypia, Stéphane Henchoz and John Arne Riise for a combined total of £10 million; others, such as Babbel, Litmanen, Arphexad and McAllister, arrived on free transfers.

But the downside to a large, experienced squad was costly wage bills. Back in May 1991, the total annual salary bill was £5.4 million, and just a year later that figure had risen to £7 million; by 1999 it had reached the dizzy heights of £36 million, and today it tops a staggering £50 million. The cost of Michael Owen and Steven Gerrard alone in 2002 is as much as the salary bill for the club's 127 employees in 1991. It was all part of the changing nature of the business. Football had transformed itself from a leisure activity into a major business.

As such, any big mistakes in the transfer market and the whole pack of cards could come tumbling down. Already the club's finances were in a poor state. In 1999 the board reported what amounted to a loss of £10 million at a time when the wages bill was soaring into the stratosphere. By the year 2000, Liverpool were heading for a financial crisis. They had made a huge outlay in the transfer market, thanks partly to the initial £22 million cash injection from Granada, but their lack of success on the field was costing them dear. There was no extra cash from any cup triumphs and their failure to make it into the Champions League meant that they were missing out on a vital source of finance. The UEFA Cup was all very well, but it did not yield the kind of cash the Champions League brought in. The latter competition guaranteed live coverage, home and away. If Liverpool were to stay among the top dogs, it was essential that they fought their way back into Europe's premier competition.

The 2000/01 season was therefore a crucial one for Houllier, and Liverpool did well, picking up three trophies, but the manager was correct to emphasise that Liverpool's final League game of the season, away to Charlton, was the most important of them all as victory would guarantee them a place in the Champions League. The match might not have had the glamour of their cup exploits, but in cold financial terms it was far more critical. A failure to get into the Champions League in 2001 would have meant the club had to face a serious shortfall of cash in 2001/02; indeed, they might never have recovered. Thankfully, Charlton provided only mediocre opposition, and two Fowler goals plus others from Murphy and Owen secured Liverpool a valuable third spot in the table. Everyone could heave a sigh of relief and give themselves a pat on the back, but it had been a close call. Parry admits that they would have survived as a club, but to have failed again to make the Champions League would have presented all kinds of difficulties. Liverpool had gambled, and could count themselves lucky that they won. Other clubs similarly chancing their arms, such as Chelsea and Leeds United, would not be so fortunate.

Liverpool went on to reach the quarter-finals of the competition and were within a few minutes of a semi-final place, and although they did not add to their already mighty collection of silverware, by the end of the 2001/02 season they had finished runners-up in the Premiership and thereby guaranteed themselves another tilt at the Champions League. They had played a total of sixteen games in Europe, most of them were televised live, and the rewards had been enormous – as much as £20 million, depending on which figures you accept.

As a result, Parry was able to get on with further off-the-field developments. The most pressing was Anfield itself. The stadium had never been the largest in the League. Even in its heyday, when 56,000 crammed into its confines, there were still larger stadia such as Goodison Park, Old Trafford, Villa Park and Hillsborough. Following its conversion to an all-seater stadium, Anfield's capacity was further reduced to a little over 43,000. In recent seasons the club had rebuilt the Anfield Road end by constructing a second tier, but it was only partly successful. The club's original ambitions had to be greatly reduced as planning permission was refused for a larger top tier when local residents complained that it would blot out light to their homes in Anfield Road. As a result, instead of increasing capacity to almost 50,000, Anfield would in the end be just 45,000.

The demand for tickets was huge and impossible to satisfy. The club had always maintained a policy of keeping the season-ticket level to no more than 30,000, even though there were many more on the club's waiting list. Parry knew full well that if they wanted to they could probably get rid of 45,000 season tickets, so it was clear that Liverpool needed to rethink its plans for the ground. They had to increase the capacity, not only to satisfy demand but also to maximise revenue, but the chances of further development at Anfield were limited. The Kop was new and offered no opportunity for expansion. The same was also true of the Centenary Stand, and of the new Anfield Road end. The only possibility for growth was to rebuild the Main Stand with a second tier, which would increase the capacity to around 55,000, but this idea posed numerous problems. For a start, in order to build upwards they would also have to build outwards, and this would necessitate buying up houses in the streets adjacent to the Main Stand. Although many properties had already been acquired by the club or were already empty, there were just as many that were still used as family homes. Buying these houses would be a tricky political problem, given the opposition they had already experienced over developing the Anfield Road end. On top of that, the Main Stand area would be reduced for a number of months to a huge construction site, which would give season-ticket holders major headaches and slash revenue. Administrative areas and dressing rooms, too, would be severely compromised. It was a nightmare scenario, in reality hardly an option.

The other possibility was to move Anfield altogether and rebuild the stadium on another site. This was clearly the favoured option of Parry and the board. It made the most sense. But even this was fraught with dilemmas, not the least of which was the additional cost. Also, many fans saw Anfield as a shrine and did not wish to leave under any circumstances. The ashes of dead fans had been scattered in the goalmouth of the Kop over the years, and there was a strong emotional tie to the ground. There were two options for the board to consider. One was to move just a few hundred yards away to a site on Stanley Park, taking in the car park. Although this looked to be the most attractive option, there were still political difficulties to be encountered, with fans and local residents soon protesting about the loss of their park and adjacent football pitches. The alternative was a greenfield site, close to motorways and rail links, with adequate parking facilities and away from residential areas. Although this had its attractions, the board deemed it too radical an idea, wanting instead to maintain its links to its spiritual home in Anfield, so the club agreed the compromise and began to draw up plans for a new stadium on Stanley Park.

But this plan was, of course, dependent on Liverpool's continuing success. It would be expensive – at least £50 million – and at the same time money had to be made available to Houllier for transfers. It was a very ambitious proposal. At least the new Liverpool website, Liverpoolfc.tv, had proved to be hugely successful. In November 2002 it was reported to be receiving 13.3 million hits a month, making it the most visited football club website in the world and the ninth most visited sporting website in the world.

The forthcoming years were going to be expensive, and if Liverpool slipped out of the Champions League they might well have to put their ambitions in abeyance. When in September 2002 Liverpool lost their opening match of the new Champions League campaign to Valencia, it understandably sent cold shivers down the spines of more than one board member. Two months later, Liverpool were out and counting the cost of lost revenue, likely to be in the region of £10 million.

9. HOU LED THE REDS OUT – HOU, HOU-LLIER!

Suddenly, Liverpool were galvanised and were pushing forward at every opportunity. Arsenal, too, were going all out in search of a winning goal. During one Arsenal attack with a couple of minutes to go, Patrik Berger intercepted the ball and lashed it upfield towards the lone Liverpool striker. Owen shrugged off the challenge of Martin Keown and powered towards goal before crashing the ball into the back of the net. It was almost unbelievable. Liverpool had stolen the cup from under Arsenal's noses, and in the seconds that remained they almost managed a third. It had been the most dramatic turnaround in an FA Cup final for years. When the final whistle went the Liverpool players pushed their injured captain Jamie Redknapp on to the podium to receive the trophy. A chorus of 'Hou Led the Reds Out – Hou, Hou-llier!' rang out around the stadium.

It was a case of yet another summer of comings and goings. Top of Houllier's list throughout most of the 1999/2000 season had been the German international defender Markus Babbel, who was available on a Bosman transfer. If Houllier could persuade him to come to Liverpool he would not cost them a penny. Not only would Liverpool have signed one of the most outstanding defenders in Europe, they would also still have enough money in the bank for other signings. It was a long, protracted process and a host of other clubs had been alerted to Babbel's availability, but Houllier had been one of the first in for him and the Bayern Munich player, impressed by the Frenchman's determination and reputation, eventually put pen to paper. An encouraging word from Didi Hamann also helped Babbel to plump for Liverpool.

The German was not the only free signing in the summer of 2000. The biggest surprise, and one which turned out to be inspired, was Gary McAllister. Houllier had talked about developing a young squad, and at 35 and 28 years of age respectively, McAllister and Babbel seemed to be bucking the trend, but Houllier explained that the young players needed some experience among their ranks. McAllister had seen it all, having played with Leicester, Leeds United and Coventry before signing his one-year contract with Liverpool. By the end of the season he would have become a legend. Also joining on a free was Pegguy Arphexad, the Leicester City goalkeeper. The previous season Arphexad had stood in front of the Kop keeping goal for Leicester and had almost single-handedly kept Liverpool at bay. Three players, and not one of them cost Liverpool a penny. It was probably just as well given that Houllier had spent over £40 million the previous season.

But there was still some money in the kitty, enough to bring French World Cup winner Bernard Diomede to Anfield. Diomede was the forgotten man of France's famous victory. He had played in some of the early games in the World Cup but had then been injured and missed out on the final run-in. It was an injury which would haunt him for life. Initially, it had taken him time to recover, and then he'd crossed swords with veteran Auxerre manager Guy Roux who seemed reluctant to offer him many opportunities. Diomede was festering at Auxerre when Houllier came in with a £3 million bid and whisked him off to Anfield.

Finally, there was Nicky Barmby, at £6 million the most expensive of Houllier's summer signings and by far the most controversial. Barmby, a former Middlesbrough and Tottenham player, had spent the last few years across Stanley Park with Everton. Houllier beat off stiff competition from Manchester United and Chelsea for his signature. It was true that Liverpool needed some width, and Barmby, along with Diomede, looked like the players to supply it, but signing anyone from Everton was always fraught with problems, and Barmby would have a difficult job proving his worth.

Equipped with their new signings, Liverpool kicked off the season on 19 August at home to newly promoted Bradford City and struggled to win 1–0. Next up was a trip to Highbury that ended in disaster: not only did Liverpool lose 2–0, new boy McAllister and German international Hamann were red-carded. Then it was off to Southampton where Liverpool strode into a three-goal lead, then contrived to throw the match away by conceding the same number in the last seventeen minutes. It was hardly championship form, and at least one fanzine raged about some of Houllier's signings. 'With £50m plus spent in the transfer market, no Liverpool manager has ever had more faith shown in him than Gérard Houllier,' claimed an editorial in *Through the Wind and Rain*. 'Certainly, we were in a bit of a state when he arrived, but worse than 1959? Hardly. If the guy turns out to be our Messiah, yours truly will be on bended knee begging for forgiveness, but if he isn't it is going to be hard for a successor to get quite the same faith (and funds).'

And just a couple of weeks into the season Houllier was at it again, this time spending £5.5 million on Middlesbrough's

German international defender Christian Ziege. Ziege, who had previously played in Italy with AC Milan, had in fact been offered to Liverpool the season before but Houllier had decided to take a rain check on him. Now he had changed his mind, and after weeks of negotiations Ziege was recruited, though not at the price Middlesbrough had been demanding, and not without some controversy.

Liverpool's season finally got under way on 6 September with a 3–1 home win over Aston Villa, thanks to a first-half hat-trick from Michael Owen, but a few days later they again contrived to throw a match away. Two goals up against Manchester City at Anfield, City pulled two back only for Hamann to force a winner. It might have been exciting for the neutrals, but it wasn't very clever. Unfortunately, it would not be the last time Liverpool let slip a comfortable lead that season.

By November, another two players had been added to the squad. The more newsworthy signing was the young Croatian international Igor Biscan, who arrived from Dynamo Zagreb for £5.5 million. Liverpool, who had been watching Biscan for over two years, had fought off a host of top European clubs to sign the 22-year-old, described as 'one of the hottest properties in European football'. The less headline-grabbing addition was Gregory Vignal, an eighteen-year-old defender signed from French club Montpellier for £500,000. Houllier saw Vignal as one for the future, a long-term prospect, and described him as a potential Bixente Lizarazu. Biscan, however, was regarded as the more immediate prospect, and he was soon introduced into the side, although by the end of the season he had drifted out of contention. The emphasis on buying young, cheap players was all part of Houllier's grand plan of building a side not just for today, but more particularly for tomorrow.

The number of foreign players at Anfield was increasing by the month. Although the club was regularly linked with various English players, their English recruits had been few and far between. At least the overseas players arrived with the right attitude. They didn't drink, they trained hard, they didn't complain and they accepted the rotation system. There were now so many foreign players at Anfield that the club programme even ran an article telling fans how to pronounce their names! However, Houllier insisted that English was the language of the club and that every player had to learn to speak it. It was wise advice, and to help matters Houllier organised for the players to have lessons.

As Liverpool headed into the new year, it was with little hope of winning the title, even though a host of commentators had tipped them for Premiership glory at the beginning of the season. Instead they found themselves in sixth spot, some thirteen points behind runaway leaders Manchester United, having already lost seven games. There had been some memorable victories, particularly the 1–0 win at Old Trafford on a bitterly cold December morning, Danny Murphy firing in a free-kick from just outside the area. The match was Houllier's hundredth game in charge; it was also Liverpool's first win at United in ten years. And a week later they thumped Arsenal 4–0 at Anfield. But any joy from those wins had been cancelled out by some sloppy losses, such as the 4–3 defeat at Leeds at the beginning of November when, again, they had led comfortably for much of the match only to throw it away.

But if Liverpool had more or less let slip any chance of winning the League, they were at least going well in two of the cup competitions. In the UEFA Cup they had beaten Rapid Bucharest, Slovan Liberec and Olympiakos to reach the fourth round of the competition. Meanwhile, in the League Cup, now known as the Worthington Cup, they had brushed aside Chelsea, Stoke and Fulham to reach the semi-finals. Houllier was philosophical about it. 'We can take encouragement from the progress we have already made,' he told fans in his end-of-year report, 'but we need to be patient.' Patience, however, was something many Liverpool fans did not possess in abundance. They had been waiting a long time for something to cheer about. Beating United at Old Trafford was all very well, but United were still streets ahead of them. First-team coach Patrice Bergues was more candid when he admitted that 'we are a bit frustrated at the moment because we know we are not too far away from being the best, but we're not there yet. This final step is the most difficult to take, but I am sure we will get there eventually.'

The tabloids were also stirring things up with stories about dressing-room rifts between Fowler and Owen, Houllier's desire to sell Owen, and the fans' hatred of the Frenchman. There were also stories about Fowler leaving, with both Chelsea and Leeds United said to be chasing his signature. In the event, nothing transpired, but it was certainly true that Houllier still had his critics, especially when it came to radio phone-ins; then again, there were plenty on the Kop who could understand his long-term plans. In the papers they called Liverpool 'boring'. It was a tag that would stick for much of the season, even though it was unjustified. Nobody, not Gérard Houllier, Arsène Wenger or Alex Ferguson, would have been able to turn things around in a couple of years. It had taken Ferguson seven years to bring the title back to Old Trafford. Slowly, though, Houllier was beginning to win over the neutrals, the victory at Old Trafford as important a milestone as any.

2001 had barely begun when Liverpool dramatically announced that they had signed the Finnish international Jari Litmanen on a free transfer from Barcelona. Litmanen, for so long one of the finest strikers in European football, had grown weary of warming the bench in Spain. Houllier had always claimed that he wanted four top strikers at the club so that he could rotate them at will. Rotation had become the buzz word around Anfield as Houllier chopped and changed his sides to meet the challenges of so many games. But for Robbie Fowler, the signing of Litmanen would make his own position all the more vulnerable.

Litmanen made his debut in the semi-final of the Worthington Cup, though it was not a fortuitous introduction as Liverpool surprisingly lost 2–1 to Crystal Palace. Apart from that, January and February turned out to be good months for the club, particularly when Palace came to Anfield for the return leg of that semi-final. They were thrashed 5–0, and Liverpool were into their first final since losing to Manchester United on that infamous Armani suit afternoon at Wembley. They began to make steady progress in the FA Cup, too, beating Rotherham 3–0, Leeds 2–0 and Manchester City 4-2, and on 15 February they enjoyed a memorable 2–0 win over Roma in the Stadio Olimpico, Michael Owen scoring both goals. 'In Rome, We Always Win in Rome!' sang the Liverpool fans. A week later, all Liverpool had to do was stop Roma from winning by two clear goals. It was to be one of those famous European nights at Anfield, and all the luck went Liverpool's way. They were even awarded a penalty (which was missed) when at the other end they'd been astonishingly fortuitous not to have one awarded against them. In they end they lost 1–0, but they were through to the UEFA Cup quarter-final.

Liverpool were the hottest favourites to win the Worthington Cup in years. First Division Birmingham surely posed no problem. Even so, neither Houllier nor anyone associated with the club was taking a Liverpool victory on 25 February for granted. And given some of their performances earlier that season, they had every reason to be cautious. It was the first time Liverpool had played at the Millennium Stadium in Cardiff, and the first time a major English cup final had been contested outside England. Liverpool fans were used to the trek to Wembley, but Cardiff police were used to local supporters rather than having to cope with thousands of fans swarming into the city from all directions. The result was traffic chaos and a delayed kick-off. Fans were still pouring in at half-time. Getting home was even more of a nightmare, but only marginally more tedious than the game itself.

Houllier decided on playing Fowler up front with Heskey, and minutes into the game it looked an inspired decision as Fowler struck a fearsome left-foot volley from outside the area into the net. It was a spectacular goal which promised much. But there was little else from Liverpool. Birmingham were no better, and as the final whistle loomed it seemed the Merseysiders were set to take the cup back home. But then, on the stroke of full time, Birmingham were awarded a penalty, which they converted. Liverpool had only themselves to blame. Birmingham might even have had a second penalty, but this time the referee thought better of it. Extra-time brought no goals either, so it was down to a penalty shoot-out in front of the Liverpool fans. The hero of the hour turned out not to be Robbie Fowler but Sander Westerveld, who made two stunning saves to bring the cup back to Anfield. Liverpool had won the League Cup for a record sixth time, and it was the first trophy they'd lifted since 1995.

And they continued to move along nicely in the UEFA Cup and FA Cup competitions, too, brushing aside Porto in the quarter-finals of one and neighbours Tranmere Rovers in a six-goal thriller in the other. To cap that, they rounded off March with a 2–0 win at Anfield against Manchester United, thanks to a long-range screamer from Steven Gerrard and a second from Robbie Fowler. In the first of their two semi-finals in April, Liverpool drew 0–0 in Barcelona before winning 1–0 at Anfield, thanks to a Gary McAllister penalty. In the FA Cup Liverpool stormed into a 2–0 lead against Wycombe Wanderers, but almost let it slip as Wycombe bravely fought back to make it 2–1. Liverpool were into another two finals. It was turning out to be quite a season.

Ambitions and expectations were now sky-high, and you could see it on the bench where every goal, every victory was greeted with as much enthusiasm by the coaching staff as by the players. It had certainly been a long time since the club had been able to look forward to such a climax-packed end of season. The FA Cup final was scheduled for 12 May, and immediately after that they would have to fly out to Germany for the final of the UEFA Cup on the 16th. Then it was home again to play, on the 19th, what Houllier argued was the most important game of the season, their final League fixture at Charlton Athletic, where a win would give them a place in the Champions League.

Liverpool had met Arsenal in three finals over the years, twice in the FA Cup and once in the League Cup. On all three occasions they had lost. The omens were not good. What's more, this might have been the English FA Cup final, but there wasn't much that was English about it. For a start, it was being played in Wales, the first time an FA Cup final had been played outside England. Secondly, it was all about the two top French managers, each competing with teams that contained only a handful of English players. But ironically it would be an Englishman who would decide the resting place of the FA Cup for the next year.

In truth, Liverpool were little less than appalling. For the majority of the game they toiled in the unusually sweltering heat. Arsenal had total control and went ahead in the 72nd minute through Freddie Ljungberg. Chance after chance had fallen the Gunners' way, and as the game progressed you did begin to get the feeling that they could well rue all those missed opportunities to put the game beyond Liverpool's reach. As long as the score stood at 1–0 there was always a flicker of hope for Liverpool. And that flicker became a flame with just seven minutes remaining when Gary McAllister lobbed a free-kick into the area. Babbel rose to head it down and there was Owen, pouncing on the ball and stabbing it into the net. The Millennium Stadium erupted. Arsenal looked on aghast. Yet again a Gary McAllister free-kick had been decisive.

Suddenly, Liverpool were galvanised and were pushing forward at every opportunity. Arsenal, too, were going all out in search of a winning goal. During one Arsenal attack with a couple of minutes to go, Patrik Berger intercepted the ball and lashed it upfield towards the lone Liverpool striker. Owen shrugged off the challenge of Martin Keown and powered towards goal before crashing the ball into the back of the net. It was almost unbelievable. Liverpool had stolen the cup from under Arsenal's noses, and in the seconds that remained they almost managed a third. It had been the most dramatic turnaround in an FA Cup final for years. When the final whistle went the Liverpool players pushed their injured captain Jamie Redknapp on to the podium to receive the trophy. A chorus of 'Hou Led the Reds Out – Hou, Hou-llier!' rang out around the stadium.

While the fans celebrated that evening, there was little in the way of festivities for the players, but by the time Liverpool reached Dortmund for the UEFA Cup final against Alavés they were high on adrenalin. 'This is your chance to become immortal,' Houllier told them. 'No team has ever won three cup competitions before.' It was Liverpool's seventh appearance in a European final.

Alavés were not considered to be the hardest of opposition and Liverpool always felt they had a good chance to win the trophy, and it didn't take long for them to pick up where they'd left off in Cardiff, racing into a two-goal lead courtesy of Markus Babbel and Steven Gerrard. Then the Spaniards hit back to make it 2–1. Just before half-time, Liverpool were awarded a penalty; up stepped Gary McAllister to make it 3–1. But Alavés were not finished yet. After the break they reorganised and pulled one back. Then suddenly it was 3–3 as Westerveld failed to stop a long-range effort along the ground. The game was shifting from one penalty area to the other as both sides threw caution to the wind in search of a winner. When Robbie Fowler pounced to make it 4–3 it seemed that surely Liverpool had won the cup, surely they would not throw it away again, but they did. With just two minutes remaining, Alavés sensationally levelled the scores, Westerveld at fault again. After Saturday's dramatic FA Cup final, you could hardly call Liverpool boring now. It was now golden goal time. Alavés were down to nine men after two sendings-off when McAllister floated another free-kick into the area. Everyone rose and the ball clipped off the back of the head of an Alavés defender and beyond the keeper into the far corner of the net. For Alavés, it was a cruel own goal; for Liverpool, it was the UEFA Cup. It might not have been the most important of European trophies, but it was important enough.

Just one game remained. Winning the three trophies was tremendous, Houllier said, but they had to win their final game of the season to qualify for Champions League football. A considerable amount of money was resting on it. Rick Parry knew just how crucial it was. 'Everything was geared to getting into the Champions League,' he said. 'Although we had made money by reaching three finals, it was nothing compared to the riches awaiting us in the Champions League.' But Parry needn't have worried as Liverpool destroyed Charlton. When the final whistle went, Houllier, Thompson, Lee, Corrigan and Bergues hugged one another in a big huddle on the touchline. It was a compelling moment. 'I have never known unity as I know here,' Bergues commented. 'This applies for every person who works for the club.'

The season's statistics took some beating. They had played a total of 63 games and had scored a staggering 127 goals. The top marksman was Michael Owen with 24. Emile Heskey, in his first full season with the club, chipped in with 22, while Robbie Fowler scored five fewer than that. All the talk was of Liverpool's young players – Owen, Heskey, Carragher, Gerrard and Murphy – all of them English.

But the success of the season was unquestionably Gary McAllister, signed on a free Bosman transfer during the summer. At 35, McAllister had reached a crossroads at Coventry: he could either look for a job as a manager somewhere or try his luck as a media pundit. Certainly no other Premiership club would want him as a player at his age. But one did, and it was something of a shock when it turned out to be Liverpool. Yet McAllister oozed experience and was just the kind of player the club needed – someone to organise and develop players such as Gerrard, Murphy, Carragher and Owen. McAllister had already won the title with Leeds United back in 1991 and had won more than 50 international caps with Scotland, but 2000/01 was his Roy of the Rovers season. It hadn't begun well for him, either. In his first game, against Arsenal, he was sent off for the first time in his career. Then, a few days later, football took a back seat when his wife Denise was diagnosed with cancer. Houllier promptly gave him indefinite leave and told him to remain with Denise, where he was most needed. It was a gesture that did not go unnoticed. When he returned, it was with renewed vigour and respect. McAllister owed Liverpool and Houllier, and they would not go wanting.

It was almost as if Houllier and McAllister were made for each other. Somewhere along the way their paths had to cross. 'If this lad had been here ten years ago,' said Houllier, 'Liverpool would have won so much more.' McAllister dripped class. He was a typical Liverpool player in style and attitude. After converting the penalty against Barcelona which took them through to the UEFA Cup final, the press badgered him to take his boot off and hold it up for a photo. After finishing all his interviews, however, he quietly declined. 'We've only reached the final,' he said, 'we still haven't won the trophy.' It was that kind of response that endeared him to Houllier. Equally, Houllier's generosity when McAllister's wife was ill, and his regular phone calls, made him feel not only wanted but respected as well. McAllister, more than anyone, would be devastated by Houllier's illness.

The Scotsman repeatedly came to Liverpool's rescue as the season wound up to its climax. In five consecutive games McAllister either scored from the penalty spot or from a free-kick. Against Everton on 16 April he scored an injury-time winner just when it seemed Liverpool's chances had been snuffed out by an equaliser, and against Barcelona he bravely stepped up to take responsibility for that penalty. By the end of the season McAllister had added three more medals to his collection. 'It doesn't get much better than this,' he said as the coach drove around the streets of Liverpool with the players displaying the three trophies to all their fans. Although he was to play a further season at Liverpool, he would never quite recapture the glory of his treble-winning season. In the summer of 2002 he left Liverpool to take over as manager at Coventry. It would not be surprising were McAllister to return to Anfield one day in some kind of backroom position.

In contrast to McAllister's glory, it had been a tough season for Christian Ziege. He had been signed in a confusion of controversy, with all sorts of accusations being made by Middlesbrough about Liverpool poaching him. At Middlesbrough Ziege had been immensely popular; he'd brought a dash of pace and flair to the left side. But he struggled to make a similar impact with Liverpool. He began well enough, and his dead-ball free-kicks regularly posed delicate problems for defenders, but after a series of lacklustre performances he eventually lost his left-back berth and was forced to accept a role as a left-sided midfielder. He didn't like that and complained bitterly. He then found himself in and out of the side, and complained even more about his lack of action. Houllier eventually grew weary of his whingeing and told him to 'shut up' and have more respect for his colleagues. It was clear that Ziege would not last much longer. Indeed, Norwegian wing-back John Arne Riise was poached from under the noses of Fulham in the summer of 2001 in order to take over Ziege's left-sided role. Riise had been expected to leave Monaco for the London club, but in a sudden U-turn he joined Liverpool for £4 million and was immediately drafted into the side to stunning effect.

As the season was coming to an end, Houllier had commented, 'Aim for the moon and maybe you land among the stars.' It was a fitting epitaph for one of the most successful years in Liverpool's history. Comparisons with Shankly were inevitable. When Shankly came to Anfield he too had initiated a revolution. He had reorganised training and facilities and had masterminded a total overhaul of the team. Dozens of new players were signed and many more were disposed of. Shankly had helped to create a team and a club for a new era of football. Similarly, Houllier was the man for another moment in a different era. He, too, had introduced new training techniques, had overseen a rebuilding of Melwood, and had set about signing new faces. Like Shankly, he wanted players fully committed to the cause and, also like Shankly, he carefully examined their motives and character before making any decision. Neither man ever criticised his players in public either, though of the two Shankly was perhaps more loyal, less inclined to dismiss a player he had signed.

Both also demonstrated their prowess in the transfer market, particularly in its bargain basement, bringing in unknown names when fans were screaming for ready-made stars. Shankly recruited the likes of Peter Thompson, Geoff Strong, Gordon Milne and Kevin Keegan, while Houllier has signed unknown quantities such as Sami Hyypia, Stéphane Henchoz and Milan Baros. Both men recognised a good player when they saw one and could spot qualities not necessarily obvious to others, and both were insistent on a core of Liverpool-born players in their side. Shankly had Tommy Smith, Phil Thompson, Chris Lawler, Gerry Byrne and Ian Callaghan, while Houllier has nurtured such local talents as Steven Gerrard, Jamie Carragher, Michael Owen and Danny Murphy.

The greatest difference, however, is that Shankly was the supreme motivator. His players would walk through doors for him. What he asked for, they did. 'If he asked you to jump in the canal, you'd jump and ask why later,' is the way Roger Hunt put it. 'You would do anything for him. Likewise, he would do anything for you.' Shankly built his players into giants. He made them believe, and even though many of them were not big names, he built up their egos so that they could turn themselves into players of the highest quality. Shankly became a god, never questioned either by his players or the fans. He could do no wrong, and he had a rapport with the public no manager has ever rivalled. He was the kind of man who would stop the team coach on the way to a game and make his players alight to shake hands with cheering fans. 'Never forget,' he would tell them, 'that these are the people who put money into your pockets, food into your mouths.'

Of course, it's a different game today and no manager will ever rival Shankly in that way. Shankly remains an icon, but Houllier has gone some way towards winning not just the minds but the hearts of Liverpool fans. He does have a genuine love for the city, its club, its history and its traditions, but where he possibly falls down is in terms of his powers of motivation, though in the mega-rich world of soccer it may be that no manager can ever motivate players as much as money can. Houllier still has plenty of silverware to accumulate before Liverpool fans will ever whisper his name in the same breath as Shankly, but if he can win the Premiership title, or even the Champions League, he will have gone some way towards emulating the great man. And it was, after all, four and a half seasons before Shankly and his team captured the League championship.

10. RECUPERATION

Houllier pulled on his dark coat, buttoned it up and wrapped a warm black scarf around his neck. Still looking gaunt and pale, he made his way up the steps, making sure to touch the THIS IS ANFIELD sign. It was the moment all Anfield had been waiting for. Everyone craned their necks towards the tunnel, then suddenly there was a burst of activity from the assembled photographers and television crews. Around the tunnel entrance there was pushing and jockeying for space and a huge flash of light bulbs. It could mean only one thing: Houllier was back. When he appeared, the entire stadium stood up to roar their greeting. 'Allez Houllier!' the Kop chorused.

The pressures on Gérard Houllier were mounting. It was not the easiest of summers, and there was barely time for a break. First he jetted off to South Korea and Japan to watch two young potential recruits playing in the Confederations Cup; then it was back to Europe to beat off the competition for their signatures and pay out £6 million. By mid-August the preliminary round of the Champions League was upon him, with Liverpool facing Finnish club FC Haka. That involved another trip abroad. After that it was the Charity Shield (now called the Community Shield) at the Millennium Stadium against rivals Manchester United. It was Liverpool's third visit to Cardiff that year, and their third win. Cardiff was fast becoming a lucky city for Liverpool. No sooner was that out of the way than the Premiership campaign began all over again, quickly followed by a trip to Monaco for the European Super Cup against Champions League winners Bayern Munich. It might not have been the most important of trophies, but Liverpool showed some majestic touches as they swept Bayern aside and raced into a 3–0 lead. Bayern pulled two goals back as Liverpool dropped a gear, but it was not enough and Liverpool had won an unprecedented fifth trophy. Not even the great Liverpool sides of the seventies and eighties could match that. As if that wasn't enough, Liverpool then raced home for a visit to the Reebok Stadium where Sander Westerveld handed Bolton a last-minute victory when a speculative long-range shot squirmed under his body. Houllier was furious, though he was not going to let anyone outside Anfield know just how angry he was. Problems, problems, problems, all the time. Within a couple of days he had organised the signing of not one but two new goalkeepers. August wasn't even over and already they had played six games, won two trophies, and signed two sixteen-year-olds and two goalkeepers. It was relentless. 'He's a workaholic,' Brian Hall observed. 'He'll work sixteen, eighteen hours a day. I've never seen anything like it, and day in, day out too.'

It was little wonder that come October Houllier was feeling weary. He'd even been to see his doctor in Paris but had been given the all-clear. He was just tired and in need of a good rest – at least that's all he thought he needed. On Saturday, 13 October, when Liverpool took on Leeds at Anfield, he discovered otherwise.

Gérard Houllier was probably not the easiest of patients. He might have had the mental strength to overcome such a major operation, but he was not one for putting his feet up, losing himself in a good novel and forgetting all about football. He was a workaholic, someone who lived for the game. His old friend Patrice Bergues admitted as much. 'Gérard's work rate is fantastic. He never stops. I have never known anyone work as hard as he does.'

Thankfully, his consultant surgeon, Mr Abbas Rashid, and consultant cardiologist Dr Rod Stables reported that the operation had been 'a total success'. The doctors in the cardiothoracic centre at Broadgreen Hospital had repaired what was described as 'an acute dissection of the aorta' and reckoned Houllier would recover sufficiently to return to work, although, they added, it might take some time. By the Monday afternoon Houllier was off the ventilator, although he would remain in the intensive care unit for a few more days.

Nevertheless, there were concerns. The medical staff might have given him the all-clear, but others were suggesting that it might be better if he was to consider a less demanding profession. That was rather like asking the Pope to become a nightclub singer. There was little chance that Houllier would put his feet up no matter what the doctors said. He lived for football, it was his buzz in life. 'Life isn't interesting unless you live on the edge,' he observed later, reflecting on his illness and convalescence. 'After my operation I was advised not to come back to work. I know I'm taking a risk, but I have taken risks all my life. I was doing it long before they wheeled me into the theatre.'

Everyone at Anfield heaved a sigh of relief when they heard that the operation had gone well. The 54-year-old's progress had been nothing short of 'remarkable'. Houllier remained in hospital for three weeks but was soon up on his feet and walking around; he even had a television installed in his room. Phil Thompson, meanwhile, had taken up the reins as caretaker manager, and media rumours that Houllier would never return refused to go away. Just weeks after his operation, however, Houllier the workaholic was on the telephone to Thompson advising him on team selection and other issues. Rick Parry also confirmed that Houllier was on the phone to him as often as half a dozen times a day, and that hardly a day passed when he did not speak to the Frenchman. He also acknowledged that Houllier had been wholly involved in the signing of Abel Xavier and Nicolas Anelka. The Paris St Germain player was even reported to have flown to Corsica to talk with Houllier while he was convalescing. The signing of Anelka was a major coup for Houllier and bucked him up enormously. It had come out of the blue and took the press by total surprise. Liverpool fans were ecstatic. Anelka might only have come on loan, but provided he settled and showed none of the tantrums and moodiness that had so far dogged his career, he could become a permanent fixture at Anfield. But, as everyone recognised, it was still something of a gamble.

David O'Leary was someone else who repeatedly had to answer the telephone to Houllier, often in the dead of night. 'There have been many occasions,' he recalled, 'when I have been driving home after an evening match at one or two in the morning and Gérard has been on the car phone. He's like an owl, working away at night. He'd just call to talk about our match and Liverpool's fixtures.' Whether such a habit was healthy or not, especially after a major operation, was debatable, although the doctors knew full well that he was never going to ease off altogether and that sometimes it can help the healing process if you have other things to deal with.

Nearly four months after Houllier had been taken ill, Liverpool faced Leeds once more, this time at Elland Road. The question of Houllier's health was once again to the fore. Earlier suggestions that he might be back by February were suddenly being re-evaluated. Houllier had returned to Liverpool from a long break in Paris and in his brother's house in Corsica for a further check-up with doctors at Broadgreen Hospital. On a visit to Melwood, he told the club that the doctors had been more than delighted with his progress but had advised a further month's recuperation at least. Phil Thompson jokingly told him that judging by his pasty face he could do with a bit of sunshine as well.

The news that Houllier would not return immediately led to further press speculation, some of which made for depressing reading, one paper again suggesting that Houllier would not be back at all. Another newspaper claimed that Jean Tigana, the Fulham manager, had already been identified as Houllier's replacement and would take up his duties in the summer. That was one of the more bizarre suggestions. Within days of his illness the tabloids had been speculating that Houllier would never return to management and that Kenny Dalglish, John Toshack, even Alan Hansen had been tapped to take over. None of it was true.

The fact remained, however, that there was no date set for a return. It was open-ended; Houllier would come back when he and his doctors felt it was appropriate. An illness of this nature was going to take time. The Liverpool management had repeatedly said that if it meant six months off, or even missing the entire season, then so be it. There was no pressure whatsoever on Houllier to race back, not even when Liverpool went through a sticky patch.

With a less than helpful intervention prior to the Leeds game on 3 February, O'Leary added fuel to the debate when he publicly suggested that Houllier should quit football management. 'I've told him,' he said, 'this job isn't conducive to coming back after an operation like he's had.' But, he added, 'If you ask me, I believe Gérard will return to Liverpool. But should he? I would love him not to.' Ironically, it would be O'Leary out of a job a year or so later.

On the morning of the Leeds match Rick Parry was forced to counter the growing speculation in a Radio Five Live interview. Asked when Houllier might be back, he replied, 'I think it will be within the time frame that we have consistently spelt out from day one, and I'm not going to be more specific. I said the day after his operation in October that it would be four to six months. It's now three and a half and everything is completely on schedule. The operation was a complete success. His aorta is fine, but it takes the body that length of time to recover from a major operation.' He then added, tellingly, 'There's one thing of which there is no doubt: he will be back.'

Of course, all the speculation achieved was to bring the drawbridge of Anfield firmly down. Liverpool slammed four goals past Leeds to give them their best win of the season. The following day Houllier himself confirmed what everybody in Liverpool already knew. At a Liverpool Echo Sports Personality of the Year dinner, he told his audience that 'there are those who say maybe I should forget about football'. He then added caustically, 'Maybe I should forget about breathing.' 'I am on the mend,' he continued, 'and it's just a matter of weeks before I get the all-clear. I want to win the championship. I say to Liverpool fans, don't always believe what you read. I am already back. I will be back again as manager in four to five weeks' time.' Houllier also publicly confirmed that he had seen the doctors at Broadgreen Hospital and that they were pleased with his progress.

Throughout the following week, most of the players came on to their own websites to confirm that Houllier had paid a visit to Melwood and that his presence had been an enormous fillip to everyone. Brian Hall saw him as well. 'He looked tired and drained when he came back to Melwood. And this was months afterwards. I remember thinking, wow, you've really been to hell and back.' Emile Heskey spoke warmly of how Houllier, after talking to all the players, had taken him aside for a quiet chat. Heskey's form had taken a dip since Houllier's illness. He spoke of how Houllier used to give him private coaching and how important this had been, and how he had missed it. Houllier was almost like a father to him, he said. After seeing and speaking with Houllier again before the Leeds match Heskey was well hyped up, and not surprisingly he gave as good a performance as he had all season, scoring twice. Four days earlier he had scored the game's only goal against his old club Leicester in a midweek clash at Anfield, and then on 9 February at Portman Road he struck twice again as Liverpool put on their best display of the season with a 6–0 win over a resurgent Ipswich. Suddenly, as if inspired by Houllier's fireside chat, Heskey was back to his best form. So, it seemed, were most of his team-mates.

Houllier had made his first return to Anfield in December 2001 when he attended the club's AGM and made an emotional speech to shareholders. Last season, he told the crowded room, we set out with the intention of winning one trophy. Instead, we brought three home, and also qualified for the Champions League one year ahead of schedule. 'Let's remind ourselves that no other club in Europe has ever won a cup treble in one season before,' he added. He also pointed out that while there was criticism in the papers that Liverpool played negative and boring football, they had scored 127 goals the previous season, the third highest total in the club's history. 'I hope we can be as boring this season,' he quipped, before concluding by saying that anyone who had any doubts about whether or not he would return could forget it. He was coming back, of that there was no doubt. As he sat down, the entire room rose to give him a standing ovation.

When Houllier had been taken ill, Liverpool stood sixth in the table and were without a manager. Rick Parry's first job was to halt any rumours or speculation within the camp, and with Liverpool about to jet off to Kiev for a Champions League fixture, it had to be done quickly. With the backing of the board, Parry and David Moores collared Phil Thompson. 'Would you take over until Gérard can return?' they asked. But there was really little need to ask; Thompson was more than happy to do whatever he could to help. 'But,' he emphasised to them, and to the press, 'when Gérard is ready to return, nothing will please me more than to go back to my old job.' Thompson did not want any tabloids putting two and two together and making five, or making any suggestions that Thompson saw himself as Houllier's successor. Nothing was further from his mind.

The morning after Houllier's collapse, Sunday, 14 October, the Liverpool squad flew to Kiev. 'Can you imagine,' Thompson remarked to Sammy Lee on the plane, 'if Gérard had been taken ill 24 hours later, either on this flight or in Kiev? Who knows what might have happened.' They both knew full well that such a scenario would have had disastrous consequences which did not bear thinking about. In the Kiev dressing room that Tuesday night Thompson was able to tell the assembled players that he had had news from the hospital: Houllier had come through his operation and had regained consciousness; the operation had been a success and the doctors were pleased. The players cheered. That night they knew what was expected of them. 'We didn't really speak about it,' Sami Hyypia recalled. 'Everybody just understood after the Leeds game that they had more responsibility.' Buoyed by the news, Liverpool went out and beat Kiev 2–1.

A few days later they thrashed Leicester 4–1 to continue an impressive run of results; on 4 November they beat Manchester United 3–1 at Anfield. The only poor result during these weeks was a 3–1 hammering at the hands of Barcelona on a night when Liverpool were overwhelmed by the Spanish side's slick passing. Still, the run was good enough to prompt the press to re-evaluate their views of Thompson. When it had been announced that he was to be in temporary charge, the tabloids had wickedly called him over-emotional, unintelligent and incapable. Liverpool, they predicted, would go to pieces. But they hadn't. On the contrary, the players had summoned fresh reserves of determination. Thompson, meanwhile, had acted with dignity and integrity. He handled himself with decorum at press conferences, listened carefully and took care not to criticise referees. He had clearly learnt a lesson or two from his tutor.

Liverpool's dip in form didn't begin until mid-December, when they slumped to a 4–0 defeat at Stamford Bridge, although there had been signs in earlier games that the team was not firing on all cylinders. The goals were drying up; since the Barcelona defeat on 20 November they'd managed just four in six games. Some claimed that Barcelona had knocked the confidence out of them, but, as Johan Cruyff had been quick to point out, Liverpool were the better side for most of the first half. The drubbing at the hands of Chelsea also had to be put into context. Although Chelsea were deserving winners, each of their chances had fallen fortuitously for them. Liverpool had actually played well for most of the game, attacking with pace and purpose, and with more luck and on another day it might have been a very different outcome. Chelsea's keeper had also had an outstanding game. So, it was not necessarily a defeat to get depressed about.

Immediately after the Chelsea game, and just two days before Christmas, Liverpool faced another uphill struggle, this time against Arsenal at Anfield. The match could not have come at a worse time. Liverpool lost 2–1 and dropped into third spot. Over the next few weeks things barely improved. There was an impressive win at Aston Villa on Boxing Day, but they struggled against West Ham and Bolton before beating Birmingham in the FA Cup by three goals to nil. That win looked as if it might regenerate Liverpool, but instead they travelled to Southampton and lost 2–0. A week later they earned a draw at Highbury when many expected another defeat, but even though Liverpool were dropping points left, right and centre, they were still hanging on to the coat tails of the leaders. Nobody seemed capable of seizing the opportunity. Manchester United, who at one stage had been eleven points ahead of Liverpool, had had their own slump in form. Just as United had been written off some weeks earlier, Liverpool were now being discounted as well, the tabloids blaming the novice Thompson for their demise. Since beating Middlesbrough back in early December, Liverpool had secured a miserly eight points from a possible 27.

The problem was hardly difficult to pinpoint: Liverpool still weren't scoring goals. Their only marksman was Michael Owen; there were no contributions coming from any other quarter. Emile Heskey was looking sluggish again and out of luck. But the real problem was not so much the strikers as the midfield suppliers. Steven Gerrard, for so much of the previous season as impressive as any midfielder in Europe, was looking tired and careless, and the two Czechs, Patrik Berger and Vladimir Smicer, were either frustratingly injured or lacking in invention. At the back, Jamie Carragher was also struggling. The pundits once again dubbed them 'boring'.

Danny Murphy, despite an England call-up, was also out of sorts. During the 1–1 draw with Southampton at Anfield on 19 January he was substituted and found himself on the end of some uncharacteristic booing by the home fans. When Houllier heard of this he was straight on the phone to the England midfielder. 'He said he'd seen many players go through the same kind of dip in form,' Murphy explained, 'and I would get through this spell because I'm a good player, and if I remember the good things I've been doing the form will come back. He said he was right behind me and knew what had gone on, and that I shouldn't worry about it.' Houllier also assured him that just because he was having a bad time, it in no way implied that his place in the side was in any doubt. Murphy was much cheered by Houllier's call, which was bolstered by some friendly encouragement from Phil Thompson.

Still, Houllier's physical absence was having a visible effect. Thompson was undoubtedly doing a sterling job keeping the ship afloat, but Houllier's tactical awareness was sorely missed in the dressing room. The side seemed to be in limbo and in desperate need of inspiration. 'When we had that blip period I think the players had to show responsibility on the pitch. I think Phil Thompson got criticism that was unfair,' Hyypia claimed. 'He was in a very difficult position.'

When on 22 January Liverpool travelled to Old Trafford for an evening game, the scene was set for a trouncing and a giant step by United towards the title. After losing four times to Liverpool, surely United would be up for this one, ready to take full advantage of Liverpool's loss of form? But Liverpool dug deep to overcome a battering in the first fifteen minutes. After that they gradually began to take control, Gerrard rediscovering his touch and dominance. As the game moved into the final fifteen minutes it seemed that only one team was going to win. Sure enough, a perfectly weighted long ball into the area from Gerrard found Danny Murphy, who raced on to it and lobbed it over Fabien Barthez into the United net. Old Trafford was stunned; it was United's fifth successive defeat by Liverpool. Suddenly, the title race was on again, United's margin over Liverpool cut to just two points.

Five days later Liverpool lost by a single goal to Arsenal in the fourth round of the FA Cup, but they followed that up in the Premiership with six wins and a draw, including emphatic victories by three or more goals against Leeds, Ipswich and Newcastle. The stage was now set for Houllier's return. Throughout February there had been rumours of an imminent return, but as yet he had not attended a game at Anfield. That would be the public signal that he was back and in charge once more.

That moment finally arrived on the evening of Tuesday, 19 March when Liverpool faced AS Roma in the Champions League. It was to be a highly charged occasion, as dramatic as any European evening Anfield had ever known. Liverpool's survival in the competition was on a knife-edge. To progress through to the quarter-finals they had to beat the Italian champions 2–0.

Despite heading their league in the first phase of the competition, Liverpool had found themselves rewarded with the severest of challenges by drawing Barcelona and Turkish champions Galatasaray along with the Italian champions. It was the group of death, scant compensation for all their earlier efforts. There was barely a wafer of difference between the four sides. For Liverpool things had begun disastrously with that 3–1 defeat at Anfield by Barcelona. That was followed by a valuable 0–0 draw in Rome, a disappointing goalless draw at Anfield against Galatasaray and two further draws in Turkey and Spain. Liverpool remained pinned to the bottom of their group, but only four points separated top from bottom. As the four sides entered the final round of fixtures any one of them could still qualify, but Liverpool faced the hardest task to be certain of reaching the last eight. To beat the Serie A champions 2–0 was an awesome task, but just the sort of challenge they had always relished in the old days of the knock-out European Cup. Liverpool had already drawn 0–0 in Rome, and the previous season they'd progressed to the semi-finals of the UEFA Cup after knocking out Roma, even though Roma had won 1–0 at Anfield.

It was again to be one of those famous European nights at Anfield. On the Kop the flags waved, banners were unfurled and a huge mosaic welcomed Houllier back. Although nothing definite had been announced, there was no doubt that night that he would be there. It might prove a testing occasion for his heart, but how could he possibly miss such a match? The fans were determined to give him as raucous a welcome as possible, the kind of reception normally reserved for their championship-winning sides. In the dressing room, Houllier sat quietly and delivered his first team talk in five months. The players listened calmly as he stirred them for the forthcoming battle. Then, as the players filed out of the dressing room towards the tunnel, Phil Thompson reminded them simply about what was expected. 'Do it for the boss!' he said.

Houllier pulled on his dark coat, buttoned it up and wrapped a warm black scarf around his neck. Still looking gaunt and pale, he made his way up the steps, making sure to touch the THIS IS ANFIELD sign. It was the moment all Anfield had been waiting for. Everyone craned their necks towards the tunnel, then suddenly there was a burst of activity from the assembled photographers and television crews. Around the tunnel entrance there was pushing and jockeying for space and a huge flash of light bulbs. It could mean only one thing: Houllier was back. When he appeared, the entire stadium stood up to roar their greeting. 'Allez Houllier!' the Kop chorused. It was as emotional and moving a moment as Anfield had witnessed in years. Houllier, both arms raised, waved to the crowd, clearly moved by the reception. Fired up by Houllier's presence and the blaring of the Kop, Liverpool rose to the challenge and presented their boss with a welcome-home present, a 2–0 win courtesy of goals from Heskey and Litmanen. It was a brave and inspired performance. Why, wondered many fans, did Houllier not play Litmanen more often?

In the quarter-final, Liverpool faced Germany's Bayer Lever-kusen, generally regarded as one of the weaker sides in the tournament; they'd already been beaten 4–1 by Arsenal. Victory against the Germans would also set up a possible all-English semi-final against arch rivals Manchester United. At Anfield on 3 April, in a dour and tense encounter, Liverpool sneaked a narrow 1–0 win, and went to Germany hopeful of holding out for a victory, but they were swept away in the tightly enclosed Bayer Arena. An early German goal set the pace, and although Liverpool equalised shortly before half-time the Germans came back to make it 3–1. A second Liverpool goal 12 minutes later from Jari Litmanen looked to have thrown Liverpool a lifeline, but with just six minutes remaining the Germans sneaked a fourth goal to take them through to the semi-final stage. For Liverpool to have scored twice and still not gone through was disappointing, but equally surprising was that they should have conceded four goals when in the previous fifteen European games they had conceded a mere eight. Michael Owen had also missed three one-on-one opportunities, chances he would normally have converted without the blink of an eyelid. On this occasion either the keeper or the post had come to the Germans' rescue. It was Liverpool's first away defeat in Europe since 1998.

Houllier, though bitterly disappointed, put on a brave face, pointing out that the only two games they had lost in the competition that season had been at the hands of sides that had just qualified for the semi-finals. He still had every confidence in his players and emphasised the enormous gains they had made in the past few seasons. 'In my first year we finished with 54 points, and the next we got 67 and qualified for the UEFA Cup,' Houllier said. 'Last season we finished with 69 points in third place, and now, this year, we've got 68 points already with five games to play. Look at other teams who have gone far in the competition in the past. Chelsea got to the quarter-finals and Leeds got to the semi-finals, but they didn't qualify for the Champions League in the Premiership table the following season. To me, consistency is a major factor in the quality of the squad, and we are there right now.' What Houllier might also have added was that Liverpool's two seasons in European competition had firmly re-established them among the Europe's top half-dozen sides. It was clear that they feared no one, and that on their day they were capable of defeating any team in Europe.

In the run-in in the Premiership, Liverpool did almost everything right. They had to win all of their final ten games to have any hope of snatching the title. Houllier firmly believed that if they did, they would be champions. It was a massive undertaking, though no more of a challenge than the one that had faced them the previous season. In truth, however, Arsenal, with two games in hand, were always favourites. Still, Liverpool almost pulled it off. The only problem was that both United and Arsenal, faced with the same challenge, matched Liverpool game for game. Everyone had expected Arsenal to implode at some point, but instead they carried on with their winning ways.

With three games to go all three sides were on a winning streak, and still Liverpool trailed Arsenal by four points. It was inevitable that Liverpool's visit to White Hart Lane on 27 April would be the crunch game of their season. They lost 1–0, their first Premiership defeat since January, and later that day they had to watch United sneak a 1–0 win at Ipswich to climb above them into second place. Liverpool's challenge for the title was over. Arsenal clinched it just over a week later, after winning the FA Cup, by travelling to Old Trafford and beating United on their own patch. They were worthy winners, and as Liverpool came out best in a seven-goal thriller with Blackburn, they once more leapfrogged United into second place. Three days later, in their final game of the season, they trounced Ipswich 5–0 at Anfield to secure the runners-up spot and automatic entry into the Champions League.

It was easy to complain that Liverpool had failed to win any silverware in 2001/02, but the fact was that they had excelled themselves. In November it had seemed that their season was over, yet they had put in an extraordinary challenge for the title, in spite of losing their manager for the best part of the season, and had ended as runners-up, ahead of United and with as many points as their north-west rivals had accrued the previous season when they strolled to the title. It was Liverpool's best ever tally in the Premiership. Houllier was thrilled. 'We have to acknowledge that Arsenal are great champions, but for us to finish above Man United is great,' he said. 'We have finished with 80 points, which is the same as Man United got last year and more than Arsenal got when they won the double four years ago. Our main aim is to win the title, but we are progressing nicely.' He also claimed that finishing second was even more remarkable considering that his ill health had taken him away from the side for so long and the fact that the influential Markus Babbel had missed most of the campaign. 'After all that has gone on at the club this season, with my illness and players' long-term injuries, for the club to be where we are now is absolutely fantastic.'

Yet Houllier's job would not be complete until Liverpool had won the title and at least reached the final of the Champions League. That was his ambition, one he shared with the fans. It needed, perhaps, one more push, one more foray into the transfer market, so a second clear-out began in the spring and summer of 2002.

It was clear that Liverpool had far too many players on the books. In all, there were 32 men in the squad, 23 of them internationals and most of them with first-team experience. Houllier had sorted out the defensive problems that had plagued the club for so many years to the extent that they now had the meanest defence in European football, the envy of every club. By the end of the 2001/02 season, the defence had a permanency about it. It almost picked itself: Dudek in goal, with Hyypia, Henchoz, Carragher and Abel Xavier strung across the back. Stephen Wright and Gregory Vignal offered back-up while Babbel recovered from his serious illness. Up front, Owen, Anelka, Heskey and Litmanen vied for the two spots while Milan Baros waited patiently, although at times not so quietly, in the wings.

But it was in midfield where the real problems lay. For a start, there were far too many midfielders on the books: Riise, McAllister, Redknapp, Barmby, Diomede, Murphy, Berger, Smicer, Gerrard, Hamann and Biscan. Eleven of them, and all bar one of them established internationals, battling it out for just four places. It was clear that some had to go. There was surely no need for more than eight midfielders. The salary bill was also spiralling; in the latest financial year it had accounted for 80 per cent of total revenue – an unacceptably high figure. There was also a danger, which must have loomed large in Houllier's mind, that some of the fringe players who were established internationals would soon become frustrated at not being given the opportunity to show off their skills in first-team football. The reality was that their international careers would also be in jeopardy if they were not playing regularly. No national manager is ever going to pick a player who isn't getting regular first-team football. Igor Biscan and Milan Baros were two such players. Although both were young and both figured in Houllier's long-term plans, neither was going to hang around for ever when they could be displaying their wares elsewhere, albeit on a smaller stage. The same was true of Richie Partridge, the 21-year-old Irish international who signed a new contract in 2002 in the hope that he might finally get an opportunity in the first team. Manchester United were known to be keen admirers of Partridge, ready to jump in at the first hint of discontent.

With all these thoughts crowding around him as he returned to the managerial chair, Gérard Houllier set about a summer clearance. First to go was club captain Jamie Redknapp. Although Redknapp was surprisingly offered a new contract by the club, he was astute enough to realise that his opportunities were always going to be limited at Anfield. He was already 28 years old. In a career that had been dogged by injury, particularly since Houllier had taken control, he knew that he came well down the pecking order. There was little or no chance of him breaking into the first team with the likes of Steven Gerrard and Didi Hamann in front of him, so he took the sensible option and in April 2002 joined Tottenham Hotspur on a free transfer. Redknapp, always a popular figure around Anfield, was married to the pop star Louise whose career was more London-centred. The club's longest-serving player, he had been one of Kenny Dalglish's last major signings, joining from Bournemouth in January 1991 for £350,000. He had made his breakthrough into the first team under Graeme Souness and had gone on to win seventeen England caps.

Next to go was the ageing midfielder Gary McAllister, whose contribution during the treble-winning season of 2000/01 had been crucial. But at 38 he had obviously seen his best days, and during the 2001/02 season it had showed. In the spring of 2002 the opportunity to become player-manager of Coventry was too tempting, and Liverpool were happy to wish him well.

Houllier had consistently shown that whenever better players appeared on the market he was prepared to be ruthless. He recognised Liverpool's weaknesses as much as any of the supporters and was never one to shirk the difficult task of moving a player on. In fact, it had long been part of the Liverpool philosophy that whenever a better player was available the club would not hesitate to sign him. Even if the incumbent player had spent years at Anfield, he would be thanked before being asked to make way for the new man. Players such as Song, Camara and Westerveld, many of them Houllier's earliest signings, had been quickly moved on in this way. Although Camara and Song had been popular with the fans, both had their limitations and there was no room for sentiment. It was the same with Redknapp and McAllister.

Surprisingly, there were no other departures. Diomede, Heggem, Arphexad and Biscan, all of whom might have expected the chop, survived for another season, possibly because there were few enquiries. Had anyone come in with a reasonable offer, almost certainly they would have gone too.

Despite missing virtually the entire season, Markus Babbel remained on Liverpool's books. He, like his boss, had been struck down by a life-threatening illness, almost from the start of the campaign. Babbel had noticed during the close season that he was unusually tired, and this in spite of the summer break. Against his old side Bayern Munich at Monaco in the European Super Cup in late August he'd felt oddly lethargic, even though Liverpool produced a stunning performance to take a 3–0 lead against the European Cup holders. Babbel had already played a few games that season in the Champions League qualifiers and the Charity Shield, and although he had felt some tiredness he'd simply put it down to the fact that it was early season and he wasn't yet firing on all cylinders.

His problem became most marked when Liverpool played newly promoted Bolton Wanderers at the Reebok Stadium on 27 August. During half-time Babbel slumped on his seat in the dressing room, totally sapped of energy. 'I don't think I can go out again,' he told Houllier. 'I feel utterly drained. I feel as if I've got the flu coming on.' Houllier was surprised, but he knew that Babbel was no shirker and that if he genuinely felt incapable of playing there was no point in pushing the matter. As a result, Babbel was substituted and Liverpool went down to their first defeat of the season. But the problem didn't end there. The following day Babbel was just as tired; even after a few more days' rest the flu-like symptoms continued to dog him. If anything it seemed to be getting worse, and he was forced to pull out of Liverpool's next fixture, a home game against Aston Villa.

The initial diagnosis at Anfield was that Babbel had some kind of viral infection, possibly glandular fever, or more likely a post-viral infection, the sort that seemed to be becoming more and more common. It often occurred after someone had had a bad bout of flu and had not been able fully to rid their body of the virus. It led to extreme tiredness. There was no obvious cure, just rest. The extreme form of it had become known as ME. At first, nobody was suggesting that Babbel had ME, but as the fatigue continued to affect him the situation became more worrying. He was sent to see a top consultant, but it is always difficult to assess the exact nature and cause of such tiredness. After a month or more it was assumed that Babbel probably did have a mild form of ME. Again it was decided that rest was the best cure; he needed to get away from anything that represented pressure. He was promptly sent back to Germany to recuperate, but by December, with no further signs of improvement, there was growing concern.

Babbel was now finding it difficult to move his legs – a symptom not usually associated with ME. As a consequence he was sent for further tests in Germany, and later that month the news came back that the illness had finally been identified: he was suffering from what was known as Guillain-Barré syndrome, a comparatively rare illness affecting the nervous system and leading to debilitation. The problem was that the illness could move up the body to affect the respiratory system, and in some cases this could be life-threatening. It was said to affect about 600 people a year in Britain. It was clear that there was little or no chance of him playing for the remainder of the season. Indeed, there were even question marks over his career, though Liverpool of course publicly played down any such fears. 'At least it has been diagnosed,' acting manager Phil Thompson told the press, adding, 'I would like to think that he won't be out for the whole of the season and that he can come back and play a vital part at the end of the campaign.' Poor Phil Thompson was becoming the harbinger of medical tidings, one minute giving the latest update on Houllier, the next a prognosis for Babbel.

But there was never really any chance of Babbel making anything like a speedy recovery. The truth was that his footballing career was in jeopardy. It would be touch and go whether he ever kicked a ball again, let alone played competitive football at the highest level.

Babbel was immediately admitted to hospital in Germany, only for matters gradually to get worse as the illness began to spread around his body. Over the next few weeks he lost the use of his legs, and for a short time he lay paralysed in his hospital bed. Fellow German international Steffen Freund found himself in the same rehabilitation centre as Babbel. Freund, then with Tottenham, was recovering from a cruciate ligament injury. 'We were in a rehabilitation centre in Donaustauf and we spent a lot of time together,' he said. 'Markus was in a wheelchair for a few months and close to . . .' He hesitated. 'Maybe, you never know with that illness. Everyone was telling me that the cruciate ligament is one of the worst injuries in the world. But then I see Markus and then I know what is really serious.' Freund admitted to being taken aback when he saw Babbel. 'It was a shock to see him, a friend, a footballer, in a wheelchair. He was so ill, overnight. Maybe he could have been finished with football, maybe he could even die, all that to a person so young.'

Every week someone from the Anfield backroom showed up at the hospital to give him support and to report home on his condition. Babbel was desperately ill, but with careful treatment he gradually began to improve. By the late spring he was out of hospital, his first steps as important a moment in his life as any, and beginning a long campaign to regain full fitness. After the first steps came the first run, then the first kick of a ball, then the first sprint, then the first training game, and finally, in the autumn of 2002, Babbel bravely returned to the Liverpool first team.

Just about the only player at Anfield with a question mark hanging over him as the season wound to its close was Nicolas Anelka, the French international on loan from Paris St Germain. After an impressive season Anelka was fully expected to become a permanent addition to the side. But then something happened to change that.

11. PLAYING WITH FIRE

Back in the seventies and eighties, when a few drinks and some nonsense were part of the pattern of football, Fowler would not have been out of order. Even the great Liverpool sides were known to be keen on high jinks. But along with saturation television coverage and wealth came responsibility, expectations and professionalism. Footballers weren't meant to be out on the booze, being the good-time boys, but when it came to Fowler, money might have taken the boy out of Toxteth but it didn't take Toxteth out of the boy.

The signing of Nicolas Anelka on loan was a stroke of genius. In November 2001 Robbie Fowler had packed his bags and gone off to Leeds United, leaving Gérard Houllier and Liverpool short of a striker. Houllier had always insisted that he wanted five strikers in his squad; the loss of Fowler left him with just the injury-prone Michael Owen, Emile Heskey, Jari Litmanen and the newly signed but still untried Milan Baros. Houllier promised that another striker would be brought in, and for a month or so various names were linked with the club, but nobody seriously mentioned the name of the out-of-favour French front man.

Since leaving Arsenal in 1999 for Real Madrid in a £25 million deal, Anelka's fortunes had nose-dived. He had helped the Gunners to a remarkable League and Cup double in 1997/98, scoring against Newcastle in the FA Cup final, and his goal tally for 1998/99 was nineteen in 46 games. At that point he was one of the hottest strikers in Europe, and it was little wonder that the Spanish giants should be interested in acquiring his services. But the manner of Anelka's departure was to leave a bitter taste in the mouths of many at Highbury.

Anelka had been signed by Arsène Wenger as an eighteen-year-old from Paris St Germain. After spending a year in the reserves, Anelka finally broke through into the Arsenal side early in 1998. His impact was immediate, but sadly Anelka, or rather his brothers Claude and Didier, who acted as his agents, had other ideas. They wanted to cash in on his talents forthwith. In the summer of 1999 they let it be known that their brother would be prepared to move if the right offer came in. Along with Real Madrid, just about every major club in Europe was interested, including Inter Milan and Juventus. Barely a day passed without some headline about Anelka's future, many of the stories no doubt planted by the brothers themselves. At times, it seemed they were more in charge of the negotiations and the decision-making than Nicolas. It was true that Nicolas was young and that his brothers were acting as his agents, but huge demands were being made. Wenger had invested heavily in Anelka, so he was none too pleased when after a short stay at Highbury he decided to leave for Real Madrid. Arsenal were left with little option but to accept his demand and negotiate a reasonable fee. Within weeks he was off on a plane to Madrid, accused by fans of being disloyal, self-centred, sulky and difficult.

It turned out not to be a match made in heaven. Anelka did not settle well, could not find an automatic place in the starting line-up, and his form dipped. He survived just one season, and although he ended it with a European Cup-Winners' Cup medal, matters had deteriorated beyond control. At the end of the season Real offloaded him back to his first club, Paris St Germain, making the same accusations Arsenal had levelled at him. It seemed the brothers were at work again, for a mega fee was extracted out of the French side. If nothing else, Anelka, not to mention Claude and Didier, was certainly a rich man by now, and he still wasn't twenty.

You might have thought a return to his home city would be the impetus for him to resurrect his career. Instead, it slumped even further. Playing in the less competitive Le Championnat, and with a side desperate for him to play, Anelka's form dipped dramatically, to the extent that he found himself sidelined and not even making the substitutes bench. Again there were the same accusations: he was controlled by his brothers, he was selfish, he was sulky, he was not deserving of his sky-high salary. Anelka needed rescuing, but although the tragic situation at PSG was there for all to see, nobody seemed intent on delivering the lad from his problems. Then, in the closing weeks of 2001, in stepped Gérard Houllier.

The Liverpool manager had barely recovered from his major heart operation and was beginning gently to ease himself back into the hot seat, his first task to think about a replacement for Fowler.

Houllier was well aware of Anelka's unrest and his difficulties with PSG. Houllier had worked with him before when he was running France's under-18 and under-20 sides and had always been impressed by the young man. It was worth an enquiry. The result was that PSG were more than happy for someone – anyone – to take Anelka off their hands, especially given the wages they were paying him. PSG anticipated a transfer deal, but Houllier, unsurprisingly, was reluctant to pay out a huge fee for a striker with a bad reputation. But what about a loan deal for the rest of the season? It was worth a try. As an enticement, he also suggested taking out a first option to buy him at the end of the season. PSG were not averse to the idea. Houllier rang Phil Thompson, who was excited at the prospect of one of Europe's top strikers linking up with Michael Owen. 'Go for it,' he replied, 'we've nothing to lose.' PSG thought about it, but with no other offers on the table they agreed.

The news of Anelka's arrival at Anfield came as a bombshell, having been unheralded by anyone in the media. It was an entertaining prospect but also one with a huge question mark. 'I've never found him difficult,' Houllier assured the doom-mongers who were predicting more surliness and awkwardness from the young man, 'but we'll just have to see.'

Anelka immediately pulled on Fowler's vacated number nine shirt and made his debut as a second-half substitute in the Boxing Day win at Aston Villa. In all, he played 21 times over the next five months, scoring five goals. Although he was clearly rusty to begin with, he looked to improve as the season wore on, even scoring twice in the final week. But a season's tally of just five goals in 21 games was hardly impressive. At times he had looked outstanding, particularly during the 3–0 win over Newcastle at Anfield in March 2002. What's more, there was no reported trouble. Player after player had gone on to their websites to reveal how pleasant and friendly Anelka had been. There had been no signs at all of the difficulties that had come to be associated with him.

As the season drew to its close, Houllier confirmed that Liverpool were interested in a permanent deal. 'We want to keep him,' the manager told the media. 'His arrival has been a good thing for us, for him and for the other strikers in the team.' He did, however, add a word of caution that was to prove significant. 'But we will see – there is the club, the player, the various interests of everyone.' For his part, Phil Thompson was insisting that Anelka had done well and that Liverpool wanted to sign him. 'He's done great by us and we are still hoping everything will come off,' he said, adding, 'Nicolas has been good for us.'

Given all the enthusiasm emanating from the Anfield dressing room, it seemed it was just a matter of setting up a deal. First, Liverpool had to agree a transfer fee with PSG, then they had to agree personal terms with Anelka himself. But Houllier was reluctant to reveal much, claiming that he wanted to wait until the season was over before negotiations got under way, although stories were already appearing that Anelka was demanding a salary of £60,000 a week. Sure enough, once the season was concluded all the signs were that a deal was being set up: a fee of £12 million was duly agreed with PSG, and it was reported that Anelka, who was desperate to stay at Liverpool, had reduced his salary demands by half. Given all the positive statements coming out of Anfield, it seemed that Anelka would shortly become a Liverpool player.

Then Houllier broke his silence to say that he wanted more time to think about it. He needed to go away, to seek some peace and quiet in order to make up his mind. Surely he couldn't be having second doubts? A week after the season had ended, Houllier announced that he would not be taking up the option on Anelka. There was outrage from the Anelka camp. 'I personally feel let down,' said Nicolas. The deal, he claimed, had been agreed a week earlier. A fee had been settled with PSG and personal terms had also been agreed between the club and the striker, but now he had been told that Liverpool would not be signing him. 'I wanted to stay at Liverpool,' he added, 'and I thought we had an agreement. I feel that Liverpool have let me down. They have not explained why they don't want to keep me.' Paris St Germain also felt cheated. Houllier had called Alain Cayzac, vice-president of PSG, to tell him that he had changed his mind and no longer wanted Anelka. 'The conversation was short and cold,' Cayzac reported. 'I told him that he was not respecting his commitments and that despite our good relationship I was very disappointed in his behaviour.' At times, he confessed, he had had doubts about the entire deal, but added, 'Houllier had always assured me that Nicolas was his first choice. Liverpool's attitude is not that of a great club. For me, everything was sorted out even if there was no written agreement.' On reflection, however, he admitted that to some extent it was their own fault for not getting anything down on paper. The Arsenal striker Patrick Vieira piped up in defence of his friend. 'It is lacking in class,' the French midfielder told the papers, 'especially as it is from a coach who has known Nico since he was a kid. Frankly, if he didn't call Nicolas to tell him the news, it is tactless.'

Generally there was confusion, even among Anelka's fellow players at Anfield. 'I think Nicolas was good for Liverpool and that Liverpool were good for him,' Norwegian full-back Vegard Heggem commented on his website. 'That's probably the best way to describe how things went. Nicolas appeared to be happy at Liverpool, and he was popular with the fans. I actually think English football suits him more than any other. Clearly he was enjoying his game again while he was with us. That's why I believe he will want to remain in the Premiership next season.' Although Anelka had been painted as a 'difficult' character, Heggem confirmed there was no evidence of any problems. 'I can tell you that the rumours about him being a difficult character are just not true. I certainly had no evidence of that, and I don't believe any of the other players had either. Nicolas was fairly reserved, but he seemed to get on with everyone.' Heggem's view was certainly not out of kilter with the rest of the squad; other Liverpool players had been repeatedly saying the same since Anelka's arrival. It was almost as if they had expected a monster to pull up outside Melwood but had been pleasantly surprised to discover that he had only one head and two ears. Both Heskey and Gerrard were among those impressed by Anelka's attitude during his time at Anfield, and both had been urging the club to make his loan deal permanent. Heskey in particular was supportive of Anelka. 'Nico has been brilliant for us. He had a bit of a reputation as someone who didn't mix, but I can honestly say that that hasn't been the case here. He gets on well with all the lads and his performances on the field have been brilliant. We want the best at this club, and he certainly falls into that category.'

By the time Anelka had sorted out a new deal, this time with Manchester City, he was less bitter about what had happened, admitting that 'my time at Anfield has given me back my appetite to play football. Liverpool allowed me to develop my all-round game and I felt good because I was being used as more than just a striker. I got on with everyone and was really sorry to leave. It was disappointing to be told I was going to be signed by Gérard Houllier and then have him change his mind, but that's life. I don't hold any grudge against Gérard because he helped me enormously during my five months there.'

Quite what lay behind the decision not to sign the agreement was, at the time, a mystery, even to those on the staff. 'I know that the manager and the board will have thought things through long and hard, and they will feel there was a good reason behind the decision,' said Heggem, 'but I'm equally sure that Gérard Houllier has something else up his sleeve. The gaffer has gone on record saying he needs another striker. A lot of names have already been mentioned, and I wouldn't bet against him springing a surprise over the summer.'

The press speculated that Houllier's late rejection of Anelka was bound up with the French player's controversial history, his alleged moodiness, his salary demands and so on, and there was some truth in this. Certainly Anelka was still prone to throwing a sulk when he was not selected. But perhaps more importantly, Anelka's brothers had not been easy to work with and had infuriated Houllier on more than one occasion. They had also set themselves up as DJs in a Liverpool nightclub. Such was their general behaviour that Houllier had taken the unprecedented step of banning them from Melwood, convinced that they were a bad influence on their younger brother. Nicolas himself had also been caught out late doing the rounds of Liverpool nightclubs. He wasn't drunk, in fact he hardly ever drank, nor was he causing any problems, but he was out late when there was supposed to be a curfew. That kind of attitude did not endear him to Houllier. You simply could not ask one player to adhere to a curfew when another was breaking it. Word also reached Houllier that Anelka had twice been offered back to Arsenal. Considering that Liverpool had thrown him a lifeline when he was warming the bench at Paris St Germain, this was hardly showing much gratitude.

But the truth behind Anelka's rejection probably had less to do with the French player's past and his brothers than with the fact that Houllier simply had someone else in mind all along. For much of the season he'd been tracking the young Auxerre striker Djibril Cissé, who ended the season as top scorer in Le Championnat and was called into the French squad for the World Cup finals in Japan and South Korea. But although Cissé was almost certainly top of Houllier's list, the Liverpool manager was not getting much encouragement from veteran Auxerre manager Guy Roux. In fact, quite the opposite. Auxerre were determined to hang on to their man for at least one more season, but 'I might not be able to hang on to him for ever,' Roux claimed, hinting that maybe in a year's time Cissé could go. Even then, he added, we are talking about £30 million. There was never any way Houllier was going to pay that kind of price. Cissé also let it be known that he did not wish to leave Auxerre for another twelve months. After that, he said, it was possible, and yes, he'd quite fancy going to Liverpool. Italian giants Roma were also sniffing around; unlike Liverpool, they were probably prepared to find the £30 million. But even they were receiving little encouragement. It was clear that a deal for Cissé was not going to happen, but that if it did it would spell the end of Anelka's time at Anfield. Nevertheless, Houllier kept an open line to Auxerre in the hope that they might decide to change their minds.

In the meantime, he changed tack and turned his attention to the young Senegalese striker El-Hadji Diouf. Diouf was the African footballer of the year, at 21 the same age as Cissé, and had scored freely in the qualifiers for the World Cup as well as hitting a dozen goals in Le Championnat for his club Lens who, after leading the title race for the entire season, had been pipped at the post on the final day. Houllier had spotted Diouf on television and was immediately impressed. He still had strong links with Lens, too: his old friend Patrice Bergues was now back at the club as director of football. It took only a phone call to Bergues to confirm that Diouf was a star in the making. Diouf also was not short on confidence, claiming that he wanted to be the best footballer in the world. 'But unfortunately,' added Bergues, 'a deal has been done to sell him to Valencia.'

Houllier was a bit annoyed with this. 'But has he actually signed yet?' he asked.

'No, not yet,' Bergues replied, 'but we have agreed a fee and he has said that he is ready to leave.'

'Look,' said Houllier, 'can you give me the chance to talk to him, to see if he would be interested in coming to Liverpool?'

Lens were not particularly happy with the situation as a late entry by Liverpool would only muddy the waters, but they had little option. Houllier was immediately in touch with Diouf's agent and the reply came back that Diouf would be very interested in a move to Liverpool, a club he had always liked. So the Anelka deal was called off and another set up with Diouf, although there would be further questions from Lens about a transfer fee not having been agreed between the two clubs. Valencia, of course, were none too pleased either. The deal had to be fully set up before the World Cup finals kicked off. It took some hurried organisation, but on the morning of the opening game, Diouf duly signed.

'El-Hadji who?' was the question on the streets of Liverpool when the deal became public knowledge. There had been excitement at the prospect of Anelka joining the club and eager anticipation at the possibility of Cissé arriving, but nobody knew who this Senegalese player was – at least, that is, until the World Cup kicked off on 31 May, Diouf appropriately taking the field to represent his country against the World cup holders France. Inside half an hour the name Diouf was on everyone's lips as he ran rings around one of the finest defences in world football. Houllier, it seemed, had pulled off another masterstroke. Even Guy Roux had to admit that Diouf was a far better player and a far better prospect than Anelka. And while Diouf set the World Cup alight, Cissé was on the next plane home as France bombed out of the tournament.

The player whose departure had prompted all this speculation and dealing in 2001/02 had been a Liverpool player almost all his life.

Robbie Fowler was said to have been an Evertonian as a youngster, but it was Liverpool who snapped him up as a schoolboy. Even as a teenager he was a precocious goal scorer, and he raced through the ranks of youth football, scoring so freely and regularly that Graeme Souness could not resist the temptation to give him a run-out in the first team. From the outset, he was sensational.

Cheeky, mischievous and popular, he was what is called in Liverpool a scallie. To the fans he was one of them, someone they might easily have gone to school with, or later in life gone clubbing with. He was the lad from down the road, Mrs Fowler's boy. He was a loveable rogue who never really meant any harm to anyone, yet when it came to it he could defend himself as well as the next lad and wouldn't cop out of any situation. He'd give as good as he got. He was the kind of lad to have on your side – well-liked, loyal, irreverent, a bit of a joker, and always good fun to be with.

He was also flawed. He enjoyed just one too many good nights out on the town, he lacked the discipline necessary to call himself an athlete, and his irreverence bordered on the disrespectful and at times overstepped the mark. He dubbed Houllier 'The Frog' and found it funny. It was typical Liverpool humour, but it now looked out of place in the new money-rich, globalised Premiership. Back in the seventies and eighties, when a few drinks and some nonsense were part of the pattern of football, Fowler would not have been out of order. Even the great Liverpool sides were known to be keen on high jinks. But along with saturation television coverage and wealth came responsibility, expectations and professionalism. Footballers weren't meant to be out on the booze, being the good-time boys, but when it came to Fowler, money might have taken the boy out of Toxteth but it didn't take Toxteth out of the boy.

Fowler had burst on to the football scene in September 1993 when he scored on his debut in the League Cup against Fulham. A couple of weeks later, in the return leg, he hit five goals and a legend was born. Few players can ever have made such a dramatic and immediate impact. By the end of the season he had bagged seventeen goals. The following year he was even more prolific, netting 25 League goals, but from then on it was downhill. There were niggling injuries and problems. He began the 1997/98 season by incurring the wrath of the England manager when he opted for a nose operation rather than an international call-up. He was then seriously injured in a pre-season friendly, returned only to be sent off, and then against Everton at Anfield suffered an horrific cruciate ligament injury which sidelined him for the remainder of the season and for the World Cup as well. By the time he was back in contention, Houllier was firmly in charge, Michael Owen had taken over as the number one striker, Emile Heskey had also arrived and the rotation system had been adopted. Once the top dog, Fowler now found himself scrabbling on the sidelines. It was not to his liking.

In an effort to stem Fowler's slide into confusion and possible lawlessness, Houllier hit upon the master plan of appointing him club vice-captain. He consulted with Phil Thompson and both men agreed that it might just provide the fillip Fowler needed to put his career on to the straight and narrow. It would focus him, argued Houllier, as well as make him feel wanted. The appointment would make him the number two at the club, behind captain Jamie Redknapp, and give him some well-needed status, at the same time sending out a signal to the rest of the club and to the public that Fowler was a much respected and appreciated figure at Anfield. Maybe he would meet the responsibility demanded by the post with a new maturity.

Fowler greeted the appointment with precisely the enthusiasm Houllier had wanted, and for a while it worked, but the one thing Fowler found difficult to stomach was that as vice-captain he should spend so much time warming the bench. If he was vice-captain, why on earth was he being named as a substitute so often? Why was he not the first or second name on the teamsheet, an automatic starter? And of course he could argue that his form would only improve with matchplay. With the reserves playing so few games, maybe one every two or three weeks, other opportunities were few and far between. Footballers want to play football. Many of them hate training and simply want to be playing in competitive games. There's nothing wrong with that, but the demands of the modern game mean it's sensible for players to take the occasional rest. Fowler was up against two problems, then: the first was this need for the occasional rest; the second was that ahead of him in the queue for the strikers' role were Michael Owen and Emile Heskey.

Owen was a total contrast to Fowler. He wasn't a Toxteth boy, for a start. He'd been born on the borders of Wales, close to Chester, where he continued to live with his parents. He was clean-cut, dedicated, sensible, a genuine professional and a fine example to any schoolkid. He didn't go clubbing, he didn't drink, he didn't get into skirmishes. But what irked Fowler most was that Owen was also a better player. On the Kop they would always love Fowler simply because he was one of them. Not so Owen. He might have been the most exciting England striker since Jimmy Greaves, but he was clinical and slightly characterless. To this day Owen has never been the focus of the same kind of affection Fowler could command. If you wanted to spend an evening with one of them, the chances were that most Kopites would plump for Robbie.

There followed a litany of incidents, both on the field and off it. At Stamford Bridge in the spring of 1999, Fowler turned his back on Chelsea's England defender Graeme Le Saux and bent down provocatively. It was meant to be funny, but few in the crowd or anywhere else found it amusing. Certainly Gérard Houllier did not. A couple of weeks later, after hitting a penalty against Everton, Fowler, in a biting response to all those cocaine rumours, celebrated by pretending to snort the touchline. It was immediately clear that not everybody would be amused. Certainly the Premiership chiefs weren't, and he was promptly fined. When asked about it after the game, Houllier claimed that he had not seen the incident, but he was growing a mite weary of having to defend his man. Then there was an incident in the toilet of a Liverpool hotel, as a result of which Fowler received a bloodied nose. It wasn't Fowler's fault, just another scallie trying it on, but you had to wonder why he persisted in drinking in such high-profile bars.

There was little doubt that Fowler, for all the affection of the Kop, was not a happy man. All too often his head would drop. Fans could visibly see his shoulders droop, could see him watching rather than participating. Time and again he failed to attack the ball, to get himself involved, to get into the six-yard box. The crowd began to groan at his apparent lack of effort and enthusiasm. In a way, that only made things worse, and the confidence drained from him. The game seemed to be passing him by and there was little he or the club could do to reverse the situation. His injury appeared to be haunting him. There were some who felt that in the year or more since it had happened football had increased its pace and Fowler had dropped a notch in the pace stakes. He now lacked that extra yard needed by the best strikers. Fowler argued that the more games he played the more likely he would be to recapture his old pace and instinct. But there was no doubt that he was given his chance, particularly when Owen was injured, and there were few signs of the old Robbie Fowler. In his final season at the club, 2000/01, he managed a mere four goals in seventeen appearances, three of those strikes coming in one game. The torrent of the mid-nineties had become a trickle; he'd netted just 34 goals in the last four seasons, and that out of a total of 171. Neither Houllier nor the club could afford the luxury of sitting back and waiting until Fowler found his cutting edge once more. It was little wonder the club preferred to select Owen and Heskey, especially as in that 2000/01 season Liverpool were chasing trophies on three fronts.

Time and again throughout those difficult months, Houllier would pull Fowler aside and have a heart to heart with him. 'In the summer [of 2000], when my head was up my backside, he just sat me down and talked about where the club was going,' said Fowler. 'He was very supportive. He was brilliant.' Houllier was trying to persuade Fowler to lead a more regular lifestyle, and when Fowler announced to everyone that he was about to become a father no one was more pleased than Houllier. That, he reckoned, might be a turning point, giving him more responsibility and more focus. But it didn't seem to be the case. On one occasion, Fowler was attacked in the city centre. There was never any suggestion that it was Fowler's fault, but the fact that the attack took place in the early hours of the morning raised further questions about Fowler's commitment to professional football. There were also raised eyebrows when it was revealed that

Fowler's wife was with him. Nothing wrong with that, except that some wondered who was looking after the baby.

Fowler might well have had a reasonable relationship with Houllier, but the same could not be said of Phil Thompson. Thompson and Fowler were too alike in many ways. They had both been brought up in hard parts of Liverpool, Fowler in Toxteth, Thompson in Kirby. They were a pair of scallies, rough diamonds out to conquer the world. Both had been with the club since their teenage years, both were loved by the Kop, and no doubt Thompson could see a bit of himself in Fowler. On paper, it looked the perfect relationship, but as so often happens in such situations, in practice they were chalk and cheese. Thompson had won it all – League titles, European Cups and a bagful of international honours. He'd grown up, become responsible and professional, and was grateful for all that had happened to him. He'd also been brought up under Shankly where there was no disrespect, no messing with the management; anyhow, the club was famed for sorting out its problems long before they ever came within the manager's earshot. Either the bootroom staff would have had a word, or more likely one of the senior players. But in this instance the senior player was Fowler himself. He had been made vice-captain of the club, and that carried responsibilities. Thompson knew that Fowler would not have lasted ten minutes under Shankly. For all his wealth, fame and cockiness, Fowler had won little and was far from being a permanent fixture in the England side, as Houllier often reminded him. More effort and less joking was the line Thompson took when it came to Fowler.

The flashpoint came in a Melwood spat between Thompson and Fowler. At the end of a practice session one morning a ball was kicked which hit Thompson on the back of the head. The ball had been kicked by Fowler. The Liverpool assistant did not take too kindly to it, accusing Fowler of deliberately striking the ball at him; Fowler claimed it had been accidental, others thought differently. Once tempers had been calmed, Houllier insisted that Fowler apologise. Fowler refused, pleading his innocence, and the row dragged on with neither side prepared to budge. Eventually it found its way on to the back pages; there was some suspicion, though never proven, that it had been deliberately leaked by the club to a sympathetic journalist. Even so, Fowler still refused to back down, even though Houllier, from his sick bed, was clearly offering his full support to Thompson. Speculation grew that it could spell the end of Fowler's Liverpool career. The story dragged on for almost a week. As a punishment, Fowler was left out of the side and wasn't even named as a substitute. Given that he was still the club's vice-captain it did not look good. It was a battle Fowler was never going to win, and eventually, after speaking with Houllier again, he backed down. Fowler and Thompson were photographed together shaking hands as if nothing had happened. Few were fooled. Something had happened, and the bad taste was not going to go away easily.

The will he go, won't he go stories gathered pace. Arsenal, Chelsea, Leeds and Blackburn were all reckoned to have their chequebooks poised, but when a transfer did happen, it came as a surprise. The deal had been done on the quiet without anybody knowing, and by the time it was announced there was no chance of a counterbid. What was surprising was that Liverpool had agreed to sell Fowler to one of their closest rivals, Leeds United. Liverpool fans were astonished. It seemed to many that they were handing Leeds the League title, giving them at a knockdown price a proven goal scorer to add to their already impressive strike force of Mark Viduka, Robbie Keane and Alan Smith. Eleven million was not a huge sum of money considering Fowler's goal-scoring record and his age, although Houllier later announced that the true figure was nearer £13 million, but even that fell short of a figure closer to £20 million many fans had hoped for. As far back as the summer of 2000 Chelsea had made an audacious offer of £12 million. Houllier and the board had thought long and hard about it and would have been prepared to accept it, but rather than make a decision they'd decided to find out what Fowler had to say. He was not keen on linking up with Chelsea's foreign legion; indeed, at that stage he wasn't keen on going anywhere.

Fowler was undoubtedly a home boy. Born and bred in Toxteth, he still maintained close ties with the community and was the popular lad about town. His marriage and newly arrived children were a further tie. He had also had a house built, all of which instinctively held him to the area. Quite simply, he did not wish to leave Liverpool. On the other hand, he did want regular first-team football. He wanted to feel loved and appreciated, too, and at Anfield, under Houllier, he felt neither.

Whether or not in the end everyone involved at Anfield really wanted rid of Fowler is debatable. Undoubtedly there were some, including Houllier and Thompson, who felt the club should cash in and that Fowler was more trouble than he was worth, that he was history rather than future. They believed that he would never recapture the pace and goal-scoring instincts of old, that he would never again be the same player he'd been between 1994 and 1997. He had become injury prone, too, and the constant battle to regain fitness was becoming a long and painful process.

But there is no doubt that Fowler did have his friends at the club. He was popular with many of the players, and even on the board he had known supporters. David Moores was one of his biggest fans and had personally vetoed an effort by Houllier in his early years to offload him. Moores had argued that transferring Fowler would not go down well on the Kop and that Houllier was too new in the job to make such a major change. It would only make him unpopular, and make his task of transforming the club all the more difficult. In hindsight, of course, it might have been better to have grasped the nettle there and then.

Still, like many others, Houllier had a soft spot for Fowler. 'I liked him as a person and we got on well,' insisted Houllier, who even telephoned Fowler prior to his Leeds United debut. 'I told him he would always be welcome at Melwood.' Fowler was always the kind of personality who would never be short of pals. There was always someone to egg him on, take him clubbing, help him spend his money. The Liverpool striker might have been incorrigible and mischievous, but he was never malevolent. Fowler enjoyed a laugh, and that was always good for team spirit. On the surface, he'd continued publicly to voice his support for Houllier, too. 'Gérard has stood by me from day one through everything,' he told the papers. 'He's got a lot of time for me and I've got a lot of time for him. I hear all these rumours about us not getting on but that couldn't be further from the truth.' Despite this, Houllier told shareholders at the club's AGM shortly after Fowler had been transferred that 'I will not keep a player at this club who is unhappy, and that applies to anybody, not just Robbie. In addition, with just eighteen months left on his contract, we could not afford a repeat of the Steve McManaman situation, which is why the timing was right for both Robbie and us. The fact that he went to Elland Road is not important.'

Still, feelings among the fans ran high and strong. There were plenty who were glad to see the back of him, reckoning that he was a negative influence. Too many headlines, all for the wrong reason, was their argument. But there were just as many who were broken-hearted to see the lad from down the road disappearing over the Pennines. Typical among them was one correspondent in the club's best-known fanzine, *Through the Wind and Rain*, who wrote: 'How do I feel? Gutted, angry and desperately sad . . . What's really galling is the way Houllier has gone about the whole business. He has orchestrated this move for the last eighteen months . . . the club accepting the Leeds offer made it crystal clear that he had no future at the club. In fact, just hours before the news of the move broke yesterday, there was nonsense on the official website that Robbie was in fresh talks over a new contract. Yet more lies from the club about Robbie. I am so angry about the whole affair.'

The saga of Robbie Fowler had indeed dragged on for the best part of two years, and in many ways it was the signing of Milan Baros, the nineteen-year-old striker from the Czech Republic club Banik Ostrava, during the summer of 2001 that slammed the final nail into the Toxteth boy's coffin. Baros was already an international with half a dozen caps when he put pen to paper. Houllier insisted he was 'one for the future', but he became Liverpool's fifth striker behind Owen, Heskey, Fowler and Litmanen. It was obvious to any seasoned Liverpool watcher that Baros was not going to be content simply to sit on the bench and bide his time for the next three years, nor was he bought to do that. Houllier might well have been speaking the truth when he claimed that Baros would have to be patient, that Fowler was well ahead of him in the queue for the striker's shirt, but his signing certainly sent out the wrong message to Fowler. His interpretation was different. He saw Baros as another obstacle, a further sign that he was not wanted and that the club was already thinking about a future without him.

When Fowler reflected on his reasons for leaving Liverpool, he put it down mainly to the 2002 World Cup. 'One of the main reasons I left Liverpool was to enhance my chance of playing for England. Realistically, if I was sat there with a Liverpool shirt on I don't think we'd be talking about the World Cup.' But the fact was that the two players still ahead of him in the England pecking order were the very same players who had been among those ahead of him in the Anfield pecking order – Michael Owen and Emile Heskey. In the end, Fowler did go to the World Cup finals in Japan and Korea, but he could only muster twenty minutes on the field. As ever, the men ahead of him were his old club-mates, Heskey and Owen.

And so Fowler wound up as a Leeds United player. But it was not to be the best of seasons for Leeds as they became entangled in an unseemly court case and their form spiralled out of control. Well out of contention in the League and out of all the cup competitions, they ended up in fifth spot, also out of the Champions League places. It was an expensive campaign that would inevitably lead to a FOR SALE sign being hung outside the ground. Nevertheless, Fowler could look back with some satisfaction on his move. He had been virtually guaranteed first-team football at Elland Road and had ended his season with a respectable tally of twelve goals from 22 Premiership games. But then an injured hip led to yet another long lay-off, and more than a third of the 2002/03 season had gone before he reappeared in a Leeds shirt. By then, the man who had signed him had also gone.

12. EASY COME, EASY GO

After the match, Houllier went into the dressing room. When Westerveld had left he asked some of the players if Sander had said anything to them. Had he apologised? They shook their heads. He had said nothing; he hadn't even bothered to explain what had happened. It was a sign of arrogance and showed no respect for his team-mates, and as far as Houllier was concerned that was it. Ever since he had been called more regularly into the Dutch squad Westerveld had seemed to grow more conceited, full of his own self-importance.

It became known as 'The Tale of Two Goalkeepers' and is still a story that baffles most Liverpool supporters. In order to tell it, we must go back to the beginning.

When Houllier arrived at Liverpool he immediately pinpointed goalkeeper David James as a weak link. Roy Evans also had his doubts, to the extent that James had been temporarily replaced by the American keeper Brad Friedel. Yet Friedel had also failed to convince, so Houllier made it one of his first tasks to unearth a new goalkeeper. In the summer of 1999 he was pleased to reveal the man chosen as the new Liverpool number one, Dutch international Sander Westerveld, who arrived as a £4 million signing from the Dutch club Vitesse Arnhem. Although largely unknown, Westerveld had played one game for Holland and was generally considered the number two Dutch keeper behind the mighty Edwin Van der Saar. In time, Westerveld would go on to win further caps for his country, although so far he has still failed to unseat Van der Saar. 'When I spoke to Gérard Houllier about signing, his first question was, "Do you want to play for Liverpool?"' Westerveld recalled. 'I just said, "Next question, please." Mind you, I was surprised that Liverpool wanted me. I'd seen David James play and thought he was an excellent goal-keeper.'

Still, once Liverpool fans had seen Westerveld in action they thought him a huge improvement on James. He might not have been as tall as his predecessor, but he was young, agile and had far more command of the box than ever James displayed. In his first season at the club he settled in well and nobody had any complaints, but during 2000/01 one or two doubts began to creep in. He could sometimes look hesitant when it came to crosses and he was not always confident on his near post. There were a number of notable mistakes, particularly at Chelsea and Barcelona, and also against Alavés in the UEFA Cup final. During the summer Liverpool travelled to the Far East, and even against mediocre opposition Westerveld managed some howlers. Still, that season Liverpool won the treble and his penalty saves during the League Cup final at the Millennium Stadium certainly contributed to Liverpool's victory. Although the Liverpool defence leaked goals during the season and regularly gave away commanding leads, you could hardly blame Westerveld alone. 'I thought I'd found my home,' he said. 'Liverpool was the club for me. I loved every minute of it. Playing in front of 45,000 at Anfield is ten times better than playing in front of 100,000 in the Nou Camp.'

Despite general approval from the fans, Houllier was far from happy with Westerveld's performances. Rumours were rife that Liverpool were looking for a new keeper, yet all the time Houllier was reassuring Westerveld that his future was secure. It now appears, however, that Houllier spent part of that summer of 2001 searching for a new keeper. 'I knew something funny was going on,' said Westerveld, 'as a couple of journalists in Holland warned me that Liverpool were dealing with [Jerzy] Dudek. His agent has since told me that they'd been negotiating for six weeks. But Houllier told me that the rumours were lies.' Houllier might have been negotiating, but nothing concrete had been sorted out by the time the 2001/02 season began in earnest. But the fact remained that Houllier had met with Westerveld's agent during the summer to discuss a new contract and had told him quite bluntly that he was not happy with Westerveld's performances. 'There will be a different keeper at Anfield this season,' he'd said, 'either an improved Westerveld or someone else.' The message was stark.

Then came Liverpool's second Premiership game of that season, away at Bolton. Bolton opened the scoring but Liverpool pulled level. Then, in the final minutes, a long-range speculative shot from Dean Holdsworth spun along the ground and squirmed past a sprawling Westerveld. It was an horrendous mistake, and Houllier was unforgiving. It was to be Westerveld's last appearance in a Liverpool shirt.

After the match, Houllier went into the dressing room. When Westerveld had left he asked some of the players if Sander had said anything to them. Had he apologised? They shook their heads. He had said nothing; he hadn't even bothered to explain what had happened. It was a sign of arrogance and showed no respect for his team-mates, and as far as Houllier was concerned that was it. Ever since he had been called more regularly into the Dutch squad Westerveld had seemed to grow more conceited, full of his own self-importance.

'The possibility of a new goalkeeper coming was going round in my head during the Bolton game,' Westerveld explained later. 'I was pleased going into the final minutes that I had coped with the pressure. I had managed to play well and not let it get to me. Then I made that mistake. On the coach home I knew I'd played my last game. That was exactly the stick Houllier needed to beat me with. If it hadn't been for that mistake, it would have been harder to justify getting rid of me.'

But what then surprised everyone was that within days Houllier announced that he had signed not just one goalkeeper but two, the second one arriving just hours after the first. He had paid out £4.5 million for Jerzy Dudek from Feyenoord, a keeper who had been on the verge of joining Arsenal during the summer, and £5 million for the England under-21 Coventry keeper Chris Kirkland. Quite why Liverpool suddenly needed two keepers when they already had Westerveld and Pegguy Arphexad beggared belief, yet here they were paying out almost £10 million without having arranged the transfer of either of the incumbent keepers. 'If Liverpool had signed one keeper, I would have stayed and fought for my place. I didn't want to leave,' said Westerveld. But with two keepers arriving it was clear that neither he nor Arphexad were part of Houllier's future plans.

Rumour had it that Houllier had only wanted one keeper and that he was chasing both men in order to sign one of them before the European deadline of Friday, 31 August. In fact, Liverpool had been chasing Kirkland for most of the previous season. They had identified him as the Liverpool keeper of the future and wanted to bring him to Anfield where they could groom him as the number two. Unfortunately, they had not been able to persuade

Coventry City to let him go. 'We'll sell him to you,' Coventry had told Liverpool, 'but not yet. When we do decide to let him go, you'll be the first to know.' Liverpool had tried to negotiate a loan deal, even a loan-back deal, but Coventry were adamant. In the meantime Houllier had also been tracking Dudek of Feyenoord, and with the European deadline date looming Dudek unexpectedly became available. At the time Dudek was playing in Russia with Poland, so securing his signature and in particular sorting out a medical before the deadline was proving to be a nightmare. Liverpool even had to send their own doctor out there.

Then, even more unexpectedly, Coventry, for one reason or another, decided to cash in on Kirkland, so Liverpool now found themselves being offered not one goalkeeper, but two. With the deadline clock ticking away, Liverpool could easily finish up with either one of the goalkeepers, with both of them, or with neither of them. Hence a decision was made to pursue both as vigorously as they could. Both deals, of course, fell into place. Far-fetched as it may seem, in football almost anything is believable. Kirkland was the first in, at 2 p.m. on 31 August. Westerveld thought he was safe, but then two hours later it was announced that Dudek had also been signed.

Westerveld was bitter at Houllier's duplicity. He maintained that all along Houllier had assured him he was not in the market for another keeper and that his position was not in any doubt. 'He spent half his time telling me that I could be the best goalkeeper in the world, that it had taken Schmeichel two years to really settle in England, and that I should ignore the rumours. But all the while he was negotiating for Dudek. At other times Houllier criticised my performances, both to me and to Joe Corrigan, and made threats about my position. Above all, a football manager needs to keep his players' confidence high. Houllier did not do this with me.'

The fact that Westerveld had been kept in the dark also meant that he had no hope now of being transferred to any club involved in European competition. What's more, Westerveld was suddenly way down the pecking order at Anfield, the number three keeper at best. For another five months he found himself kicking his heels around Anfield until he was eventually transferred to Real

Sociedad in January 2002 for £3.5 million. As far as Houllier was concerned, it was simply that Westerveld was not good enough and he had gone out and found someone better. It was a case of easy come, easy go. On the evidence of the abilities of both Dudek and Kirkland, you had to admit that Houllier was probably correct.

After four years in the job, Houllier had built up the most impressive squad of players in English football, even better than Wenger's Arsenal and without a doubt with far more depth than Manchester United. Houllier could boast some 34 players, the vast majority of whom he would have been quite happy to have playing in the first team. Only seven of those players had not yet had any first-team experience. Little wonder they had to build new facilities at Melwood; they would have been forced to fight for a peg for their clothes of a morning. Twenty-one of them were internationals, too, mostly current internationals.

But of course that number of players created a number of problems. For a start, there was the cost. Liverpool had one of the highest wage bills in the Premiership. Certainly businessman and major shareholder Steve Morgan always argued that the club was overburdening itself. 'I agree with 95 per cent of what Gérard Houllier has done,' he stated, 'but the squad is definitely too big and the wages bill needs to come down.' Houllier's second problem was that a dozen different nationalities were now represented at Anfield. Long gone were the days when just men from the four home nationalities, all speaking one language, crammed into Melwood. Now there were Germans, Frenchmen, Poles, Portuguese, Finns, Swiss, Czechs, Norwegians, Croatians, Irish, Senegalese, Danes and, of course, a few Englishmen. Whatever happened to the Scots, whose accents were once so dominant in the Liverpool dressing rooms?

Inevitably there was a language problem, despite Houllier's insistence that the universal language of the club must be English. Milan Baros, for one, struggled; it was a good nine months before he was anywhere near confident. So many nationalities and so many languages also made the bonding process between players more difficult. Foreign players could not always understand the nuances of the English language, the subtlety of its humour and its culture. And as any professional will tell you, the humour of the dressing room can be crucial to building team morale. 'We had enough problems understanding the likes of Dalglish and Stevie Nicol's humour, let alone Polish or Senegalese humour,' said former player Alan Kennedy. Others testify that few players ever understood what Bob Paisley was going on about either.

Nor was it easy for overseas players to settle in Merseyside, especially the younger ones. Sometimes they brought family with them, but it wasn't always possible. They needed to make friends quickly, and in a multicultural dressing room they inevitably stuck with their own nationalities, and that led to cliques. Houllier understood that one way around this difficulty was to loan players back to a team in their own country, not only to get first-team experience but to have more time to learn English, to mature, and to become more capable of adapting when they returned to Liverpool. Djimi Traore returned to Lens, and Alou Diarra went to Le Havre; the two French youngsters Anthony Le Tallec and Florent Sinama Pongolle were also allowed to remain in France for a couple of years until they were eighteen and mature enough to cope with the problems of moving. Even those who were older and with families of their own had to take into account even more than usual how wives and children were settling in a city like Liverpool, which is not always the easiest of places to live. Wives and families also had to adapt and learn a new language, and once children reached a school age there was the natural dilemma of whether they really wanted their children to be educated abroad or at home.

Perhaps it is little wonder, then, that not all Houllier's signings have been successful. Indeed, of the 33 players signed by him, a dozen have moved on for one reason or another. The net deficit on trading in the transfer market stands at a staggering £80 million. 'Sure, he's made a few bad signings,' admitted Jan Molby, 'but what manager hasn't? Seventy or so per cent of his signings have been excellent. He has the ability to spot a player he likes. And there is a difference there. We are not just talking about good players, but players who give something else as well.'

Houllier has always looked for players who are fully committed to the cause. They have to be players who not only accept the discipline of the club, but are also prepared to accept such things as the rotation system. They need to be prepared to sit on the bench or to play in the reserves; they mustn't expect to make the first team every week. A Houllier player has to be a team player, someone who puts the team before himself. As he argued in *Entraîneur: Compétence et Passion*, 'the great players are those who want to win more than the others. But the group always has to be more important than the individual.' 'He likes players who are strong, one hundred per cent committed, mobile and so on,' Molby agreed. 'But he is also demanding something else from them. That something extra which is upstairs.'

Former players from the sixties will tell you that this philosophy is very similar to Shankly's, the only difference being that Houllier's philosophy is more intellectually defined. Shankly simply did it by instinct. 'When Shankly went to sign a player,' recalled Willie Stevenson, who in many ways epitomised a Shankly player, 'he would always look at the player's background. He wanted to know if he was married, if he drank, if he trained hard, if he was a womaniser, and so forth. All his players had to be prepared to give one hundred per cent to the cause. And they weren't always the best players, you know, but they did have that something extra.' Stevenson himself was no star and Glasgow Rangers had just let him drift off to Australia, but Shankly brought him back to Britain and turned him into one of the most stylish and committed half-backs of the era.

Jean-Michel Ferri was one of Houllier's first signings, in December 1998, but he worked no similar magic here. Ferri was off almost before anyone had had time to say 'bonjour'. He made only two appearances, both as a substitute. But he had arrived on Merseyside with an injury which took some time to sort itself out, and for much of the time he was sitting on the sidelines being treated, something that did not really help his integration into either the Anfield or Merseyside community. By the time he was fit he was surplus to requirements, and he wanted to return to France.

Titi Camara was a far more complicated affair. Camara had arrived on Merseyside as part of the large batch of players signing up in the summer of 1999. Camara was a powerful attacking midfielder, bursting with ability. He was signed from Marseille for

£2.6 million having spent much of his time there on the bench, despite being voted the club's most popular player by the fans. It was to be much the same story at Anfield, even though it all began with such promise. He made an immediate impact with his clever trickery, spectacular goals and powerful runs, but seemed less keen to tackle back and could often drift out of games. There was an undisputed lack of consistency about his play, and although many Liverpool fans were sorry to see him leave, it was inevitable given the signing of Emile Heskey. Camara might have been a Kop pleaser, but former player Alan Hansen probably voiced the opinions of those at Anfield when he summed up, 'He'll score a wonderful goal and then for ten minutes give it away. I'm not quite sure you would play him from the start. He flicks it all the time, and if he's played up front you've got to get hold of the ball.' And that was the problem, in a nutshell. One Anfield insider said that the Melwood staff reckoned he was 'lazy'. In training he didn't give as much as he should, he'd opt out, he was never quite fully committed. That would never do for Houllier. In December 2000, fewer than eighteen months after he had joined the club, he was sold to West Ham United for £1.5 million. He failed to make the grade at Upton Park, too, and soon returned to continental football.

Another summer 1999 signing who spawned one of the most memorable chants at Anfield of the past decade was Rigobert Song. Song was an athletic right-back who liked nothing more than a few sprints upfield, but while his charges sometimes opened up possibilities for attackers, more often it left his own defenders having to cover for him. Once or twice he was caught out, most memorably against Manchester United at Old Trafford when a ball lobbed over him as he retreated back into defence led to a United goal. Houllier noted that one. As captain of his country Song was desperate for first-team football, so with Houllier unable to guarantee him his place he, too, was offloaded to West Ham, for £2.5 million in November 2000.

Dutch striker Erik Meijer also arrived in the summer of 1999 on a free transfer from Bayer Leverkusen. Meijer was never intended as a first-choice striker, simply as an occasional stand-in for Owen or Fowler, but more was expected of him. Meijer was as big a failure at Anfield as any player who has served under

Houllier. Although he had bagfuls of enthusiasm, he failed to score even one goal and soon returned to Germany, joining Hamburg.

But perhaps the most puzzling of all Houllier's signings was Christian Ziege, the much-prized German full-back. Houllier could have signed Ziege in 1999. At that time AC Milan were offering almost all of their players to Liverpool, but Ziege went to Middlesbrough. A year later, with Song moving out of the equation and the German putting in some exhilarating perform-ances, Houllier changed his mind and decided that perhaps Ziege was the answer to the left-back role. Interestingly, some six months before the deal was clinched, one unofficial Liverpool website carried an email predicting that Liverpool would sign Ziege that summer. The writer claimed that he had been told by a young Middlesbrough player he knew that the word at Boro was that Ziege would be leaving for Anfield. At the time there had been no hint that Ziege might join Liverpool, but the writer was adamant, and certain of his information. Over the following months the same caller came online a number of times to repeat his prediction. In the late summer of 2000 Ziege finally made it to Anfield after a drawn-out deal that cost Liverpool £5.5 million.

The German, however, turned out not to be the solution – at least as far as Houllier was concerned. He began well enough, but after a nightmare of a game at Leeds in early November, when Liverpool threw away a comfortable lead, his form steadily deteriorated and he was dropped. He never really regained his place. He was clearly unhappy not to be playing first-team football, and said as much to the press. It brought a stinging response from Houllier. 'The first thing I said to him was to shut up,' he said, 'because speaking out the way he did showed a lack of respect for other players. I have just advised him to keep his mouth shut in future. He is not going to attract my attention or demonstrate his commitment to the cause by complaining in the media and making comments like these.' It was typical Houllier, outraged that any player should go whingeing to the media. It was effectively the end of Ziege's association with Liverpool. 'If someone is not committed or not prepared to give his all, you have a problem,' said Houllier. 'Believe me, though, it is one I will not tolerate for long.'

Ziege's signing had already caused enough trouble with the FA, who were now investigating the deal. It was alleged by Middlesbrough that Houllier had discovered a clause in Ziege's contract allowing him to leave the north-east club if anyone came in with an offer of £5.5 million. Middlesbrough, who must have been kicking themselves for ever allowing such a clause to be inserted into his contract, were left wondering how Houllier had ever managed to discover this little-known fact. They suspected skulduggery, but Liverpool denied any such allegations. In the summer of 2001 Ziege was offloaded to Tottenham Hotspur for £4 million, but that wasn't the end of the affair. Middlesbrough, determined to recoup some of the cost of losing Ziege, applied to the courts. Initially they lost, but then in November 2002 the Court of Appeal gave them leave once again to pursue a compensation claim for £8 million.

Perhaps one of the abiding mysteries of Houllier's reign has been his reluctance to sign French players. He had joined Liverpool in the wake of France's memorable World Cup victory, and there were high hopes that at least a few of the World Cup side would find their way to Anfield. After all, Houllier had himself been heavily involved in the formation of that side. As coach of the under-21s he had been responsible for bringing in talented young players such as Nicolas Anelka and David Trezeguet. He had seen and worked with not only the entire World Cup team but many others as well, especially those on the periphery of the squad. With the possible exception of Aimé Jacquet, Houllier knew as much about French football as anyone.

In 1998/99 a whole host of these French players were still competing in the French league. Robert Pires was at Metz, Laurent Blanc and Christophe Dugarry were both at Marseille, Fabien Barthez, David Trezeguet and Thierry Henry were all at Monaco, and Stéphane Guivarc'h and Bernard Diomede were at Auxerre. Of the rest, most were playing in either Italy or England. Yet instead of snapping up the residue of those still playing in France, the only player from that generation of Frenchmen to arrive at Anfield was Bernard Diomede, who was signed a year after the World Cup and who failed to come anywhere near making the grade at Anfield. Diomede had been injured in the World Cup and had struggled ever since, but at £3 million Houllier probably thought he was worth a gamble. Injury certainly did not help his cause, and a disallowed overhead-kicked goal against Sunderland in September 2000 also did nothing for his confidence. Had that goal been allowed – TV replays clearly showed that it had crossed the line – then Diomede's career might have been kick-started. As it was, he returned to irregular reserve-team football, and with no further opportunities coming his way was later made available for transfer. Unfortunately, nobody seemed to want him. Diomede had played just five games for Liverpool; taking into account his salary, he had cost Liverpool something like a million pounds a game. Admittedly Anelka arrived on loan from Paris St Germain, but it was never made permanent. None of the stars of the 1998 World Cup victory ever found their way to Anfield. There were rumours about David Trezeguet, but nothing ever transpired, and probably they were no more than wishful thinking on somebody's part.

Houllier would argue that it was not a case of missing a trick but a considered decision that if he was going to sign French players they would have to be young, cheap and better than any of the homegrown players in his squad. By the autumn of 1998, the price of any French player had more than doubled after their success. Even allowing for that, it is still surprising that Houllier has brought in so few Frenchmen. After the unfortunate signing of Ferri, the next Frenchman to join Liverpool, early in 1999, was the unknown teenager Djimi Traore. For some time it looked like Traore might not make the grade, but a lengthy loan spell with Lens gave him the necessary experience to break into the Liverpool first team at the start of the 2002/03 season. It wasn't long before Houllier and the media were heaping praise on him, calling him the new Lilian Thuram. Traore's signing set something of a trend. Next in was another teenager and another cheap buy, Gregory Vignal. Then came the much-hyped signing of French super-kids Anthony Le Tallec and Florent Sinama Pongolle.

At the end of 2000, the signing of Igor Biscan from Dynamo Zagreb for just over £5 million was heralded as a major coup by Liverpool, and when in December he came on as a substitute at Anfield to make his debut he looked an exciting prospect. In many ways Biscan resembled the emerging Steven Gerrard. He was well built, strong and fast. He could pass the ball with some skill while making powerful, surging runs upfield. Nor was he afraid to have a shot at goal. With Hamann, Gerrard and Biscan it looked like Liverpool had found themselves the toughest midfield in the Premiership. But then, almost as quickly as he had arrived, Biscan faded from the scene. A year or so later and he was struggling even to secure a place in the reserves. Perhaps it was problems with acclimatisation, language, or simply an inability to keep his place in the first team. Whatever it was, by the autumn of 2002 he was beginning to look like an expensive flop and was set to leave Anfield, his career never having really started.

Biscan had always been something of an unknown quantity; the same could not be said of Nick Barmby. Merseysiders had had enough opportunities to see Barmby play, but it was difficult to know exactly why Houllier had decided to bring him in. Although Barmby might be described as a wide player, he was never quite as wide a player as Liverpool needed, nor was he any better than Berger or Smicer. But in August 2000 Liverpool paid Everton a handsome £6 million for the former Middlesbrough and Spurs player. Like so many others Barmby began well enough, but he could not acclimatise to Houllier's rotational system. He also had problems with an ankle. After seeing a consultant he was told that there was some floating bone in it. An operation was required, which of course posed a dilemma. 'At Liverpool there are so many good players that if you get injured it's difficult to get back in,' he later claimed. And he was right. Although Barmby made one or two further appearances for Liverpool as a substitute, exactly two years after arriving at Anfield he left for Leeds United.

But perhaps the strangest of all Houllier's easy come, easy go signings was Jari Litmanen. When it was announced that the Finnish striker was coming to Anfield in early January 2001, it was like a belated Christmas present. What's more, Litmanen was joining on a free transfer. He was surely the bargain of all time. He might have been just a month off his thirtieth birthday but his reputation as one of Europe's top strikers was secure. Litmanen had been plying his trade with Barcelona since bursting on to the scene with Ajax, but a combination of injuries and the dismissal of Dutch coach Louis Van Gaal had limited his appearances at the

Nou Camp. He was known to be a lifelong Liverpool supporter who bored his team-mates by reciting the entire Liverpool championship side for almost any season they cared to name. It was an attitude that certainly endeared him to Houllier, not to mention Koppites.

Yet for all his fanaticism, ability and determination to remain at Anfield and win a regular place in the side, Litmanen was another who was gone within eighteen months of signing. When he did play he showed touches and skills that had fans drooling with appreciation. Perhaps the problem was that nobody seemed quite sure where to play him. If he was up front, it meant that two out of Fowler, Owen and Heskey had to be relegated to the bench; if he was played just behind the two front runners, then someone in the midfield had to sit out the game. He also seemed to be more of a 30-minute player than a 90-minute one, someone more likely to come on and turn a game rather than influence it from the start. Liverpool fans would debate at length the Finn's virtues, regularly urging the manager to give him a prolonged spell in the side, but Houllier was more inclined to see him as a substitute, bringing him on for a final burst, if at all. The result was inevitable. It was a role Litmanen had already played for a couple of years at Barcelona and one he had grown weary of. While he showed commendable patience for a player of his ability and reputation, he finally snapped and demanded more. Houllier could promise nothing, so Litmanen was soon on his way, returning to his old club Ajax and leaving Liverpool fans wondering what might have been.

Diomede was undoubtedly the odd man out in this group of players. Litmanen had not cost a penny, apart from his salary, and had certainly been a gamble worth taking. The same could be said for Meijer, and Camara, Song, Ferri, Barmby and Ziege had all left for roughly the same as had been paid for them. Most of them had come anticipating first-team football but had been disappointed to find themselves some way down the pecking order. The emergence of so many young players at Anfield had also reduced their opportunities. But selection must ever have been a headache for Houllier, who most of the time was spoilt for choice. For a start, there were five goalkeepers. Two of them were top-class keepers, and a third was not that far behind. In defence it was almost a case of perm any four from eight, while the midfield was so crowded for choice that you had eleven contenders for four spots. Up front, too, there were four players vying for two places. And when it came to substitutions there was usually a problem as well. It was all very well having the luxury of such choice and knowing that no matter how many injuries you had you could always be certain that the replacement was as good as the person being replaced, but keeping everybody happy was a serious problem. You could keep some of the people happy some of the time, but not all of the people happy all of the time. No player likes to sit on a bench, or to play reserve-team football. The question that has faced so many at Anfield over the last few years is this: is it better to be a member of a highly successful squad and play the occasional game, or to play regularly for a lesser side?

During his early years at Anfield, and in particular during the treble season, Houllier was more than inclined to swap and change his side around. He called it the rotation system. Houllier argued that with so many games, players needed to be rested, especially young players who could not be expected to play week after week. You could see the sense in his reasoning, but it was also clear that at times the players looked as if they had not seen one another for weeks. The sides never seemed to be the same from one game to the next. 'You can have too many idle hands,' argued Steve Morgan. 'It happens in any business. When people aren't involved they get frustrated . . . You've got to keep people busy. For instance, there are five goalkeepers at the moment. Now, why do we need five goalkeepers? Two of those keepers are exceptional. I do feel sorry for Chris Kirkland, and I wonder how he's ever going to get the chance to play when ahead of him is Jerzy Dudek, one of the best goalkeepers in the world.'

Does Houllier know his best side? was another question being asked, and with some justification, by many fans. In the past Shankly and Paisley, when asked what their side was for a game, usually answered, 'The same as last week.' During the 1983/84 season Liverpool used just fifteen players during their League campaign, and they won three trophies, including the First Division title. It is also true that Liverpool sides in the seventies and eighties regularly played as many games in a season as Houllier's sides, and they never complained about tiredness.

Admittedly, some of those sides had not boasted as many young players. Perhaps there is a genuine need to take better care of the youngsters today, especially the likes of Michael Owen and Steven Gerrard who were injury prone before the age of twenty.

In *Entraîneur: Compétence et Passion*, Houllier argues in favour of the rotation system but emphasises that 'you should warn them [the players] at the beginning of the year what you are going to do. They will accept rotation better, a choice dictated by particular tactical considerations, when the rule is for all the group and for all of the season. The players generally know, with one or two exceptions, which is the best team . . . You usually have seven or eight players who play almost all the time; the problem is with the other players who are competing for the other places.' Certainly Houllier has had more than his share of problems with idle players, although perhaps not as many as other managers have had. It was a difficult rule to apply.

Many players became unhappy even though they knew the deal when they arrived. Neither Robbie Fowler nor Jari Litmanen quite came to terms with being played only once every four or five games. What's more, there were many on the Kop who felt that the two of them deserved more opportunities. But while Fowler complained, Litmanen learnt to bite his tongue – but only temporarily. 'Liverpool might have a problem keeping everyone happy at the club if they are not playing regularly,' he said. 'I wanted more out of this move, but when you are not playing it is difficult to remain enthusiastic.' You could understand his distress. He simply wanted to play football. Houllier's response was cutting. 'I am the protector of the team and the club,' he thundered. 'I don't tolerate people sulking and chipping away. We have a massive squad because players like Liverpool and the atmosphere is good. Providing the attitude is right, there won't be a problem, but if it is not I can be extremely ruthless.'

The younger players felt the strain too. Vignal was apt to complain at not being given an extended run in the side, and Traore might well have gone elsewhere sooner had Houllier not thrown him into the side at the beginning of the 2002/03 season. David Thompson similarly wanted away because he desired more regular football. Stephen Wright, too, might still be a Liverpool player had he been given more opportunities. There were many sad to see the young full-back join Sunderland for the knockdown fee of £2 million, including some of his team-mates who simply could not understand why Liverpool were selling a player of his calibre. He was a promising prospect, but the reality was that he was at the back of a long queue for the right-back berth, ahead of him the likes of Markus Babbel, Jamie Carragher and Abel Xavier. In the end he decided it was better to play regularly for another club than to play occasionally for Liverpool. It wasn't just a matter of winning trophies and playing on the European stage; it was also essential to feel part of a team and to believe that you were making a genuine contribution. From the subs bench, you did not always get that feeling.

Houllier admits that the management of substitutes is one of the most delicate problems for any trainer to resolve, that it's one of the commonest areas of conflict. 'The substitute shouldn't feel excluded from training,' he preached, 'and you need to show him that you are following his efforts even if it doesn't immediately result in selection. You shouldn't have two groups when you're training, one which is playing and one of subs, just one.' The problem is that not only will those players who are not being regularly selected begin to complain, they will also tend to gang together with others who are receiving similar treatment. And of course they will then reinforce one another's opinions. There's another problem, too, as Houllier appreciated: 'Conflict within a group almost always comes from substitute players rather than those playing as they sometimes find a sympathetic ear in certain journalists looking for sensational stories.'

There were always a handful of players at Anfield ready to grumble. Even Vladimir Smicer, generally the most patient of players, on occasion expressed his desire for more first-team football. During his first six months at Anfield Milan Baros was also prone to moan and to let the papers know how he felt; Houllier even considered letting him go to Lens in exchange for El-Hadji Diouf during the summer of 2002. His answer to those who groused was simple: perform better and get yourself noticed. For the youngsters, however, that was easier said than done, especially when seasoned internationals stood before them.

13. BUILDING FOR THE FUTURE

That Houllier should even have considered Bowyer as a Liverpool player was in itself astonishing. It seemed so out of character. He'd set about ridding Liverpool of its Spice Boy image. Known troublemakers had been shown the door, and Houllier had spent much time attempting to re-educate some of the English players with a more professional attitude. Drinkers, clubbers and gamblers had been told to clean up their act or else, and they'd soon learnt that Houllier was not just threatening them. When he said something, he meant it. There was no second chance.

Perhaps one of the most important and often overlooked aspects of Houllier's four years in charge has been his unstinting search for new young players. While big-name signings have appeared on a regular basis, Houllier has also been quietly signing up a host of young players from across Europe, many of them from France. In effect, Houllier has been fashioning not just the current squad but the next Liverpool side, the one that will be gracing Anfield in the middle and latter part of the decade.

One of the first youngsters in was Djimi Traore, who arrived as an unknown from French side Laval in February 1999 for a give-away £500,000. At the time he was just eighteen years old. He might only have played a mere five games in the French league at the time, but he'd already attracted the attention of a host of top European clubs. It took weeks of secret negotiations to bring off the deal, and when he finally secured his signature Houllier told fans that one day 'you'll thank me for signing him'. That day finally arrived in the 2002/03 season when Traore was given his place from the start of the season and began to show the promise that had spurred Houllier into signing him in the first place.

Another young Frenchman joining the club was Gregory Vignal, a defender who came from Montpellier for £500,000 in September 2000 and who made his debut at the age of 20 in January 2001 in a third-round FA Cup tie with Rotherham. Houllier thought his Premiership debut, the following month against West Ham, the most impressive he had ever seen, and few disagreed with him, but it was still not enough to secure a regular spot in the first team. When he did make something of a breakthrough, injury cruelly robbed him of his place after only a handful of games, leaving him on the sidelines yet again. Vignal wasn't always the most patient of players, but no way was Houllier going to let him drift off to another club.

It was often frustrating for the youngsters, but Houllier has been determined not to introduce young players too quickly to the rigours of the Premiership. You only have to examine his kid-gloves approach with Michael Owen and Steven Gerrard to see that even the best are left out of the side from time to time. Houllier had to be sure they were capable of holding their own before letting them loose, and for no one was this policy more frustrating than Richie Partridge, the young Dubliner who spent years honing his skills in the reserves. Still, with only 22 reserve games a season and many of those used by the manager as a means of getting injured players fit again, his opportunities were limited. Partridge was a regular Irish under-21 international long before he appeared for the Liverpool first team. He wasn't a Houllier signing, but the manager was determined to keep him involved, and even loaned him out to Gary McAllister's Coventry City during the 2002/03 season.

But perhaps the most high-profile youngsters to join up were Florent Sinama Pongolle and Anthony Le Tallec from French club Le Havre. So determined was Houllier to sign them that in the summer of 2001 he flew to Japan and South Korea just to watch the pair playing in the Confederations Cup – a trip, of course, that later exacted a toll on Houllier's health. Although only sixteen years of age, the two youngsters were already being chased by half a dozen of the world's top clubs including Real Madrid, Barcelona, Bayern Munich and Manchester United. The two players, rated as probably the best pair in world football for their age, cost Liverpool a staggering £3 million each in September 2001, but Houllier reckoned it money well spent. So, too, did United manager Alex Ferguson, who generously called Houllier to congratulate him. Typically, though, rather than bring them to Anfield as soon as possible, Houllier loaned the pair back to Le Havre for a further two seasons and pencilled in the summer of 2003 for their arrival, when they would both be eighteen. In the meantime, with their help Le Havre were promoted to the French First Division where the two lads would go on to gain valuable experience.

Also joining them at Le Havre was Alou Diarra, an eighteen-year-old signed from Bayern Munich in July 2002. Diarra had gone to Bayern Munich from France when he was sixteen but had failed to break through into the first team. He'd played one or two games and had impressed, but with Stefan Effenberg the incumbent midfielder it was going to be a long wait. Diarra's contract was soon up, and although Bayern offered him a new one and pleaded with him to stay, Diarra had already decided that his future lay elsewhere. Again, Houllier fought off a host of top continental clubs for his signature, and was able to promise him a year out at Le Havre where he would be playing regularly in top-flight football. Like Le Tallec and Pongolle, Diarra is due to arrive at Anfield in the summer of 2003.

Although some of these signings failed immediately to make the grade, or weren't considered mature enough for the demands of Premier League football, there were others drafted in who were promptly thrown a red shirt. John Arne Riise, a £4 million signing from Monaco in June 2001, was considered good enough for a first-team place even though he was only 21, and by the end of his first season he was voted player of the year by many of the fans. But Riise was slightly older and certainly more experienced, having already played a few seasons at the highest level with Monaco and as an international with Norway. Certainly Houllier regarded him as a player with a long-term future at Anfield.

Milan Baros probably fitted into the same category. The eighteen-year-old, signed from Banik Ostrava in August 2001, had already played five times for the Czech Republic and was a regular player in the Czech league, yet when he came to Anfield he found himself relegated to the reserves, where he didn't impress. He took time to settle in Merseyside, put on weight, had difficulty with the language and did not look at all happy. But Baros was determined to make his mark, and after a summer of intense training and weight loss in 2002 he was drafted into the side and immediately made an impression.

Daniel Sjolund was another teenager Liverpool had been watching for some years. Even before he joined West Ham United, Liverpool had tried to bring him to Anfield, but that attempt had fallen through. When West Ham made overtures to Liverpool about the possibility of signing Rigobert Song, however, it opened up the way for some wheeler-dealing. Rather than an outright fee, Liverpool instead suggested a player-plus-money deal, and in November 2000, in a £2.5 million swap deal, the seventeen-year-old Finnish under-21 international signed at Anfield while Song went in the opposite direction. Goalkeeper Chris Kirkland was another youngster to arrive at Anfield having already played Premiership football, this time with Coventry City. He was just twenty years old.

And, of course, on top of all these imported youngsters Liverpool were developing their own at the academy under the tutelage of Steve Heighway. Steven Gerrard, Stephen Wright and David Thompson had all emerged from there and been given opportunities by Houllier, and a new batch of up-and-coming youngsters such as Neil Mellor, John Welsh and Jon Ostemobor are patiently awaiting their opportunity. Putting all these players together, it's easy to see that Houllier is ensuring some kind of success at Anfield in the forthcoming years. The problem, however, as always, will be how to keep them all happy.

As ever, the summer of 2002 turned out to be a busier time for Gérard Houllier than he'd ever intended. While many of his Liverpool squad packed their bags and jetted off to the World Cup finals in Korea and Japan, Houllier took the decision to remain at home. He'd wanted to go, but after the long season and his serious illness he decided that travelling to the other side of the world was not such a good idea. For Houllier, it marked a major shift in attitude. Prior to his illness he had worked some sixteen hours a day, always the first into Melwood and the last to leave; holidays, similarly, had usually been spent dashing across the world to take in some football competition. Nor was it usually just a question of watching a few matches; given his FIFA and UEFA commitments, he was often obliged to take on honorary and diplomatic duties. But in the summer of 2002 Houllier decided to stay at home and have a short holiday before concentrating on the business of bringing new players to the club. The 2002 World Cup was the first major tournament he had missed in 22 years.

He was feeling tired. He still had not fully recovered from his operation. Most men in his position would have taken considerably more time off work. 'I probably came back two or three weeks too early,' he later confessed, 'because at the end of the season, I really paid for it. It was difficult. I didn't show it to the players. If you struggle, they can feel that. But I was tired, I was struggling, I didn't have any strength. I was doing too much, I wasn't looking after myself the way I should have been. In hindsight, it was a mistake.' If second thoughts about travelling to Japan and Korea ever emerged, his wife Isabelle would have quickly put an end to them. There was already plenty to be done around Anfield, tying up the loose ends of contracts and new transfer deals.

Phil Thompson also urged him to rest up that summer and applauded his decision to remain at home. As he watched him each day, he too became increasingly concerned at the amount of work his boss was taking on. For one thing, he said, 'I just wish Gérard would ditch his mobile phone,' adding that it was his life. 'After an hour switched off, he has 25 messages, and he calls most of them back. Since returning to Anfield, he still gets stuck into his duties one hundred per cent, all of the time. I have to keep an eye on him.' It was said mischievously, but his worry was genuine. He feared further health problems. 'Gérard is a workaholic. He'll watch videos of opposing players into the wee small hours. He can look after himself but he still needs guidance, and that's what I'm there for. We have to make sure he doesn't overdo things.'

Outside his inner Liverpool circle, nobody was ever quite sure which players Houllier was interested in. Certainly the press weren't. Newspaper headlines linked him to dozens of players, the vast majority of whom he had never even considered. Usually it was just agents either attempting to suggest that their client might be interested in a move to Merseyside or trying to up personal terms or a fee with another club by cheekily implying that Liverpool were competing for someone's signature. Once the 2001/02 season had finished, the focus shifted on to the on-loan Nicolas Anelka, then, of course, on to the young Auxerre striker Djibril Cissé, and finally on to El-Hadji Diouf. Lens had their eye on Milan Baros as part of the Diouf deal. Baros had not settled well in Liverpool and had made little impression; he was not too popular either, and many at Anfield were questioning the wisdom of his signing. His only appearance for Liverpool had been for ten minutes as a substitute in Barcelona. He was not even a regular reserve player, and the hype that had accompanied his signing had proved to be just that – hype. Houllier sounded out one or two staff members at Melwood where the general consensus was to let him go if it meant getting Diouf, but Houllier still wasn't convinced and decided to have a word with Baros himself to gauge his reaction. Baros was totally opposed to the idea. He wanted to stay at Anfield. Liverpool was the club he wanted to play for, not Lens, and he was ready to battle for his place. Houllier was impressed by his attitude and decided to back him, so he went back to the negotiating table. Rick Parry was also prepared to back his manager's judgement. The two of them told Lens that Baros was not for sale and that anyhow he was not interested in a transfer to Lens. The French club then decided to pass on Baros and instead reluctantly thrashed out a £10 million deal to sell Diouf to Liverpool. By the time the deal was agreed, Diouf had burst on to the World Cup scene, almost doubling his price overnight. In the light of this, Lens claimed that the deal had not been agreed and that with other clubs now looking to sign him they wanted a figure nearer £20 million. But with Diouf stating days later that he was going to Liverpool no matter what, Lens were finally forced to accept Liverpool's £10 million.

Houllier also snapped up one of Diouf's Senegal team-mates, Salif Diao, who also played his football in France, with Sedan. Diao, a strong midfielder, had been earmarked by Liverpool scouts as a man who could stand in for the injury-prone Steven Gerrard. The manager's old friend Michel Platini had urged Houllier to sign the young player. 'He's a very strong, pacey player,' he'd advised, 'so like Patrick Vieira at Arsenal, and one day he'll be every bit as good as Vieira.' That was enough to convince Houllier.

The third addition to the squad was a further recruit from a French club, Bruno Cheyrou, a 24-year-old left-sided midfielder who had just enjoyed a highly successful season with title challengers Lille. Within a couple of months of joining Liverpool, and before he had made his Premiership debut, he was awarded his first international cap. The new France manager, Jacques Santini, called him his 'new Tigana'. The only other additions to the squad that summer were a new goalkeeper, the 22-year-old Patrice Luzi, signed on a free transfer from Monaco, and Alou Diarra.

In all, Houllier had spent a modest £20 million on his five recruits, but there were others who never quite made it to Anfield.

One was Lee Bowyer, one of the undoubted stars of a Leeds United side that under David O'Leary had pushed for silverware over a number of years. Although they had failed in their endeavours to bring trophies back to Elland Road, they had nevertheless challenged on all fronts and had impressed many with their aggressive but exciting blend of football. They were a young side, and chief among their collective talents was Bowyer.

He'd begun his footballing career with Charlton Athletic, and after just 46 League games with them and some headline-catching goals he became one of the most sought-after youngsters in the game. It was inevitable that one of the bigger clubs would pick him up, and in July 1995 he moved to Leeds for a giveaway fee of £2.6 million. It would prove to be a career-making move. Bowyer was powerful, a strong tackler, had pace and liked to push forward in search of goals. He was just the kind of player any club, let alone Liverpool, needed.

But there was just one problem: Bowyer was indisciplined, not just on the field but off it as well. At Charlton he'd been fined and banned after testing positive for marijuana in a random drug test. Eighteen months later there were further complaints as he was caught on video throwing chairs around a restaurant. He was also convicted for attacking Asians at a McDonald's restaurant in east London.

But it was the court case arising out of an incident in January 2000 which caused the biggest headlines. Bowyer, Jonathan Woodgate, Michael Duberry and other Leeds United players had been arrested and charged with various offences following an attack on the Najeib brothers outside a Leeds nightclub. After the attack, which was said to have involved repeated kickings, Sarfraz Najeib was left with a shocking catalogue of injuries including a broken leg, broken ribs and a fractured nose, as well as a bite to his left cheek. He subsequently spent a long period recovering in hospital. His brother, although not as badly injured, nevertheless suffered severe bruising to the head, face, leg and chest, and, like Sarfraz, had to be treated for post-traumatic stress. Bowyer always maintained that he had not been involved in the assault.

During the first trial an untimely article in the *Daily Mirror* brought a swift halt to proceedings, the judge ordering a retrial. During that retrial some months later the grim facts of the case were once more detailed. They included admissions of heavy drinking as well as the assault. At the end of the trial, the jury found Bowyer not guilty of grievous bodily harm; Woodgate and one other were cleared of GBH but convicted of affray; another defendant was convicted of both GBH and affray and was jailed for six years. Sarfraz and his family were shocked at the verdict, maintaining that Bowyer had been involved in the assault and that justice had not been done.

After the verdict, Leeds fined Bowyer a record four weeks' wages, around £70,000, for breaching club rules by being under the influence of alcohol. At first Bowyer refused to accept the punishment and was promptly transfer-listed by the club, but two days later, and after some gentle persuasion, he agreed to dig into his pocket. That tiff seemed to leave more of an indelible mark on Bowyer than on the club, as he subsequently refused to agree a new contract, though that situation was certainly not helped when Leeds chairman Peter Ridsdale said that he would not have signed Bowyer from Charlton had he known at the time what he now knew. Talks went on for months, and although Leeds did offer an improvement to his contract and were clearly eager to keep the young man on their books, Bowyer decided that he had had enough. He wanted out.

That of course alerted a number of clubs to his availability, but oddly enough the only ones that showed any interest were two clubs one might have thought would have wanted nothing to do with him, namely Arsenal and Liverpool. After all, both clubs had highly intelligent, sophisticated French managers whose attitude to alcohol was well known. Arsenal's interest, however, was short-lived. They put in an enquiry to his agent but were told that Bowyer's preference was Liverpool. His determination to seal a deal to go to Anfield ended Arsenal's involvement. They didn't even bother to enter the auction.

The initial asking price was £15 million, but typically, Houllier was never going to pay anything like that. He valued Bowyer at a smaller figure, and even though he was determined to get his man he was quite happy to sacrifice the deal if the price was too high. Houllier decided to play a waiting game. He knew that Bowyer wanted to come to Liverpool; he also knew that he had only one more year left on his contract. Sooner or later Leeds would panic and sell at a more realistic price. The other factor in Houllier's favour was that Leeds were heavily in debt. They had failed to qualify yet again for the Champions League, despite spending heavily in the transfer market over the previous few years. Simple economics stated that unless you qualified for the Champions League you could not finance the kind of spending spree on which O'Leary had embarked. Leeds chairman Peter Ridsdale had announced that the club would have to sell players in order to raise £15 million to satisfy the city, and Bowyer was clearly one of the players he had in mind. All Houllier had to do was be patient and wait for the price to fall.

In the months that followed, Houllier's friend O'Leary, much to the surprise of many, was sacked by Leeds, which raised the question as to whether the new manager, whoever he may be, would veto the sale of Bowyer. In the event, Terry Venables was appointed, but with the proviso that he would still have to raise £15 million. His first task was to speak with two players who looked set to leave. One was Rio Ferdinand, who seemed bound for Manchester United; the other was Lee Bowyer. Although both men were impressed by Venables' enthusiasm and knowledge of the game, neither indicated any change of heart. As Houllier had suspected, the price for Bowyer had fallen from £15 million to £7 million, with a further £2 million to be paid to Leeds depending on appearances and so forth. Liverpool had a bargain – or had they?

Bowyer's anticipated signing promptly set off a fierce debate among fans. He was a 'bad boy' with an appalling reputation both on the field and off it. Black supporters of the club were outraged that Houllier should even think of recruiting him. Other Liverpool fans remembered the elbow he'd stuck into Gary McAllister's face, as well as a reckless challenge on Jamie Carragher that had almost split the Liverpool defender in two; Carragher had been fortunate, but on another day against another defender Bowyer could have caused serious injury. Liverpool might have had fearless midfield tacklers in the past, but there'd always been a modicum of restraint. The debate raged on the club's many unofficial web pages as well as in the fanzine magazines. One poll on Koptalk showed a small majority in favour of signing him; most other polls reflected that majority, albeit always marginally. But almost all Liverpool fans were agreed on one thing: Bowyer was an outstanding player, just the kind of man Liverpool needed to win the title. Still, concern over his track record remained. 'Will he be the rotten apple in the barrel?' asked one website columnist, who feared that Houllier had 'put his neck on the block'.

That Houllier should even have considered Bowyer as a Liverpool player was in itself astonishing. It seemed so out of character. He'd set about ridding Liverpool of its Spice Boy image. Known troublemakers had been shown the door, and Houllier had spent much time attempting to re-educate some of the English players with a more professional attitude. Drinkers, clubbers and gamblers had been told to clean up their act or else, and they'd soon learnt that Houllier was not just threatening them. When he said something, he meant it. There was no second chance.

All the evidence was there that Bowyer was a 'bad boy'. He might have been found not guilty, but during the trial he'd admitted to some appalling behaviour, especially heavy drinking. And that notorious trial was not just a one-off. Bowyer had form. Whether Houllier genuinely believed he could transform Bowyer is anyone's guess. Others had tried, including the law, and failed. A simple phone call to David O'Leary would have elicited some of the truth about what had gone on that night. Certainly there was room for doubt given that Michael Duberry had revised his own plea to the court and had detailed an attempted cover-up to the jury.

The signing of Bowyer, however, turned out to be nowhere near as simple as everyone had anticipated. Once Leeds had accepted Liverpool's offer and permission had been given for the Merseysiders to talk to him, Bowyer was over to Anfield like a shot. He was clearly keen to join the club. Talks began, and although they continued into the next day, all the right noises were made. Then came a problem over personal terms. Much of it seemed to hinge on the repayment of Bowyer's financial debt to Leeds, who had paid out on the player's behalf more than a million pounds in legal fees. The deal was that Leeds would pay that debt if he remained at Elland Road, but if he moved he would have to foot the bill himself. It seemed a reasonable demand. Given that Bowyer did not appear to have the funds to pay such a debt, the question was whether Liverpool would pay it or loan Bowyer the money. There was also said to be a question over Bowyer's salary. At Leeds he had been paid some £17,000 a week, but he'd been offered a new contract by the Yorkshire club at £40,000 a week. Liverpool were offering £35,000 and were refusing to go any higher. Bowyer was arguing that he could have stayed at Leeds and got a better deal. Fine, said Liverpool, if that's what you want, go back.

After a second day of talks there was stalemate; it looked as if the deal was about to founder. A third day of discussions followed, and still no resolution was on the table. Liverpool remained confident that a deal would happen, but Houllier was not going to be held to ransom. It was really a question of how much Bowyer wanted to be a Liverpool player. If he was simply coming for the money, then they could do without him. He had to be prepared to compromise, to demonstrate his commitment to the cause.

By Friday, 19 July it looked as if a deal had been agreed. Certainly Peter Ridsdale was suggesting as much. As far as Leeds were concerned, he said, everything was finalised and Bowyer was going with their blessing. Bowyer, he predicted, would sign immediately after the weekend. But then something happened that scuppered the deal once and for all. As Bowyer left Anfield that Friday afternoon, he was served with a writ as part of a civil action by lawyers representing Sarfraz Najeib and his brother. The following morning the story of the writ was the front-page headline in at least two of the tabloids. ASIAN BROTHERS ISSUE BOWYER WITH WRIT OVER ATTACK was how the *Daily Mirror* put it. Memories of the original trials were regurgitated, and it became clear that if anyone at Anfield had been assuming the matter was over, that a line could be drawn under the whole episode, they were sadly mistaken. There was little doubt that a further trial would now take place; the other defendants in the original trial were also expected to be served with similar writs. Sarfraz and his father had not simply been threatening when they'd said that this was not the end of the affair.

The point in bringing a civil action is twofold. First, the case is not heard before a jury, only a single judge. Secondly, in a civil action it is not necessary to prove the case 'beyond reasonable doubt', as is required in a criminal action, but only 'on the balance of probability'. The odds were suddenly in favour of the Najeib brothers. When the civil action would be heard was anyone's guess; it might be months away, maybe well into 2003. But of one thing everyone was certain: all the nasty details would now be pored over again. It would be a huge embarrassment for Liverpool, for a club that had previously taken pride in its good image. And what about Bowyer, wouldn't he find himself just a touch preoccupied? And how would Houllier respond when asked by the media, as he surely would be, if he supported Bowyer?

It's tempting to say that it was a dilemma for Liverpool, but in fact it was nothing of the kind. There was only one option. Indeed, Houllier should never have got himself into such a position in the first place. It had been clear to most people that a civil action was on the cards. It might have been that Houllier did not fully appreciate the workings of the English legal system, which would be understandable, but if that was the case surely someone at the club should have ensured he was better informed. Furthermore, a television company was already planning a drama documentary about the incident and the trial; they were hardly likely to be going ahead with it if they did not have some 'interesting' evidence to produce. Nor was the documentary likely to be in Bowyer's favour, even if that TV company was Granada who held a 9.9 per cent stake in Liverpool Football Club. People would be bound to ask why on the one hand Granada were exposing Bowyer while on the other helping to pay his wages.

Finally, and possibly most importantly, how would all the black players and fans at Liverpool respond to the signing of Bowyer? The answer to that is that the players would probably have reacted with seasoned professionalism. Most of them had, after all, played alongside him in the England squad. But they could hardly have been happy at the possibility. Nothing was said around Anfield by any of them, but it was widely known that some of them had their private opinions. As for the fans, they remained divided, though you didn't have to be a rocket scientist to assume that black fans would have been outraged.

It was also true that Bowyer was dithering. One minute he wanted this, the next minute he had found something else to discuss. The negotiation of modern contracts had admittedly become far more complex since the days of Shankly when players had simply asked how much they would be getting and where the pen was. Modern contracts run to hundreds of pages covering a million and one eventualities from time off to promote kit to which country their salaries are banked in to whether or not they can stoop to play in the reserves. But both Houllier and Parry were becoming anxious and angry at the length of time it was taking. Is he really committed to us? wondered Houllier. Every time we seem to be getting towards an agreement something new crops up. Does this man really want to play for Liverpool?

Houllier had left for Le Havre that Friday morning; Liverpool were due to play a friendly match against the local side, who had just been promoted to the French First Division, part of a deal set up following the transfer to Liverpool of Le Tallec and Pongolle. That evening and through into the Saturday, Rick Parry and Gérard Houllier spoke frequently on the telephone. Both men agreed that Bowyer was continuing to throw spanners into the works. Houllier was disappointed with his attitude; Parry, perhaps the more politically astute of the two by virtue of his knowledge of the English legal system, was also becoming highly concerned at the damage that might be done to the club. As the two men talked it became apparent that neither of them had much more of an appetite for the deal. So, at lunchtime on the Sunday, a statement was released: Liverpool were pulling out. There were a number of reasons for their reluctance to continue, foremost among them that as far as they were concerned Bowyer was not one hundred per cent committed to Liverpool.

It was typical of Houllier that he should refuse to sign such a player, but what still confused many was why he'd ever contemplated recruiting Bowyer in the first place, especially given that Anelka had been sent packing for a far flimsier reason. On the pitch Bowyer would undoubtedly have added a further dimension to the side, but off it, who knows what trouble he might have caused? And would he ever have been able to win over Liverpool fans, especially given that Liverpool were acknowledged as something of a cult club among the Asian community. It was, and remains, something of a mystery.

Another player who didn't quite make it to Merseyside was the Blackburn winger Damien Duff, who had enthralled football fans with his explosive running during the 2002 World Cup finals. Duff looked like just the kind of player Liverpool needed – someone with the ability to take the ball wide to the byline. He also had pace and skill, and would undoubtedly have been a tremendous addition to the squad. Unfortunately, Liverpool left it too late. Although they had shown interest prior to the World Cup, they had made no offer, and once the finals were over Duff's valuation doubled. Not only were Blackburn offering him a highly lucrative extension to his contract, they'd also slapped a £20 million price tag on him. After much consideration, Houllier made an enquiry; a £10 million bid was dismissed as 'derisory', and a follow-up bid of £12.5 million received the same treatment. It turned out that Duff wasn't particularly keen on moving anyway and had agreed to sign the new deal with Blackburn.

The one other player who escaped the Houllier net was Hugo Viana, a young Portuguese midfielder who had captained his country's under-21 side and had been called up for the national squad in Japan and South Korea. Houllier was particularly keen on him, but somewhere along the line Newcastle's Bobby Robson showed more fleetness of foot and before Liverpool could get their act together Viana was on his way to St James's Park. Houllier was annoyed but had no one to blame but himself. Robson's close connections with Sporting Lisbon, whom he'd once managed, had no doubt helped to smooth the deal. At least Houllier showed good grace by calling Robson to congratulate him.

'You bugger,' he complained.

14. WINE FOR MY MEN, THEY RIDE AT DAWN

Houllier and Thompson would hand out pieces of paper to each player in the squad and tell them to write down their personal goal for the team. Afterwards the pieces of paper would be collected, analysed and carefully placed into piles. That summer of 2002, to the management's surprise, almost all the players opted to win the Premiership. That was the one thing they wanted above all for that season. Houllier had thought more of them might have gone for some sort of glory on the European stage; that was certainly his preference. But no, they wanted to win the title. So be it, he said, that is now our collective ambition. Now, go out and win it.

As the 2002/03 season got under way Liverpool could boast 22 internationals, all but one of them current, and a further four under-21 internationals. It was obvious that not everyone was going to be satisfied, and although they were all well paid, no footballer wants to sit on the sidelines and watch his side, no matter how good they are or how many trophies they are winning. Daily training and top-class coaching is all very well, but the true test of a player's ability, the only yardstick for improvement, is competitive football on a regular basis. Although Houllier would stress time and again that the team came first, players do set their own standards, especially international players, who need to be fully involved if they are to be selected by their nation. Sitting on a bench every week does not attract attention. It was a problem that would come to haunt Houllier over the opening months of the season.

Liverpool began their close-season preparations at a trans-formed Melwood, redeveloped along the lines of the French football training headquarters at Clairefontaine which Houllier himself had created, which in turn had been based on the facilities he'd installed at Lens in 1982. The bootroom might have gone, but every morning the staff still meet for an hour between 8.15 and 9.15 during which they chew over recent results, receive injury updates and scouting reports, and decide on the training schedule for the day. 'It's pretty much the same as happened in the old bootroom,' said Phil Thompson, 'it's just slightly more formalised and the surroundings are more congenial.' Houllier agreed. 'The tradition and spirit of the bootroom has been perpetuated,' he said. 'Every morning all the technical staff gather together for an hour or so, with no phone calls and no interruptions, just to talk about training, the team, the players and so on. That's day in, day out. Even if there is no training there are always three or four of us here. So the bootroom tradition still exists. I am very keen and insistent on keeping that. We still keep a diary, and my colleagues could tell you that this time last year we did this session, those players were there, and so forth. It is important if you want to improve, because sometimes you try things that don't work and at some stage you are confronted with poor results or difficult situations. It is important to find out what happened before, and having a record does help. But we do not meet after a game. That tradition has gone.'

Houllier had introduced a new ritual, though. At the beginning of every season he would call all the players into the large room at Melwood where they normally held team talks and discuss the forthcoming year with them. He had just one question for them: what do you want to achieve this season? He told them to be realistic, not to suggest something Liverpool had little hope of realising. Do you want to win a trophy, and if so which one, or do you simply want to reach the final of a competition or finish higher up the Premiership? Together, they had to make a decision, and once the decision had been made it would become the collective ambition. There was a reassuring element of democracy about it. The players set their own goals and then, as a team, had to apply themselves in order to achieve them.

Houllier and Thompson would hand out pieces of paper to each player in the squad and tell them to write down their personal goal for the team. Afterwards the pieces of paper would be collected, analysed and carefully placed into piles. That summer of 2002, to the management's surprise, almost all the players opted to win the Premiership. That was the one thing they wanted above all for that season. Houllier had thought more of them might have gone for some sort of glory on the European stage; that was certainly his preference. But no, they wanted to win the title. So be it, he said, that is now our collective ambition. Now, go out and win it.

The pre-season friendlies, however, produced a mixed bag of results, and they were followed on 11 August by defeat in the

Community Shield against Arsenal at Cardiff. Liverpool barely competed and were totally overwhelmed in midfield by a strident Arsenal. If these matches were anything to go by, the season was set to be something of an uphill struggle. Nevertheless, a week later Houllier travelled to Aston Villa for the season's first game full of confidence. El-Hadji Diouf was given his first outing, and he showed enough skill and endeavour to suggest that Houllier had unearthed a gem of a player. Liverpool won 1–0 thanks to a John Arne Riise goal, but they could have had four. The encouraging sign at least was that Liverpool were creating chances. The Villa victory was followed a few days later by an even more impressive victory, Liverpool brushing aside Southampton by three goals to nil at Anfield. This time Diouf was on the scoresheet with a couple of goals and an imperious performance that had his name ringing around Anfield. Two games, two wins.

The problem of too many quality players reared its ugly head only a couple of weeks into the season with several players grumbling about non-selection, most notably Jari Litmanen, who by the end of August was back in Holland with Ajax. But the Premiership fixture list ground on relentlessly, and next up was a trip to Blackburn, the game before which Liverpool target Damien Duff announced that he was going to sign an extension to his contract with the Lancashire club. He clearly had something to prove to the Merseysiders for he proceeded to run Abel Xavier ragged time and again. A Duff cross brought the first goal. Liverpool then equalised through Murphy, and Riise later put them ahead, only for Blackburn to snatch a late draw thanks to some nifty footwork from that man Duff again. In truth, a draw was as much as Liverpool deserved; throughout much of the match they had failed to get out of second gear, and when they had taken the lead they'd failed to close the game down.

Astonishingly, they did exactly the same again on 2 September when they entertained Newcastle at Anfield. In what in the past had always proved to be an exciting encounter, Liverpool stormed at their opponents and by half-time could easily have been three goals ahead. In the second half more chances followed, and Liverpool soon found themselves with a two-goal lead. With ten minutes remaining, however, and with Liverpool still tearing

Newcastle apart, the Geordies scored from a rare attack. Panic set in, but still Liverpool went in search of a third goal. Then the inevitable happened, Alan Shearer putting an end to Anfield dreams of topping the table. Houllier was not dispirited. It had been an exhilarating performance from Liverpool who had played some of their most attractive football at Anfield in years. Instead of the usual ponderous defensive attitude that had dogged the previous season's performances, Liverpool had gone out with a win-at-all-costs attitude and had played with flair and pace. He knew they would play a lot worse and still win before the season was over. What's more, it was difficult to criticise any of the players, all of whom had shown tremendous commitment to the cause. It was one of those games where you simply had to shrug your shoulders and say, 'Well, that's how it is when we play Newcastle at Anfield.'

But on 11 September Liverpool threw away another two-goal lead, this time against Birmingham City, and in the last quarter, too. It was barely believable. The draw left Liverpool trailing Arsenal by two points. It wasn't that Liverpool were playing badly and not creating chances, far from it. The root of the problem was simply that the strikers were not putting those chances away. Emile Heskey had failed to score all season, and Michael Owen had visibly lost his confidence in front of goal. Against Newcastle he had fluffed three clear chances, and against Birmingham he was gifted four one-on-one opportunities, but with each of them he looked for a second, even a third touch of the ball instead of just lashing it into the back of the net like the Owen of old. It was as much a headache for Houllier as it was for Owen. The dilemma was whether to drop him or stick with him: dropping him might only further erode his confidence; sticking with him might cost the side more points. Any critic could justifiably claim that Owen had already cost Liverpool four points. Had he put just half his chances away, both Newcastle and Birmingham would have been dead and buried by half-time.

As he sat in the dugout during that Birmingham match, Houllier pondered his dilemma. With 20 minutes remaining, despite Liverpool leading 2–0 Owen was visibly anxious. He could bring on Milan Baros in a straight swap, or simply stick with Owen.

Baros had been scoring regularly for the reserves and had netted two for his country a few days earlier. He was desperate to get on, too. Then Birmingham struck. Houllier had to make a decision. If he brought off Owen it would be a public signal that he was not happy with him; he felt he needed to protect the youngster, and there would have been nothing more likely to add to his woes than to be substituted. And what would he do then? Select him for the next game, rest him, play him in the reserves? Houllier decided to bring off El-Hadji Diouf instead and opt for an attacking midfielder by introducing Patrik Berger to the fray. It didn't work. With the last touch of the game, Birmingham snatched an undeserved equaliser.

It was inevitable that there would be criticism the next day, and sure enough the web pages were full of questions. Why hadn't Baros been introduced? What did he have to do to get a game? How much longer would Houllier stick with an out-of-form Owen? Why didn't he rest Owen? It was the biggest barrage Houllier had faced for some time, and on top of that he now had to make a decision about the forthcoming game, away to Bolton. Should he put Owen on the bench and give Baros an opportunity, or select Owen and perhaps be more ready to bring Baros on should Owen again look anxious in front of goal?

In the end, Houllier opted for Baros, leaving Owen, Heskey and Diouf on the bench and, strangely, playing new French recruit Bruno Cheyrou as a second striker, tucked in behind the Czech – strange because Cheyrou was essentially a midfielder. It didn't take Baros long to show why he was worthy of his place. He struck a goal in the first half, hit a post, then nipped in between two defenders in the second half to score another. Liverpool ran out 3–2 winners, Emile Heskey grabbing a late winner immediately after Liverpool had conceded the lead for the second time that afternoon. All the headlines were about Baros, but they might just as easily have been about the Liverpool defence which had again given up a lead and had again conceded two goals. Liverpool had won, but they'd hardly been convincing, which was something of a worry considering that the Champions League campaign was about to kick off.

Liverpool had been drawn in a group with the Spanish champions Valencia, the Russia champions Spartak Moscow and the Swiss champions Basle. On paper it did not look too difficult, and there were satisfied smiles around Anfield when the draw was made. Valencia were certainly a tough proposition, but there seemed no reason why Liverpool shouldn't take second spot and win through to the next stage.

Valencia overran Liverpool in Spain with a first-half display of powerful running, slick passing and clinical finishing. By half-time Liverpool were two goals down, lucky not to be four down, and all but wiped out. They improved in the second half but never looked likely to threaten Valencia's comfortable lead. In truth, Liverpool were poor.

Houllier had gone into the game announcing that Liverpool were now adopting a more attacking approach to their game. In the past, he claimed, they had been inclined to be too defensive, but now they would be more positive. Given that Liverpool were up against one of the best sides in Europe – Valencia had not only beaten Real Madrid to the title but had been Champions League finalists in two out of the past three years – it was perhaps a foolish suggestion, or at least badly timed. Just as worrying was the fact that Houllier decided against starting with the striker in form, Baros, with Owen, opting instead for Diouf and Heskey. At half-time he withdrew the two Senegalese players, Diouf and Diao, later claiming that Diouf had looked tired and out of sorts, and replaced them with Owen and Cheyrou. Owen's introduction certainly gave the Reds more impetus, but by then they were always chasing a lost cause. Baros, inexplicably, was left warming the bench. Liverpool also suffered the further indignity of having Dietmar Hamann sent off for a second offence.

It was an embarrassing defeat for Liverpool. It certainly gave the newspapers an excuse to fill plenty of column inches with pieces about Liverpool's lack of conviction. 'Humiliated', 'outclassed' and 'inept' were just a few of the adjectives adorning the following morning's back pages. That left Liverpool smarting, but they knew they were capable of better, and given the way they had played they could count themselves lucky not to have lost by a wider margin. There was still everything to play for; all they had to do was make sure they won their home games and maybe took a point from their away matches in Switzerland and Russia. But that first defeat certainly left a few directors nervous. If Liverpool failed to qualify for the second stage, it would cost them something in the region of £10 million. That was a considerable amount of money and would clearly mean a tightening of the purse strings around Anfield. And the person most likely to feel the pinch if that happened was Gérard Houllier, whose transfer treasure chest would suddenly look a little bare. 'If it comes to that, someone will have to go,' warned one Liverpool boardroom insider. 'That's the only way you can really raise money now.' Quite who that person might be was anyone's guess, although with Real Madrid said to be sniffing around Michael Owen many fans began to put two and two together. 'Owen is not for sale,' warned Houllier. 'Thirty million would not even buy one of his legs.'

But there was some way to go before any reassessment of the balance sheet was called for. A week later, however, such a prospect became a little more real when Liverpool could manage no more than a draw at Anfield against Basle. Liverpool peppered the Swiss goal with some 27 shots, three times striking the woodwork and once having the ball kicked off the line, while the keeper saved at least three certain goals. It was a deeply depressing result, but the team's form was little different in the Premiership. The previous Saturday, against a workmanlike West Bromwich Albion, they had not been able to settle the game until the final minute. In the first half Owen, who had been rugby-tackled by the keeper, managed to miss yet another penalty, his sixth miss in twelve. Liverpool continued to create chance after chance but neither Owen nor anyone else seemed capable of putting the ball into the back of the net. Although Liverpool scored in the second half through Milan Baros, it was a nail-biting final few moments as West Brom attacked, looking for an equaliser. Then, in the final moment, John Arne Riise converted some neat work by Owen to put the game beyond doubt. It was Liverpool's first clean sheet in five games.

After the Basle match there were long faces in the boardroom. Liverpool had just been booed off the field, although somewhat unfairly it has to be said. They had played some delightful football, it was just one of those nights when the ball simply won't go into the back of the net. Rick Parry moved nervously around the room, trying to make small talk and to impress on others that it was far from over, but privately he was well aware that Liverpool had now made things very difficult for themselves. They could still qualify, but they would now have to win their next couple of matches against Spartak Moscow. Nothing, it seemed, was ever easy at Anfield.

By late September rumours were also beginning to circulate around the city that all was not well at Melwood. Morale was said to be low, and the whinge register was reckoned to be at an all-time high, though they were mainly emanating from the fringe players. No names were ever mentioned, but everybody could guess that young players such as Richie Partridge, Gregory Vignal, Chris Kirkland and Igor Biscan must be getting increasingly fed up with sitting on the sidelines. A chance never seemed to come for them. Biscan was a full international, and the others were all under-21 internationals; they might have expected by now to have made the grade. It was only youthful ambition, and there was nothing wrong with that. Indeed, if you have young players, what you want is to have them banging on the manager's door.

It was a problem Houllier had all along been stoking up for himself. Since his arrival at Anfield he had signed some outstanding young players; they were now, naturally enough, demanding an opportunity to shine. Stephen Wright had already decided that playing in a first team was more important than who you played for and had taken his leave. Now, Partridge, the young Irish winger, was also set to leave, initially on a month's loan to Coventry but with a view to a more permanent deal. At one stage Manchester United were said to be keen to sign him, but nothing had happened.

At least the problem of Michael Owen was soon solved. Owen had failed to score in open play so far that season. It was the longest he had ever gone without scoring, and the papers were full of criticism and unfair questions. There were suggestions that he was no longer the player he had been, that he had been found out by defenders, that he was burnt out, that he'd suffered too many injuries. It was all nonsense, yet when Ian Rush came to his defence, arguing that all strikers go through lean spells and that Owen's approach work had improved as a result, he too was ridiculed. But while fans and the world's media became edgy, behind the scenes at Anfield there was no such panic. Houllier remained confident that Owen had the quality to emerge from his barren patch. He, too, insisted that the loss of form was 'temporary' and that all strikers went through such difficult patches. 'There is no problem with Owen,' he told them. 'He will score goals again.'

Sure enough, against Manchester City at Maine Road on 28 September the goals flowed. In the first few minutes Owen found himself in a one-on-one situation with Peter Schmeichel, but when the giant City keeper stood tall and managed to push the ball out of play with his foot, it seemed that the Owen nightmare was to continue. The City crowd howled with delight, but from the resulting corner Owen hooked the ball into the back of the net. He was on fire again. In the second half he hit a second, then in the closing moments he chased a long ball to notch up a hat-trick. It was little wonder that he gave his boss the thumbs up. Further wins followed in October over Chelsea, Leeds and Tottenham, and with other results going in Liverpool's favour they suddenly found themselves topping the table with a four-point lead over Arsenal. Sandwiched in between were two comfortable wins over Spartak Moscow which set up nicely the return home game against Valencia in the Champions League. Although a win was not essential, Houllier knew that anything less would mean pressure on the final group game.

On 9 November Liverpool were in Middlesbrough, who were beginning to piece together a decent run themselves. It was never going to be an easy game, but again Houllier decided to start with the same defensive midfield of Hamann, Gerrard, Diao and Murphy which had failed to overwhelm both Chelsea and Spurs. True, Liverpool had won those games, but more by good fortune than good play. Goalless at half-time, the fans anticipated the manager going for some more attacking flair. But no, it wasn't until late in the game that he finally replaced a sluggish-looking Gerrard with Vladimir Smicer. Almost immediately, Middlesbrough scored. Smicer, however, added pace and invention to the midfield, and when Milan Baros also came on Liverpool finally took the game to the home team. But it was all too late. Liverpool had lost their first premiership game of the season.

They now faced an uphill task against Basle. At Anfield earlier in the season Liverpool had cursed their bad luck; now they travelled to Switzerland knowing that nothing less than victory would take them through to the second phase of the Champions League. Houllier was confident that they could do it, and once again stressed that they would be more positive than they'd been in recent games. As proof of that he left out Diao in favour of Smicer. But given that Basle had managed a last-minute draw with Valencia on their home ground as well as beating Celtic, a result in the Reds' favour was never going to be anything like a foregone conclusion. Within just 90 seconds Liverpool's task became even more daunting when a sudden breakaway put them a goal behind. That meant they now had to score two. Twenty minutes later the Swiss team added a second, and just before the half hour they tore Liverpool apart again to add a third. It was an almost unbelievable avalanche of goals; Liverpool's normally rock-solid defence had been dented three times in less than 30 minutes. Gerrard again looked out of sorts, while Didi Hamann was finding it impossible to cope with the cut and thrust of the Basle attack. Djimi Traore was showing his inexperience, Sami Hyypia clearly looked unhappy.

In the second half, however, Houllier replaced the tiring Gerrard with Salif Diao, and suddenly Liverpool began to look like a different team. They were winning the ball in the midfield now, and all those who had underperformed in the first half were looking considerably more impressive. The goals came, too, the first from Murphy, the second from Smicer, the equaliser from Owen after he had yet again failed to convert a penalty. With ten minutes remaining Liverpool pressed for the fourth goal that would take them through, but it never came. It had been a remarkable game and a brave fightback by Liverpool, but in truth they should never have got themselves into a position of needing to score four goals.

For a club that had been counting itself among the top half dozen in Europe, only to fail to reach the last sixteen of the Champions League, it was a bitterly disappointing night, even though third spot in their group put them into the UEFA Cup. Houllier knew they were a far better team than that, but the one trophy he longed to win would have to wait for at least another season. More worrying for the directors was the loss in revenue, which would have to be recouped elsewhere. At least with the size of his squad Houllier probably never had any intention of going on another massive spending spree. At most he needed only one or two players, especially with the two French kids due in the summer, and there were a number of players being lined up for an exit within the next six months or so, among them Patrik Berger, Bernard Diomede and Vegard Heggem.

Liverpool were still atop the Premiership, of course, still on target to achieve their stated collective ambition, still with everything to play for, but on Radio Five over the next few evenings, especially after Newcastle barged their way into the second phase of the Champions League, listeners were ringing up ready to lynch Houllier. He couldn't motivate the side, his tactics were strange, why had they never signed a wide player, why did he play such a defensive side, why did he bother with Heskey, why didn't he play Baros . . . the questions were endless. It was all predictable, though the comments were as venomous as any over the four years of Houllier's stewardship.

A day later, after Houllier had chewed over the defeat, he pointed the finger directly at Steven Gerrard, taking the unusual step of issuing a warning to the 22-year-old midfielder in the newspapers. Gerrard, he said, must not fall into the trap of believing his own hype. 'I hope he doesn't believe everything that is written about him because then you start going downwards. Maybe it's a question of himself and his environment. It is not physical. An athlete always has to think he must do better. If he thinks he has reached the top he goes down, and in this game you go down quicker than anyone else. You saw what happened against Tottenham when I took him off. We started to play better. Stevie was not at the races against Basle. Once a player starts to think "I am king of the world" then there is difficulty and danger. I am frustrated with him. I have given him my trust and my faith, but talent without work is frustrating.' Houllier's statement was even carried on the official website, no doubt sanctioned by the manager himself.

It was most unlike Houllier to make his views so public, and to talk to the press so openly. In his book he had written that 'when a player is not at his best, when he's going through a bad patch, there's no point in "slagging him off" as long as he is making every effort to improve.' Obviously in this instance Houllier felt that Gerrard was not making the required effort. During the summer Gerrard had missed the World Cup through injury. He had returned and seemed to have overcome his problems, but he'd then sustained a hip injury. He'd returned again, but his form had deteriorated. By speaking out, Houllier had decided to take a calculated risk, alienating the player in the hope that it might jolt him into action. Although Gerrard had never been a problem in the way that Fowler had, he was known to enjoy himself a little too often. He'd been warned in the past against excessive clubbing, and this public warning was clearly a yellow card for the 22-year-old. Gerrard had to buckle down and focus on further improvements to his game to avoid a second caution.

Going out of the 2002/03 Champions League at the opening hurdle was the first backwards step Liverpool had taken since Gérard Houllier had arrived on that warm summer's day in 1998 to throw his beret into the ring. In his first full season in sole charge at Anfield Liverpool had finished fourth in the Premiership. In his second season they'd finished third and had won an unprecedented cup treble. In his third season, he'd recovered from a serious illness to see his team reach the quarter-finals of the Champions League and then clinch the runners-up spot in the Premiership. But as the damp of November descended, he was left wondering if perhaps he'd reached the end of the road.

Worse was to follow. The 9 November loss at Middlesbrough came after a run of 29 Premiership games with only one defeat, and it began a dreadful sequence that spilt into 2003. A goalless draw with Sunderland on 17 November was followed a week later by Liverpool's second defeat of the season, at Fulham; then an injury-stricken Manchester United, minus Beckham, Ferdinand, Veron and Keane, came to Anfield and walked off with a 2–1 win. Both Charlton and struggling Sunderland beat Liverpool in December, and Everton snatched a draw at Anfield. By Christmas Liverpool had thrown away a seven-point lead at the top of the table and had slumped to fifth place, seven points adrift of new leaders Arsenal. Even Everton had climbed above them. It was hardly championship form; if anything, it was relegation form. Houllier clung to the belief that Liverpool would pull themselves out of this catastrophic slump and that the championship race was still far from over, but the fans were getting restless. There were even rumours that Houllier would soon be moved upstairs to be replaced by either Martin O'Neill or David O'Leary. Over the next week they managed only two more draws, against Blackburn and Arsenal, and at St James's Park on New Year's Day they were beaten 1–0. Four points from a possible 30 was Liverpool's worst run in almost 50 years – you had to go back to the 1953/54 relegation season to get near it – and serious questions were now being asked, principal among them whether Houllier could really take Liverpool any further. Only time would tell.

On Houllier's office wall at Melwood is a photograph of Bill Shankly. It's a reminder of the past and the traditions of the club, but some might say it's also a burden. Many managers would shudder at the thought of so much history and the pressures it invariably brings, but Houllier doesn't see it that way. 'You learn from the past,' he says. 'This club has achieved so much that it creates a feeling of expectation that is incomparable to other clubs.' For him, it's a past which also has to be the future.

Brian Hall has seen them all at Anfield, both as a player and now as a club employee: Shankly, Paisley, Fagan, Dalglish, Souness and Evans. He's worked with them all in one capacity or another. 'Don't compare Gérard Houllier with Bill Shankly,' he urges. 'That does Houllier a disservice. Both are great men. Both understood the relationship between the fans of this club and the manager. But what Gérard Houllier has to offer is Gérard Houllier. When Bob Paisley took over from Bill Shankly, how did he do it? Well, he did it because he was Bob Paisley. He did not try to be Bill Shankly. You have to be your own man. If you're not yourself, you'll be found out, and it'll be the players who find you out first. And not many managers have won five trophies in a year. Gérard Houllier is Gérard Houllier. That's it. Full stop.'

INDEX